"UNRULY" CHILDREN

How do we become moral persons? What about children's active learning in contrast to parenting? What can children teach us about knowledge-making more broadly? Answer these questions by delving into the groundbreaking ethnographic fieldwork conducted by anthropologists Arthur and Margery Wolf in a Martial Law Era Taiwanese village (1958–60), marking the first-ever study of ethnic Han children. Jing Xu skillfully reinterprets the Wolfs' extensive fieldnotes, employing a unique blend of humanistic interpretation, natural language processing (NLP), and machine-learning techniques. Through a lens of social cognition, this book unravels the complexities of children's moral growth, exposing instances of disobedience, negotiation, and peer dynamics. Writing *through* and *about* fieldnotes, the author connects the two themes, learning morality and making ethnography, in light of social cognition, and invites all of us to take children seriously. This book is ideal for graduate and undergraduate students of anthropology and educational studies.

JING XU is an anthropologist at the University of Washington and the author of *The Good Child: Moral Development in a Chinese Preschool* (Stanford University Press, 2017). She pursues interdisciplinary research, bringing together humanistic and scientific perspectives to study how humans become moral persons.

NEW DEPARTURES IN ANTHROPOLOGY

New Departures in Anthropology is a book series that focuses on emerging themes in social and cultural anthropology. With original perspectives and syntheses, authors introduce new areas of inquiry in anthropology, explore developments that cross disciplinary boundaries, and weigh in on current debates. Every book illustrates theoretical issues with ethnographic material drawn from current research or classic studies, as well as from literature, memoirs, and other genres of reportage. The aim of the series is to produce books that are accessible enough to be used by college students and instructors, but will also stimulate, provoke and inform anthropologists at all stages of their careers. Written clearly and concisely, books in the series are designed equally for advanced students and a broader range of readers, inside and outside academic anthropology, who want to be brought up to date on the most exciting developments in the discipline.

Series Editorial Board

Michael Lambek, University of Toronto
Laura Bear, London School of Economics and Political Science
Naveeda Khan, Johns Hopkins University

"Unruly" Children

*Historical Fieldnotes and Learning
Morality in a Taiwan Village*

JING XU
University of Washington

CAMBRIDGE
UNIVERSITY PRESS

Shaftesbury Road, Cambridge CB2 8EA, United Kingdom

One Liberty Plaza, 20th Floor, New York, NY 10006, USA

477 Williamstown Road, Port Melbourne, VIC 3207, Australia

314–321, 3rd Floor, Plot 3, Splendor Forum, Jasola District Centre,
New Delhi – 110025, India

103 Penang Road, #05–06/07, Visioncrest Commercial, Singapore 238467

Cambridge University Press is part of Cambridge University Press & Assessment, a department of the University of Cambridge.

We share the University's mission to contribute to society through the pursuit of education, learning and research at the highest international levels of excellence.

www.cambridge.org
Information on this title: www.cambridge.org/9781009416276

DOI: 10.1017/9781009416269

© Jing Xu 2025

This publication is in copyright. Subject to statutory exception and to the provisions of relevant collective licensing agreements, no reproduction of any part may take place without the written permission of Cambridge University Press & Assessment.

When citing this work, please include a reference to the DOI 10.1017/9781009416269

First published 2025

A catalogue record for this publication is available from the British Library

Library of Congress Cataloging-in-Publication Data
NAMES: Xu, Jing, 1983– author.
TITLE: "Unruly" children : historical fieldnotes and learning morality in a Taiwan village / Jing Xu, University of Washington.
DESCRIPTION: Cambridge, United Kingdom ; New York, NY, USA : Cambridge University Press, 2025. | Series: New departures in anthropology |
Includes bibliographical references and index.
IDENTIFIERS: LCCN 2024001559 | ISBN 9781009416276 (hardback) |
ISBN 9781009416269 (ebook)
SUBJECTS: LCSH: Children – Taiwan. | Moral development – Taiwan. |
Child psychology – Taiwan. | Children – Research – Taiwan.
CLASSIFICATION: LCC HQ792.T33 X82 2025 | DDC 155.4/1823–dc23/eng/20240526
LC record available at https://lccn.loc.gov/2024001559

ISBN 978-1-009-41627-6 Hardback
ISBN 978-1-009-41625-2 Paperback

Cambridge University Press & Assessment has no responsibility for the persistence or accuracy of URLs for external or third-party internet websites referred to in this publication and does not guarantee that any content on such websites is, or will remain, accurate or appropriate.

In Memory of Arthur Wolf

Contents

List of Figures	page ix
List of Tables	xi
Foreword Stevan Harrell	xiii
Preface	xvii
Acknowledgments	xxvi
Notes on Transcription and Terminology	xxviii
List of Abbreviations	xxix
Introduction: Learning Morality in a Taiwan Village	1
1 Fieldwork beyond Fieldwork: Reconstructing an Ethnography of Children through Historical Fieldnotes	36
2 Crime and Punishment: Parenting and the Disobedient Child	72
3 Playful Creatures: Learning Morality in Peer Play	103
4 Gendered Morality: Fierce Girls and Naughty Boys	138
5 Care and Rivalry: An Untold Tale of a Sibling Dyad	176
Epilogue: Taking Children Seriously	212

Contents

Afterword   224
    Hill Gates
Appendix: Topic Modeling List (Corpus: Child Observation)   231
Glossary   232
References   234
Index   253

Figures

1.1	Village sketch map	*page* 42
1.2	Children playing at the irrigation canal in Shulin	43
1.3	Village houses and paddy fields	43
1.4	The Wang family house that Arthur Wolf lived in	45
1.5	MC with a girl	58
1.6	MC with young children	59
2.1	A boy in a fighting pose	86
3.1	A group of children playing	105
3.2	Child Observation co-occurrence network	107
4.1	Doll Play (DP) test materials	148
4.2	TAT Drawing #4	152
4.3	TAT Drawing #1	155
4.4	TAT Drawing #7	159
4.5	A girl contemplating	165
4.6	An adopted girl's (#193) behavioral-interaction network	170
5.1	Child observation subset (#49 and #50) union network	187
5.2	(a) #49's ego network of behavioral interactions, (b) #50's ego network of behavioral interactions	189
5.3	Top 100 high-frequency words in the Child Observation subset (#49 and #50)	190
5.4	Top 50 high-frequency words in Child Observation subset (#49 and #50)	191
5.5	Word co-occurrence network in the Child Observation subset (#49 and #50)	192

List of Figures

5.6	A boy carrying his baby brother	194
5.7	TAT Drawing #5	201
5.8	TAT Drawing #2	204
5.9	TAT Drawing #8	204

Tables

2.1	Answers to the physical assault scenario in Child Interview Question 8a	page 83
2.2	Older children dominating younger children through coercion, according to behavioral grading of Child Observation texts	89
3.1	Number of behavioral-interaction entries grouped by age status and behavioral direction	108
3.2	A sample of high-frequency behaviors	122
4.1	Total number of behaviors by gender and interactional direction	142
4.2	Gender differences in initiated behaviors, two-sample proportion test, $df = 1$	143
4.3	Gender differences in received behaviors, two-sample proportion test, $df = 1$	144
5.1	Wang Yi-kun and Wang Mei-yu's family, Household #7	181
5.2	Wang Yi-kun (#49) and Wang Mei-yu (#50) in children's co-occurrence network	188
5.3	Behavioral grading results (Child #49 and #50)	193

Foreword

Anthropologist Arthur Wolf died in 2015, fifty-seven years after he and his then wife Margery Wolf had arrived in the north Taiwan village of Xia Xizhou to begin field research on the lives of children there. They stayed two years, collecting a huge trove of descriptive and quantitative data, including timed observations of child behavior, projective tests, parent interviews, and school questionnaires, all recorded on paper in that predigital age. Then those data sat. Margery Wolf clearly drew on some of the fieldnotes, although only a small part, for the three books she wrote based on that stay, and Arthur used some of them as background for his doctoral dissertation and his later research on the incest taboo. In his final years, Arthur returned to these data, beginning to digitize and analyze some of them, but he did not live to complete his analysis.

After Arthur died, his widow Hill Gates approached me asking if I could suggest a scholar who might make use of the data from the Wolfs' stay in Xia Xizhou. As it happened, I knew the perfect person: XU Jing had recently arrived at the University of Washington as a postdoctoral researcher studying social cognition in American infants and toddlers. A native of Hunan in central China, XU Jing had never been to Taiwan, but she was a native speaker of Chinese, the mother of a young son, and the author of a recent book on moral development in a Shanghai preschool. She also, like Arthur, combined insights from psychology and

Foreword

anthropology and was not afraid of supplementing ethnographic observation with quantitative analysis. I recommended her to Hill, who cautiously agreed to consider XU Jing for the job.

Arthur had built his dream house – mostly out of locally sourced lumber and with his own hands – on his family's ranch in the hills of Sonoma County, but he succumbed to prostate cancer before he could enjoy retirement there. The house became a library, data repository, and workspace for scholars interested in Arthur's legacy, and Hill invited XU Jing to visit in 2018 and look through the materials. Passing the five-day "probation," XU Jing came away with the trove. She quickly set to work analyzing, with the help of research assistants, data science consultants, and a few people, now old, who had participated in the Wolfs' original research.

The result is *"Unruly" Children*, a unique and valuable book that addresses important issues, both substantive and methodological, for ethnography, Taiwan studies, family dynamics, and most importantly the anthropology of childhood. How does an anthropologist who has never been to the place she writes about reconstruct the local world of six decades before? How would her account have been different if she instead of her predecessors had made the observations and written the notes? What did they put in that she would have left out, and vice versa? How does the child-centered approach of the Wolf archive give us different insights into of childhood and learning from the parent-oriented, "socialization" approach of most ethnographies of childhood? How did growing up under martial law imposed by a military dictatorship, a factor that the Wolf's did not write about (perhaps to protect their research subjects) affect children's experiences? How did children's process of moral learning in the Taiwan of that day, when the typical woman bore five or more children who took care of each other and spent most of the day outside, differ from the experience of today's single children who spend solitary hours in front of a screen? Finally, what might be universal in the experience of Xia Xizhou children of the 1950s, and how might analyzing the meticulous and detailed records of their everyday lives inform our understanding of how human children everywhere learn to be moral beings?

XU Jing addresses all these important questions and more. Although she cannot, nor can anyone else, offer definitive answers, her perceptive analysis and innovative methodology can refine our understanding and point the way forward for future ethnographers, psychologists, and historians of childhood. They also bring to life a world that is no more, adding history to psychology and anthropology as disciplines to which she has something important to say.

Delayed by the COVID-19 pandemic, XU Jing was finally able to visit Xia Xizhou at the end of September 2023.

Stevan Harrell[*]

---

[*] Stevan Harrell, a student of Arthur Wolf, taught at the University of Washington from 1974 to 2017.

Preface

Human children present a great mystery. Humans have a longer childhood than all other primate species. Our children are the most voracious learners the universe has ever seen, beating cutting-edge artificial intelligence in many respects. They take their time to learn about the world they live in, and they eventually change that world. One fundamental question especially intrigues me: How do children become moral persons? Or according to Chinese traditions, which take moral cultivation as the ultimate goal of learning and human development (Xu 2017), how do we "become human" (*zuo ren*)? This question is rendered more complex, and to me, more interesting, if we look at moral development in real life, with all its messiness, in cultural and historical contexts, instead of fixating on philosophical musings or neatly controlled laboratory studies. Several years ago, an unexpected but outstanding opportunity found me, concerning a rare archive of fieldnotes about childhood in rural Taiwan. These precious materials belong to the late anthropologist and sinologist Arthur Wolf, who conducted fieldwork in a Taiwanese village called Xia Xizhou, about thirty minutes by train from Taipei, from 1958 to 1960. Since I got access to this archive in August 2018, I have been fascinated by the sociomoral life of Xia Xizhou children represented in these texts and devoted myself to rediscovering these children's stories.

The earliest immigrants from Fujian, on the southeast China coast, settled in this village of the Taipei basin during the eighteenth and

Preface

nineteenth centuries, when Taiwan was ruled by the Qing dynasty. Taiwan was ceded to Japan after China lost the first Sino-Japanese war (1894–95). Following the end of WWII and after five decades of Japanese rule (1895–1945), the Republic of China (ROC) regime, led by the Chinese Nationalist Party or the Kuomintang (KMT), took over Taiwan. In 1949, the KMT imposed martial law on Taiwan.[1]

The protagonists of this book, Xia Xizhou children, were born in and grew up in the Martial Law Era. Most of the villagers were Hoklo people, a group of Han ethnicity. They were part of what's called *benshengren*, in contrast to *waishengren* who fled to Taiwan from mainland after the Chinese civil war.[2] The village children all spoke Taiwanese Hokkien, their mother tongue. But unlike their parents, who grew up speaking Japanese as well as Hokkien, these children were among the first generation who were taught Mandarin (*guoyu*) and learned about the great motherland of China at school. In this Cold War context, the authoritarian KMT regime promoted itself as the legitimate ruler of China and the authentic embodiment of Chinese traditions. The regime redefined "Chineseness" by emphasizing an anti-communism element. It imposed Chinese nationalist education on the island.

When we think of the year 1958 from today's vantage point, what do we remember? The United States launched Explorer 1 satellite, a quick response to the Soviet Union's launch of Sputnik 1 in the previous year. In the People's Republic of China (PRC), my home country, Mao Zedong commanded the Great Leap Forward movement and a horrific famine was inflicted on China between 1959 and 1961. In Taiwan, the

---

[1] Martial law was finally lifted in 1987, by President Chiang Ching-kuo.
[2] Hoklo and Hakka are two main Han ethnic groups in Taiwan whose ancestors migrated from coastal China's Fujian and Guangdong provinces largely during the Qing dynasty. After the end of Japanese rule, when the ROC regime, led by the KMT, retreated to the island in 1948–49, it brought massive migration of people from mainland China, which constituted another ethnic Han group. The labels *benshengren* and *waishengren* emerged after the KMT had taken over Taiwan: the former referring to Taiwan-born Hoklo and Hakka people and the latter referring to new immigrants from mainland China.

year 1958 was known to the world for the Second Taiwan Strait Crisis,[3] a conflict between the Communist PRC and the Nationalist ROC on and around the small islands of Jinmen (Quemoy) and Mazu (Matsu).[4] Childhood in the frontline of this conflict zone became a *New York Times* headline in 1958: "Children Live in Caves," many children living underground in Little Jinmen, short of food, with no medical supplies (see Szonyi 2008: 74).

With such geopolitical dramas unfolding in the wider region during the Cold War era, the life of my protagonists seemed quite ordinary to the adult eye. The strangest event in 1958, for Xia Xizhou children, was perhaps the arrival of an American couple, an anthropology graduate student at Cornell University named Arthur Wolf, and his wife at that time, Margery Wolf, an aspiring novelist. They lived there until summer 1960, for Arthur's dissertation fieldwork. His research was an improved replication of the Six Cultures Study of Child Socialization (hereafter "SCS"), a landmark project in the history of anthropology and cross-cultural research on childhood (LeVine 2010). With aid from their excellent Taiwanese research assistants, the Wolfs accumulated thousands of pages of fieldnotes, including systematic observations, interviews, projective tests, and demographic information.

From this field trip, Arthur and Margery Wolf launched their distinguished careers in anthropology and sinology. Through them, the ordinary life of Xia Xizhou children entered into an extraordinary intellectual history. The children had no idea that their everyday games, dramas, tantrums, and moments of boredom were all meticulously

---

[3] The First Taiwan Strait Crisis was 1954–55, see https://history.state.gov/milestones/1953-1960/taiwan-strait-crises.

[4] On August 23, 1958, Mao, to deal "directly with Chiang [Kai-shek] and indirectly with the Americans" (see Szonyi 2008: 67), ordered the PLA (People's Liberation Army) to bomb Jinmen (Quemoy) and Mazu (Matsu) areas, small islands under ROC rule but only within a few kilometers of the southeast Chinese coast. ROC forces returned fire, and the Eisenhower administration provided aid. This event set the stage for a bizarre system, with both sides shelling each other on alternate days, which lasted until 1979 (Szonyi 2008: 76).

Preface

documented by the white, foreign anthropologist's team, as the first ethnographic research on Han Chinese children in the world. Nor did they anticipate that their village would become an iconic landmark in the map of sinological anthropologists (Freedman 1968: xii). Readers of anthropology and Chinese studies are familiar with this village, under the pseudonym *Peihotien* in Margery Wolf's classic ethnographies, such as *The House of Lim* (1968), *Women and the Family in Rural Taiwan* (1972), and *A Thrice-Told Tale* (1992). From Arthur Wolf's foundational works on marriage and kinship (A. Wolf and Huang 1980),[5] readers know that this village is a patrilineal, patriarchal community, with an entrenched son preference and a historical tradition of minor marriage, adopted daughters as "little daughters-in-law" (*sim-pu-a*). Many, however, did not know that the main research subject of the Wolfs' first fieldwork in Taiwan was young children, because the bulk of the Wolfs' 1958–60 fieldnotes, although well preserved in the past decades, have not seen the light of the day until now.

Six decades later, through the introduction of Stevan Harrell at the University of Washington, Hill Gates, the holder of Arthur Wolf's library, invited me to the library up in the hills above Healdsburg, northern California, and generously gave me permission to analyze this fieldnotes archive, which I call "the Wolf archive." I dived into this rich mine of past children's worlds with great excitement. But I was also haunted by a question: How can one even write an ethnography without first-person fieldwork experience? Childhood in mid-twentieth century Taiwan is certainly a less familiar world to me than childhood in early 2010s PRC, which I have studied "in the field." It is also a less familiar world than my own childhood in the 1980s and 1990s, postreform China. Venturing into history and rediscovering previous anthropologists' fieldnotes,

---

[5] For a bibliographical list of research and publications by the Wolfs and their students and associates on the Haishan area, including this village and several neighboring villages and towns, see Harrell (1999) and A. Wolf and Huang (1980: Appendix B).

however, my interest in this archive was inevitably shaped by my own experience and expertise.

In the process of reading these fieldnotes, a familiar song rang in my mind again and again. Entitled "childhood" (*tongnian*), this nostalgic song likely portrayed the songwriter and Taiwanese cultural icon Lo Ta-yu's own experience, of growing up in the Taipei area during the late 1950s and early 1960s. Ever since it came out in the early 1980s, this song has enjoyed phenomenal popularity in the entire Mandarin-speaking world. It became part of my own childhood memory. I have long wondered what the childhood described in that song was like: With cicadas chirping in the humid summer heat, children were climbing the banyan tree, catching dragonflies in the lush green rice paddies, playing on the swing in the schoolyard, reading comics after school,[6] or whining for pocket money.

The song finally came alive when I read the fieldnotes and encountered the same scenes and landscapes of the hot Taipei Basin summer in the text. I was fascinated by the various games and pretend play that children ingeniously created, enacted rules for, and indulged themselves in, by their pervasive sense of humor across various playful scenarios, and by their mysterious capacity to find joy, however mundane the situation. Episodes in these fieldnotes posed a stark contrast to the grand, geopolitical narratives of that time. The scenes depicted in the fieldnotes also differed from what I saw in September 2023, at the site that used to be Xia Xizhou but was now part of the urbanized and industrialized New Taipei City: There were no children running around in alleys or climbing trees all by themselves. Children had all moved into segregated apartment units, and their free time was heavily structured and supervised by adults.

---

[6] For example, the song mentioned a Taiwanese comics series, Yeh Hong-jia's *Jhunge Shiro*, which was first published in 1958 and enjoyed unprecedented popularity among children. According to Wolf's fieldnotes, children in Xia Xizhou liked comics. I wonder if they were reading *Jhunge Shiro* too.

Preface

Reading these fieldnotes, I kept thinking about my own parents, who were born in the mid-1950s, just like the Xia Xizhou children. In a Chinese village about 600 miles away from Xia Xizhou, my father, then a small child, almost died from malnutrition in the famine during the Great Leap Forward years, the famine that he later remembered as "Three Years of Natural Disasters" (*sannian ziran zaihai*). At the height of Taiwan's Martial Law Era, Xia Xizhou children were learning anti-communist propaganda, such as "Eliminating Communist Bandits" (*xiaomie gongfei*) and "Maintaining Secrecy and Preventing Espionage" (*baomi fangdie*), as some of them still remembered when I interviewed them in 2023. They did ask political questions at the time, as were recorded in these fieldnotes, a few examples include, "Who do you think will win, the Chinese or the Communists?" and "Why don't we ask the Americans to fight the Communists?"[7] In the meantime, my parents were taught about "liberating Taiwan" (*jiefang taiwan*), among many slogans during China's high socialism era. My mother vividly recalled that they would cite a quote from Chairman Mao before engaging in a fight with other children.

Beneath all the geopolitical abstractions and ideological slogans, however, Taiwanese children in the fieldnotes must be similar to my parents, or to children in many other preindustrialized societies, in some fundamental ways. They were all playing around in courtyards, rice paddies, or by the river, while taking care of their younger siblings and sometimes fighting with other cliques of children. They were exploring all sorts of ways to have fun, despite lacking fancy toys or comfortable material conditions. They were growing up while playing, working, and learning, and in all this, constructing a sense of self. To me, the purpose of anthropology is not just about studying a particular society. We study a particular society in order to understand humanity more broadly. Childhood provides a unique lens to explore fundamental dimensions of human experience.

[7] See Chapter 1.

Preface

Plowing through these fieldnotes six decades later in Seattle, at a time of rising geopolitical tensions, I have been bombarded by the American news cycle on cross-strait relations, or more accurately, on the grand drama of the United States–China–Taiwan triangle. I couldn't help but wonder: What about the "human" part? How much do we know about people's everyday life, actual people who are or were living through those turbulent times? Even more rare is record of young children's world. Unlike many other historical accounts of childhood, the Wolf archive provides such systematic materials on the actual life of children, instead of representations and discourses about children, or adult recollections of childhood memory. Regarding the existential question of "becoming moral," which means the very essence of "becoming human" in the long tradition of Chinese thought, these fieldnotes offer precious insights into how young children in the past, on the margins of history, develop moral understandings and sentiments in their ordinary life.

As a Han Chinese daughter and mother, I couldn't help but insert myself into this narrative. I was intrigued by parent–child relationship and especially the question of punishment. For example, the tropes of "discipline" (*guanjiao*) and "obedience" (*shuncong*) are so popular in discourses and precepts about "traditional Chinese families." As a child, I was never truly obedient. As a mother, I have learned that, however much I want my son to listen to me, he is a little person of his own will, reason, and feeling. Were children of the past generation so different from us? Did they not have a rich inner life and some sort of agency too? It turns out that Xia Xizhou children were not docile either, even though their understanding of authority and justice was influenced by the historical context.

My point is that once we shift our attention from "parenting" discourses to children themselves a whole different picture of moral development emerges. One fascinating part of this new picture is Xia Xizhou children's peer play, as the rich repertoire of peer play encapsulates all sorts of moral dramas and lessons: They were learning tirelessly about the social worlds. They were learning about particular norms and rituals, power relations, and cultural values in local society at that time. But more than that, they were also learning about common problems across societies, about cooperation and care, about authority and dominance, and all the gray areas in between.

I was also drawn to the gender question. Like quite a few mothers in this Taiwanese village, my paternal grandmother grew up as a "little daughter-in-law" (*tongyangxi* in Mandarin). She was adopted into my grandfather's family when she was young and got married to my grandfather at the age of fourteen. The last time I spoke to her, not long before she passed away, she was remembering her younger years and how badly she was treated. My father, like many Chinese men in his generation, preferred boys, but his hope for a son was dashed by the One-Child Policy in China. As a singleton child, I enjoyed all the love from my parents. But still, the idea of "proving myself as worthy" that haunted many Han Chinese daughters also shaped who I am. Encountering numerous young girls in these fieldnotes, most of whom had brothers, I was curious to learn how gender affected their sense of right and wrong, good and bad, in ways similar to or different from what I had experienced. I was wondering how these young girls thought about their often-times disadvantaged situations, and how they might assert their own voices in those situations. I was eager to witness their moments of joy and sorrow, anger and pride – witness vicariously, through texts.

The life of young boys, too, sparked a great level of curiosity in me. I am raising a boy, a Chinese American boy. He was a special "interlocutor" in my first book, *The Good Child*. When I was doing fieldwork in a Shanghai preschool a decade ago, he was a student in that school, a toddler. When I was working on these historical fieldnotes, he was about the same age as the oldest protagonists in this book. During the long COVID-19 pandemic, working from home and sharing the space with my son, many magical moments occurred to me, in which text blended into reality and history became present: When I encountered episodes of mischievous boys defying parental orders or teasing each other, I could hear my own child's voice, literally and figuratively. In short, exploring the story of these Taiwanese boys and girls is to experience an alternative life that is remote yet intimate.

Writing *through* and *about* historical fieldnotes, this book also traces how I discern the multiple voices that shaped these texts, make sense of behavior via texts, and give new life to these old texts. Drawing from diverse methodologies and adopting a human–machine hybrid mode of text reading, I interrogate core questions of ethnography, from making sense of social encounters to producing and interpreting fieldnotes. For example, the book cover photo encapsulates the intersubjective nature of ethnography, as it captures a moment of mutual gaze between the anthropologist-photographer and his research interlocutors, in the context of children's play. I connect these reflections to children's social cognition and explore the limits and possibilities of knowing and meaning-making. Children's social world, within and beyond their familial realms, provides a fascinating window into the development of human morality, the subtleties of human relatedness, the complex processes of learning and cultural transmission, and ultimately, what it means to be human.

Acknowledgments

First and foremost, I am deeply grateful to Hill Gates for her incredible generosity and trust. She welcomed me at the Wolf ranch and gave me unique access to her late husband Arthur Wolf's precious fieldnotes. Our fun conversations have taught me a lot, not just about these materials but also about passion for knowledge. My gratitude also goes to Stevan Harrell, who introduced me to this hidden treasure of fieldnotes, helped me in each and every step of this research, and provided invaluable comments on earlier drafts of this manuscript. I am very grateful to my collaborators and research assistants who contributed to the digitization and analysis of these fieldnotes, Gladys Wang, Lu Zhou, Jose M. Hernandez, Chang Liu, Yanchen Wu, and many others. Several funding agencies supported my research, including the Chiang Ching-kuo Foundation, National Academy of Education/Spencer Foundation, Wenner-Gren Foundation, and Rockpile Foundation. Communications with Arthur Wolf's friends and students, especially Myron Cohen, Huang Chieh-Shan, John Shepherd, and Maria Duryea, shed light on several puzzles in this research. Many colleagues at the University of Washington helped me at various stages of this project, especially Patricia Ebrey, Ben Marwick, Madeleine Yue Dong, Ann Anagnost, and James Lin. When I finally visited Taiwan in September 2023, Mr. Wong Min-Liang – the son of Arthur Wolf's good friend Wang Shiqing, academic colleagues from various institutions, as well as former villagers at

Acknowledgments

Xia Xizhou – some of them participated in the original fieldwork – all welcomed me with open arms. I really appreciate their hospitality, help, and kindness.

I must extend my gratitude to my editor Michael Lambek and to Charles Stafford who introduced me to Cambridge University Press. I must also acknowledge my great intellectual debt to Pascal Boyer and James Wertsch at Washington University and Xiaojun Zhang at Tsinghua University, who always answered my questions with patience and guided me with kindness. In the past years while I was juggling between work and family and navigating a precarious academic system, lovely friends from all over the world gave me much-needed support. My very special thanks to Yang Zhan, Ming Xue, Chunyan Su, Chaoxiong Zhang, Helina Solomon-Woldekiros, Mary Wertsch, Bambi Chapin, and Lihong Shi. Finally, much love to my husband, my son, and my parents. Through them and with them I came to understand what really matters.

Notes on Transcription and Terminology

Romanization of the names of Taiwanese people in this book is done according to the Wade-Giles system, in respect of the choice made by Arthur Wolf, the original researcher whose fieldnotes this book is based on. I used pseudonyms for all research participants. Romanization of other Chinese characters, including place names, is done according to the Hanyu Pinyin system. A few exceptions, that is, local idioms, are marked by an H (Hoklo Taiwanese) in Glossary.

In terms of writing system, I used traditional Chinese characters according to the convention in the historical context of postwar Taiwan.

Throughout the book, I use the term "Chinese" in the broad sense of cultural heritage.

Abbreviations

CCP	Chinese Communist Party
CI	Child Interview
CO	Child Observation
DP	Doll Play
KMT	Kuomintang, Nationalist Party
MI	Mother Interview
MO	Mother Observation
PLA	People's Liberation Army
PRC	People's Republic of China
ROC	Republic of China, Taiwan
SCS	Six Cultures Study of Child Socialization
SI	Spontaneous Interview
SO	Situation-elicited Observation
TAT	Thematic Apperception Test

Introduction

Learning Morality in a Taiwan Village

To Divide an Orange

When we look at the apparently simple actions in children's world, we see even the most abstract concepts of human morality emerging from such concrete, seemingly trivial experiences. One example for children in the Taiwanese village Xia Xizhou, well documented in the Wolf Archive, is the scene of dividing an orange. In this impoverished community where families scrambled to feed multiple children, oranges were a pleasant treat for many youngsters. With some pocket money they got after persistent whining toward mothers or grandparents, children were excited to visit the little stores in the village to buy oranges, among other snacks. On a February evening, six-year-old girl Wang Shu-yu, an adopted daughter, offered to "help" her little sister, two-year-old Wang Shu-lan:[1]

Shu-yu walked out of her house, holding her little sister Shu-lan's hand. Shu-lan had an orange.

Shu-yu asked Shu-lan: "Let sister open the orange for you [break it up for you]." Shu-lan didn't say anything. Shu-yu took it and broke it up into six

---

[1] CO #685, 2/7/1960. Throughout this book, each episode of fieldnotes, an observation, an interview, or a projective test transcript is indexed by the initials of its data type, followed by its unique ID assigned to each episode within that data type. All unique IDs were generated in Python programming environment and therefore begin with #0. For example, "CO" refers to the data type "Child Observation."

Introduction

pieces and kept two pieces [sections] for herself. Shu-lan didn't comment. She walked over to the adults who were gambling in front of her house and watched them.

When Shu-yu finished the orange [the two pieces], she went back to Shu-lan and said: "Let me divide it for you." Shu-lan let her and Shu-yu kept one piece. Shu-yu went back over to watch the gamblers.

Shu-yu finished the orange and went back to little sister. Her little sister had only three pieces [of orange] left. Shu-yu: "Let me divide it." She took the orange from Shu-lan and Shu-lan whined and said: "No! No!"

Shu-yu broke it and kept a piece. Shu-lan whined and said: "No!"

Shu-yu: "Never mind." She stuck the piece in her mouth [anyway].

During the tedious process of transcribing fieldnotes one page after another, I burst out laughing when I noticed this episode. My eyes lit up in moments like this. Gathering clues to identify individual personalities from countless fragments of random observations, I was intrigued by this episode. Shu-yu's maneuver blurred the boundaries of the most basic moral categories, care, fairness, and reciprocity[2] on the one hand, and selfishness, dominance, and aggression on the other hand. Her successful maneuver depends on her perceptive analysis of the social situation.

Another episode of dividing an orange introduces yet more puzzles:[3]

Huang Ah-fu (six-year-old boy) and his younger brother Huang Hsin-yu (three years old) ran into the store to buy an orange. Ah-fu wanted to peel the orange and Hsin-yu wanted to do that too. Ah-fu wouldn't give it to him. Hsin-yu started to cry and ran home, saying: "I'm going to tell somebody, I'm going to tell somebody!" He ran to the corner and Ah-fu said: "I'm not going to give you any."

Hsin-yu ran back, whining: "I want to peel the skin. I want to peel the skin."

Ah-fu: "What does it matter whether you peel it or I peel it? You can't eat the skin. Do you want to eat the skin?"

---

[2] Reciprocity in the sense that Shu-yu might have thought herself entitled to getting part of the orange as fair reward for "helping" her little sister.
[3] CO #382, 12/07/1959.

Hsin-yu: "Alright, you peel half and I'll peel the other half."
Ah-fu: "Alright." Hsin-yu watched. Ah-fu peeled until there was only a little left.
Hsin-yu jumped up and down: "Let me peel that! Let me peel that!" Ah-fu gave it [the orange] to him. Hsin-yu peeled it and gave it back to Ah-fu.
Ah-fu: "Each one gets half." He was counting the sections over and over again.
Hsin-yu to Ah-fu: "Don't let Sister Chen see."
Huang Shu-feng, a boy from another family, had come up and they [all the children who were present at the store] huddled around.
Ah-fu: "Aiyo! [Oh!]" He shoved them away.
Ah-fu: "What is so much fun to look at?" They all laughed. Ah-fu slowly and carefully divided the orange in half. They walked away.

Unlike the mischievous Shu-yu, big brother Ah-fu acted in a fair manner, dividing the orange in half. We might be baffled by Hsin-yu's wining though: What is there to fight about in peeling the orange skin? Was it about fairness, whatever you do, I need to do it too ("You peel half and I'll peel the other half")? Was it also about having fun, a kind of joy that our adult minds cannot fathom? Or on the little brother's part, besides fairness and joy, there was yawning for a sense of autonomy and agency? Simple vignettes of dividing an orange point to profound mysteries of learning morality. It is unlikely that parents explicitly taught their children how they ought to divide an orange. Even if parents did so, in reality some children violated the normative prescription, or manipulated it to their own advantage. It is even more unlikely that parents had any moral instructions or opinions on peeling the orange skin.

So how do children acquire moral motivations and sensibilities? This is the primary theme of my book. The book title, *"Unruly" Children*, captures my main argument: From an adult perspective, I see disobedient children defying parental commands and not deterred by punishment. This points to the limits of parenting and socialization, the conventional framework through which we understand the project of learning morality. But shifting to the vantage point of a developing child and zooming

Introduction

into their own world, I see the opposite of "unruly": Children navigate cooperation, conflict, and the gray areas in between, creatively negotiating their own rules, with complex moral reasoning, emotions, and gendered expressions taking shape in a specific historical context. I trace how children learn morality through playing with other children, including their siblings, and highlight peer learning in moral development.

Han Chinese societies are particularly interesting places to study how children become moral persons. Moral cultivation, or *zuo ren* ("becoming human"), has long been a central concern of Chinese philosophy (Jiang 2021), at the nexus between ethical thoughts, family values, and educational traditions (Bai 2005; Cline 2015; Kinney 1995). Although the imagery of "the child" has assumed a symbolic significance in understanding Chinese morality and family, children themselves are often rendered invisible in actual studies. By bringing to light the story of these "unruly" children from the shadow of classic works in sinological anthropology,[4] this book unsettles prior assumptions about "the traditional Chinese family." For example, children's defiance and maneuvers challenge some entrenched discourses in the academy and beyond: The idea of "the innocent child" in Chinese studies and the stereotype of obedient, docile Asian children – especially girls – in Euro–American popular imagination.

The secondary theme of this book is fieldnotes, from the making of fieldnotes through ethnographic encounters with children to reconstructing an ethnography of children through making sense of historical fieldnotes. I did not have first-person fieldwork experience to orient myself. I was not present at these hilarious scenes of dividing an orange. As an ethnographer, I couldn't help but wonder about the

---

[4] See James L. Watson's explanation of this term: "'Sinological anthropology' is a term of convenience; it is generally used to designate all anthropologists who work in the field of Chinese studies" (Watson 1976: 355). Many of the foundational studies in sinological anthropology, including Watson's own research, were conducted outside mainland China.

original experience *in the field*. Six decades ago, did the observer on the spot also laugh out loud, when she saw Shu-yu "helping" her little sister to break an orange? Was the observer also baffled, in an amusing way, when she saw the little brother Hsin-yu insisting on peeling the orange skin? The person who observed these children and took notes was Arthur Wolf's research assistant, a Taiwanese teenage girl recorded as MC, who became children's trusted "Older Sister Chen" (MC is shorthand for "Miss Chen"). How did children feel about being observed during intimate moments of their social life, for example, sibling disputes?

As these vignettes show, children are acutely attuned to their social partners' behaviors and intentions. They are also keenly sensitive to what others might think of them: Hsin-yu did not want the observer MC to see what they were doing. Ah-fu shooed other children away from the scene. They might feel embarrassed. They care about reputation. These little gestures, the most human experience, prompt us to reflect on the nature of ethnographic knowledge, knowledge based on concrete social encounters and psychological inferences. Anthropology has ignored the theoretical significance of childhood learning (Blum 2019; Hirschfeld 2002). I would add that studying children can also offer methodological and epistemological insights to our discipline. We should learn *from* children. Perhaps we should also strive to learn *like* children.

These two themes intersect at children's social cognition, a broad set of mental processes and skills that enable individuals to make sense of and respond to the social world, including emotional situations. Therefore, the analytical approach of this book differs from mainstream works in anthropology and Chinese studies: Instead of centering adult social life, as in most ethnographies, I take children's developing minds as a point of departure. For the study of morality, I switched the question from learned patterns of social norms and moral values to the very process of learning. For those interested in childhood, contrary to the conventional perspective of "childrearing" in Chinese studies, which emphasizes how parents and educators shape the moral personhood of youngsters, my

Introduction

book focuses on children's active learning. Due to the unconventional nature of this book, a reanalysis of other anthropologists' fieldnotes, I can only rely on textual records, for the most part, to reconstruct children's lives. Based on ethnographic close reading, I use computational "distant reading," which has become increasingly popular across social sciences and humanities, to systematically examine these texts. I also interpret the meaning of textual patterns through the lens of children's developing social cognition. Taken together, a new look at the Wolf Archive can address three questions: The question of learning morality in childhood; the place of children in the study of Chinese culture and society; and the contributions of new methodologies to anthropological knowledge.

The Wolf Archive and Intellectual History

The Wolf Archive is a unique, unpublished set of fieldnotes that occupies a significant niche in multiple streams of intellectual history, at the intersection of anthropology and the study of Chinese and Taiwanese societies. In the 1950s and 60s, without access to mainland China, many anthropologists went to Taiwan or Hong Kong for fieldwork and used these sites as a proxy for understanding "Chinese society and culture." Arthur Wolf was among the first American anthropologists who did fieldwork in Taiwan. His first field trip to Taiwan marks a milestone in the "Golden Age" of sinological ethnography (Harrell 1999), as the works of Arthur and Margery Wolf and their students and associates made long-lasting contribution to the study of Chinese and Taiwanese kinship, family, women, gender, and religion. What became lost in this intellectual history, however, was the original intention of the Wolfs' Xia Xizhou field trip (1958–60).

In Arthur's own words, the purpose of this field research was to "add a Chinese case" to the Six Cultures Study of Socialization (SCS) (Wolf Unpublished manuscript:[5] 9). Based on comparative fieldwork in

---

[5] Hereafter "Wolf n.d."

six societies, Kenya, Okinawa, India, the Philippines, Mexico, and the United States,[6] the SCS was a landmark study in mid-twentieth century American anthropology and an unprecedented endeavor of field research on childhood in cultural contexts (LeVine 2010). Led by Beatrice and John Whiting, anthropologists at Harvard, Yale psychologist Irvin L. Child, and Cornell psychologist William W. Lambert, the SCS project focused on children between the age of three and eleven (with a total sample of 136 children from six sites). This large-scale, cross-cultural research utilized a standardized design that combined anthropological and psychological methods. It produced a series of theoretical, ethnographic, and methodological publications as well as documentaries on culture and child development.[7] A product of collaboration between anthropologists and psychologists, the SCS's legacy on psychocultural study of human development cannot be overstated (Amir and McAuliffe 2020; LeVine 2010).[8]

As an anthropology graduate student at Cornell University, Arthur Wolf became interested in psychology. Under the supervision of psychologist William Lambert and anthropologist Lauriston Sharp, Arthur started his dissertation fieldwork in Taiwan, intending to replicate and expand the SCS template. His project was the first anthropological research on Han Chinese and Taiwanese children. The research had a larger sample size and more complete data than any individual case in SCS. Yet the Wolfs never published any systematic analysis on childhood from this research. A main reason is that during the fieldwork,

---

[6] The six communities studied were the Nyansongo, a Gusii community in Kenya; the Rajputs of Khalapur, India; Taira, a village in Okinawa; the Mixtecans of Juxtlahuaca, Mexico; the Tarong in the Philippines; and New Englanders in Orchard Town in the United States (all pseudonyms).

[7] The most influential publications include B. Whiting (1983); B. Whiting, Whiting, and Longabaugh (1975); J. Whiting (1966); B. Whiting (1963); and B. Whiting and Edwards (1992).

[8] For a collection of articles on the legacy of the SCS, see a special issue in the *Journal of Cross-Cultural Psychology* (Lonner 2010).

Introduction

Arthur discovered the institution of minor marriage, *sim-pu-a*, and his interest shifted to marriage norms and incest avoidance. Besides, at a time with no personal computers, it was hard to process such a large amount of data, which also delayed the analysis. But he always appreciated the unique value of this project that these data could generate "dramatically greater systematic knowledge about Chinese childhood than we have ever had before" (A. Wolf 1982: 4).

In his final stage of life, Arthur returned to this project, started writing a book manuscript, and left behind a couple of introductory draft chapters. He reflected on how his own thinking had evolved over the decades: "Had I written in the 1960s as intended, I would have focused on testing the hypotheses formulated by the Six Cultures Study. I now pay more attention to reporting as accurately as possible the data I collected" (A. Wolf n.d.: 36). The shift in attitude is related to his experience of revisiting the fieldsite in the 1990s – which is no longer the village Xia Xizhou but part of New Taipei city. He realized that his research could never be replicated, due to drastic changes in the community (Duryea 1999).

A New Look at the Wolf Archive: Theoretical Framework

Six decades after the original fieldwork, my reanalysis of the Wolf Archive has more than "documentary historical value" (Edwards 2000: 318).[9] This book is not just about recovering disappeared childhood and obscured intellectual history. It is also an attempt by a female Chinese anthropologist to establish a dialogue with Western specialists of an earlier generation. To animate this conversation, I brought in my own intellectual vision that cuts across anthropology, psychology, and Chinese studies, drawing from new conceptual interests and empirical findings. First, trained in cognitive anthropology and developmental psychology, I examine

---

[9] Edwards (2000), entitled "Children's Play in Cross-Cultural Perspective: A New Look at the Six Cultures Study," revisited SCS data on children's play.

everyday childhood learning through the perspective of children's developing social cognition in cultural contexts. This theoretical stance differs from the SCS' behaviorist paradigm that treats the human mind as a black box. It also goes beyond the "human nature versus learning" dichotomy that framed Arthur Wolf's vision when he resumed this project later in his life. Moreover, while the SCS and Arthur Wolf set out to study childhood and childrearing in a general sense, this book puts morality as an explicit focus and in light of a naturalistic perspective.

What Is Learning? From Behaviorism to Cognitive Anthropology

The SCS project, as ambitious and significant as it is by today's standard, was motivated by a behaviorist understanding of childhood learning. The SCS theorized learning as stimulus–response processes and emphasized external reward and punishment in shaping behavior. The SCS's behaviorist hypothesis was clearly stated in its "field guide": "reward by socializing agents for behavior of any given system will increase the habit strength of behavior in that system" (J. Whiting 1966: 11). Since the 1950s, however, the study of childhood learning has undergone significant paradigm shifts, the most prominent shift being the "cognitive revolution" (Miller 2003) and the interdisciplinary study of the mind. Scientists have accumulated a vast body of knowledge about children's developing minds: Young children have a much more complex mental capacity and richer emotional life than the behaviorists once assumed, and they are not mindlessly responding to environmental stimuli. Whereas behaviorists treated the human mind as a black box, cognitive scientists today consider how the mind works as central in any meaningful understanding of learning and behavior. In the case of studying children, this means taking cognitive development seriously. This especially matters for understanding social learning – learning from interacting with other people (Gweon 2021) as well as the transmission of human culture (Hirschfeld 2002; Tomasello 2016).

Introduction

Arthur Wolf's own understanding of child development evolved, reflecting his ambivalent attitude toward the SCS theoretical paradigm: At the beginning, he intended to test the SCS hypotheses. The decades he spent studying incest avoidance and proving the Westermarck hypothesis[10] (A. Wolf 1995, 2014) changed what he wanted to know about children. As he recounted in his draft manuscript, he was still interested in explaining children's behavior, but his interest had drifted away from the earlier behaviorist paradigm and toward a nativist view: "It [my interest] simply shifted from what people learn to what they are born knowing. I now take more seriously than I once did the possibility that behavior is not very malleable. It might be that while human-beings learn quickly they do not modify their behavior as a result" (A. Wolf n.d.: 28–29). Without taking into consideration how the child's mind works (which is similar to the SCS framework), here my predecessor resorted to the strict dichotomy of learned versus inborn knowledge. In contrast, many cognitive anthropologists today have come to view this as ultimately a false dichotomy (Boyer 2018).[11]

I find the cognitive neuroscientist Stanislas Dehaene's book, entitled *How We Learn: Why Brains Learn Better than Any Machine … for Now*, helpful for understanding the basic concepts of nature and learning: "Pure learning, in the absence of any innate constraints, simply does not exist. Any learning algorithm contains, in one way or another, a set of assumptions about the domain to be learned" (Dehaene 2020: 24–25). Dehaene's definition of learning applies to multiple levels of empirical reality: "In cognitive science, we say that learning consists of forming an internal model of the world. Through learning, the raw data that strikes

---

[10] The Finnish anthropologist Edward Westermarck (1894, 1921) posited, in *The History of Human Marriage*, that siblings who have close physical proximity during childhood are expected to experience sexual indifference toward one another.

[11] The debate on innate and acquired characteristics of biological organisms has a long and complicated history; for a review, see Griffiths and Linquist (2022).

our sense turns into refined ideas, abstract enough to be reused in a new context – smaller-scale models of reality" (2020: 3).

The opening vignettes of dividing an orange, for example, allude to several internal models of the social world, models that have moral significance and can motivate behavior: Models about ownership, for example, in the first vignette, the orange belonged to the little sister, about fairness in resource distribution and exchange, for example, in the second vignette, the two brothers ought to divide the orange equally, and even about dominance, for example, in the first vignette, the older sister clearly exploited the little one, perhaps because she was older. Different internal models can cohere or stand in contradiction. Learning means that children not only construct these models, but also weigh and evaluate different models according to the concrete situation. Taking advantage of a younger sibling might override a sense of respect for ownership, if the older sibling predicted that she could get what she wanted. Learning also means that children constantly update these internal models of the social world, based on their prior experience, and alter their predictions about others' behavior: Next time the little girl might not be easily tricked by her older sister's seemingly altruistic offer.

This idea of "forming internal models" is related to but different from the concept of "cultural models" that has been discussed extensively in American cognitive anthropology during the earlier decades.[12] According to the classic definition, "A cultural model is a cognitive schema that is intersubjectively shared by a social group" (D'Andrade 1987: 112).

---

[12] "Cultural Models Theory" (CMT) includes a cluster of theories concerning the relationship between cultural knowledge, language, and mind. It was systematically developed in the 1980s (D'Andrade 1981; Strauss and Quinn 1997; Holland and Quinn 1987). Cognitive anthropologists are reviving this theoretical tradition today (de Munck and Bennardo 2019). But as Claudia Strauss (Forthcoming) points out, compared to classic definitions of cultural models as shared cognitive schemas, recent formulations of CMT (Bennardo and Munck 2020) lack conceptual clarity, that is, including too broad sets of cultural knowledge, such as cultural themes that are not mentally represented in interconnected associative networks.

Introduction

For one thing, proponents of cultural models theory (CMT) tend to follow the dichotomous view of nature versus learning and understand cultural models as "learned." In contrast, some "internal models" in the dividing-an-orange scenario, for example, notions of fairness, are likely constrained by innate predispositions. Moreover, forming internal models does not mean that children simply "absorb" or "internalize" cultural knowledge. While some CMT theorists do emphasize the importance of childhood learning, they tend to simplify the process of learning and reduce it to "socialization" or "internalization." My research challenges this framework and draws attention to the complex psychology that underpins how children actually learn and negotiate cultural models (Xu Forthcoming). In the Taiwanese historical context, certain cultural models of social hierarchy and kinship, for example, girls yielding to boys, older children yielding to younger ones – especially for siblings, might feed into children's evolving internal models of how to divide an orange. But an important part of learning morality is active evaluation and judgment as to whether one should conform to these cultural norms or not. This often requires paying attention to a variety of situational factors, such as authority's presence or absence, personal relationships, and previous social interaction histories. Among these complex inferences and calculations, some might require deliberate effort while other processes might operate automatically without one's awareness. To better understand the process of learning, that is, "forming internal models," I advocate a cognitive anthropology approach that engages with latest psychological research and takes seriously how the mind works.

Childhood Learning in Cultural Contexts: A Reviving Interdisciplinary Program

Within the past decade or so, new conversations between anthropology – mostly evolutionary anthropology – and psychology brought forth a revived interest in studying child development in cultural context. A recent article (Barrett 2020), *Towards a Cognitive Science of the Human: Cross-Cultural Approaches and Their Urgency,* identified "children" as the most common title word across all empirical cross-cultural studies since 2010 (a sample of 249 papers). This new wave of research is partly a response to the persistent sampling bias in cognitive science – populations predominantly from WEIRD (Western, Educated, Industrialized, Rich, Democratic) societies (Henrich, Heine, and Norenzayan 2010). It is also an effort to examine the universal and variable aspects of human cognition, as well as the mechanisms that guide the interaction between the two. Note that cognitive anthropologists have cautioned against a mechanistic dichotomy of "universal versus variable" in the study of culture as well as the conceptualization of "WEIRD" societies (Astuti and Bloch 2010). But we need increased participation from sociocultural anthropologists to further this critical conversation.

These new studies value the SCS's enduring legacies on interdisciplinary collaboration, cross-cultural comparison, and field research (Amir and McAuliffe 2020). But compared to mid-twentieth century, we have made substantial progress. The most exciting progress is occurring in the domain of social cognition, especially in identifying human children's extraordinary, universal capacity to learn from others (social learning) and to acquire and transmit culture (cultural learning), which supports the highly variable behavioral and cultural repertoires (see Barrett 2020 for a review). Taking advantage of new theories and findings on cognitive development, and using sophisticated methods across cultures, researchers have established a more nuanced and accurate understanding of the relationship between mind and culture. These psychological foundations have significant implications for understanding how we organize societies and cultures, yet so far sociocultural anthropologists have rarely engaged with this line of interdisciplinary study. My work addresses this problem through examining children's moral development, one of the most important topics in this new research program.

Introduction

Mind, Culture, and Moral Development: The Missing Child in Sociocultural Anthropology

My reanalysis pursues a key question that the Wolfs never asked, that is, how children become moral persons. This conceptual focus is shaped by booming new interest in morality across anthropology and psychology. My research facilitates critical conversations between sociocultural anthropology, a field in which research on childhood learning is marginalized (Hirschfeld 2002), and the increasingly synergetic constellation of psychology and evolutionary anthropology, a research program that takes children more seriously. My work aims to, metaphorically, rescue "the missing child" in sociocultural anthropology.

According to classic moral development theories (Piaget [1932] 1997; Kohlberg 1984), a sense of morality does not emerge until after early childhood. But recent research has established a new consensus that young children have more complex moral cognition and emotions than previously assumed (Turiel 2018). Psychologists have found that various foundations of morality, such as empathy, fairness, care and harm, and coalitional sentiments, emerge early on, even in infancy (Lucca, Hamlin, and Sommerville 2019; Woo, Tan, and Hamlin 2022). Thanks to collaboration with evolutionary anthropology, recent cross-cultural comparative experiments have identified universal and culturally diverse aspects of children's prosocial development, for example, acquiring a sense of fairness in resource distribution (Blake et al. 2015) and learning cooperative norms (House et al. 2020).

In the past few decades, sociocultural anthropology has also witnessed a flourishing interest in morality and ethics, and has made it into an explicit theoretical focus.[13] In this new scholarship, anthropologists have either elaborated their critique of psychological studies of morality or included conversations with psychologists in general reviews of

---

[13] For reviews of the field or comprehensive edited volumes, see Lambek (2010a); Fassin (2012); Laidlaw (2017, 2023); and Mattingly and Throop (2018).

A New Look at the Wolf Archive

the anthropology of morality and ethics (Fassin 2012; Laidlaw 2023). Anthropological and psychological approaches to morality have their respective limits: Psychologists tend to prioritize western-centered concepts and samples, without addressing the rich diversity of human moral experience. They are also prone to micro-level explanations that can hardly account for the complexity of human action in context or processes of social change. Many anthropologists, on the other hand, despite an explicit attempt to go beyond a Durkheimian framework that conflates "moral" with "social" (Yan 2011), still commit to the Durkheimian paradigm of disregarding human psychology when explaining behavior.

My work emphasizes the perspective of child development and learning that is rarely addressed in the new anthropology of morality and ethics. Sociocultural anthropologists' bias against studying childhood learning is closely related to the field's entrenched antipathy toward psychology and psychological explanations of human behavior.[14] Due to such persistent biases, mainstream anthropological accounts of learning are psychologically implausible: "How people actually learn (as opposed to how societies organize learning) is scarcely understood by anthropologists" (Stafford 1995: 11). Sociocultural anthropologists have largely approached children as "passive assimilators" who simply "absorb whatever testimony the environment throws at them" (Astuti 2017). Such a simplified view of learning, like the analogy of a sponge absorbing water, reflects outdated assumptions: The child's mind is a black box and "mind internal" processes are irrelevant, or the child's mind is a blank slate, with no initial guidance or constraints on learning. If we start from these assumptions, we have flattened, obscured, or even erased the complexity of children's mental life.

That is why, as cognitive anthropologist Charles Stafford (2013: 21) points out, "psychologists and anthropologists clearly have a great deal to learn from each other when it comes to the study of child development

---

[14] Quinn (2005); Quinn and Strauss (2006); and Stafford (2020).

Introduction

in general and children's moral/ethical development in particular." By studying children, we can begin to appreciate the full complexity of learning, the basis through which human morality is established and negotiated. This is not to say that a sociocultural anthropology perspective is not valuable or that we should blindly follow psychologists. In fact, through studying children, we can bring deep cultural knowledge to challenge Western moral psychology concepts, such as popular constructs of individualism versus collectivism and autonomy versus conformity. We can provide ethnographic insights on children's spontaneous social life and address macro-level factors and processes such as social change and transformations of moral values.[15] Along these lines, my book does more than present an ethnographic account on Taiwanese children, as opposed to laboratory studies of predominantly Western children. It goes beyond the focus on prosocial behavior in recent psychological literature to also delve into the dark side of moral experience, that is, dominance, punishment, and violence. It explores the intertwinement of cooperation and conflict in children's everyday life, that is, the gray area of teasing, and illuminates the inherently messy dimensions of moral life. Lastly, as part of what the anthropology of morality and ethics has emphasized, this book highlights the ethical action of fieldwork experience itself (Lambek 2010b), but with a special reference to children as our interlocutors and in light of children's socio-moral cognition – "cognition" as a general term that also encompasses emotional and motivational processes. Reanalysis of the Wolf Archive provides a unique opportunity to inject reflections on the intersubjective nature of field research, ethnography and knowledge production more broadly. These kind of reflections are still lacking in cross-cultural studies of child development (Broesch et al. 2020).

---

[15] My own work brought a sociocultural anthropology voice into these conversations with psychologists (Chapin and Xu Forthcoming; Xu 2014, 2017, 2019, 2020a, 2022a).

Learning Morality ... Like a Child: A Naturalistic Approach

Synthesizing these interdisciplinary conversations on morality, I adopt a naturalistic view that has become increasingly visible in anthropology, cognitive science, and philosophy:[16] The capacity to learn morality is a defining feature of humanity because humans evolved as a cooperative species. In other words, human children are born to learn morality. An important open question concerns *how* children acquire morality: Some researchers advocate that morality is based on an innate "moral core," rather than active learning (Woo, Tan, and Hamlin 2022); others emphasize the role of domain-general learning mechanisms in acquiring morality (Railton 2017).[17] But many researchers on both sides share a common assumption, that is, a strict dichotomy of nature versus learning, or what is biologically prepared versus what is "learned." I use quotation marks for "learned" because my theoretical starting point is to reject this dichotomous framework.

I envision the relationship between nature and learning as mutually constitutive: Learning morality is simultaneously universalistic and pluralistic. Moral development "is originated in our species' natural history of cooperation and coordination and actualized in our holistic social history" (Xu 2019: 657). Besides the evolutionary roots of human morality, there is a universalistic dimension to learning morality because cultivating morality and raising children as socially valued members is a basic goal across all societies. The pluralistic nature of learning morality manifests at various levels: From a cultural perspective, understandings of moral learning, the desirable moral values, socialization strategies, and

---

[16] For example, Tomasello (2019); Curry, Mullins, and Whitehouse (2019); Boyer (2018); and Wong (2023).

[17] The nativism–empiricism debate on the origins of morality includes a variety of theoretical stances together forming a full spectrum. For example, the journal *Cognition* published a special issue on "moral learning" (Cushman, Kumar, and Railton 2017), a collection of papers that introduce diverse viewpoints regarding the types of learning mechanisms and the respective roles of innate constraints.

Introduction

social agents vary across diverse communities (Fung and Smith 2010). From a cognitive perspective, children's moral intuitions are underpinned by multiple mechanisms of social cognition, motivated by solving different types of problems and/or regulating different sets of social relations. From a normative perspective, due to the inherent complexity of human cooperation and diversity of basic moral intuitions, there is no "single true or most justified morality" (Wong 2023) that is not context dependent. To be human, even for young children, is to learn how to deal with conflicts or contradictions between different moral concerns.

At a time when artificial intelligence (AI) is captivating popular imagination and stirring up controversy, writing this book in the IT hub Seattle, I find it helpful to compare human children to AI, in this naturalistic framework. At the moment of writing this chapter, ChatGPT frenzy is sweeping the world. Machine-learning power seems to overshadow human learning. Artificial intelligence appears far superior to human intelligence in many respects. Computer scientists are so ambitious that they are training AI systems to learn human morality (Metz 2021). However, cognitive scientists remind us that it is human children who hold the real key to deciphering the mystery of learning and intelligence (Gopnik 2022). I am intrigued by what is so special about human children. Like an ethnographer chatting with her interlocutor, I asked ChatGPT what it thought of itself in comparison to human children:

To my question "who is better at learning, ChatGPT or a human child?" ChatGPT did not give a definitive answer, but it did point out some crucial differences: ChatGPT was trained on a large amount of data, what is called "training data" in the field of machine learning, but it may lack the ability to understand emotions and social cues that are crucial for human interaction and communication.[18] When I further

---

[18] ChatGPT March 6, 2023 entry, via https://chat.openai.com/chat. A recent study (Kosinski 2023) suggests that the newest version of ChatGPT might possess some capacities of Theory of Mind (ToM), but to what extent it is truly humanlike ToM is still debatable.

specified my question, asking "Who is better at learning morality, AI or a human child?" ChatGPT returned several paragraphs of overlapping, sometimes repetitive answers, which I summarized as follows:[19]

Morality is a complex and multifaceted concept that involves a wide range of cognitive and emotional processes. ... While AI systems can be programmed to follow moral rules and principles, they lack the ability to understand the nuances of moral decision-making and the importance of context and personal experience. In addition, AI systems do not possess the same level of empathy and emotional intelligence as human children, which are essential for moral reasoning and moral decision-making. ... Human children have the capacity to develop a deep understanding of moral values and principles through socialization, moral reasoning, and moral emotions such as empathy, guilt, and shame. They can learn from a variety of sources, including parents, teachers, peers, and their environment, and their moral development is influenced by a range of factors, including culture, religion, and personal experiences.

This fairly reasonable answer highlights the complexity of learning morality. Artificial intelligence systems are not well designed, at least so far, to learn human morality. But for human children, this task seems intuitive and much easier. The child's mind is not a blank slate. Children's moral acquisition, which starts very young, requires limited input (Ayars and Nichols 2017). This stands in stark contrast to the "big data" approach in AI systems. At least in the domain of morality, children's "learning algorithms" must be superior to prevalent AI architecture, shaped by our species' natural history. Cognitive scientists have made substantial progress in tracing the developmental emergence of moral knowledge. But a great deal of learning morality remains a mystery, for example, how exactly it unfolds in real life, due to the scarcity of systematic ethnographic studies. The Wolf Archive can shed precious light into this mystery.

---

[19] ChatGPT March 6, 2023 entry, via https://chat.openai.com/chat.

Introduction

The Invisible Child in "The Chinese Family"

My reanalysis of the Wolf Archive is not only motivated by renewed conversations between anthropology and psychology. It also aims to address popular biases in Chinese studies from a new angle, concerning the place of children. The imagery of "the child" has assumed a significant and evolving role in Han Chinese culture, due to its importance in various branches of philosophical thoughts (Hsiung 2005: xi), its place in cosmological order (Topley 1974), and its connection to educational desire and political governance (Bakken 2000; Kipnis 2011). "The child," family, and morality are closely intertwined, a tradition that dates back to early China (Cline 2015): Family values are an integral part of moral order (Jiang 2021), family relations constitute an important space to cultivate morality (Kinney 1995), and childhood is a critical phase in the lifelong project of moral cultivation – the ultimate goal of education (Li 2012).

However, despite such symbolic significance, the experience of children – children as agents with a rich inner world, not passive objects of representation, recollection, and moral discourse – remains largely invisible in sinological anthropology. This is true even in a key domain, the study of Han Chinese family and kinship.[20] From the formative time of this subfield, when the Wolfs' works helped establish the parameters for studying the traditional Han Chinese family, to the present era when family life has undergone complex transformations, children exist merely in the shadow of parent–child ties or childrearing ideologies.

Based on their Xia Xizhou fieldwork, Margery Wolf pointed out the lack of systematic study of childrearing at a time of a growing interest

---

[20] The anthropological literature on the Chinese family system is incredibly rich. As a part of kinship studies, it was a foundational theme in sinological anthropology (G. D. Santos 2006). The early work was mainly influenced by the British social anthropology paradigm, especially Maurice Freedman's lineage model, and also informed by conversations with sinologists. For a review of early work, see Ebrey and Watson (1986). For recent developments in the field, see Brandtstädter and Santos (2011); G. Santos and Harrell (2016); and Yan (2021).

The Invisible Child in "The Chinese Family"

in "the Chinese family"[21] among Euro–American anthropologists: "The Chinese family has been examined in many contexts – from its place in the economy to its role in ancestor worship. Only in passing has it been considered in terms of the family's basic function: the training of future adult members" (M. Wolf 1978: 224). But even in this seminal paper entitled "Child Training and the Chinese Family," her central focus was childrearing, whereas children are mere objects of training: Children get deterred, conditioned, and molded by adults' discipline. This "child-training" paradigm has dominated anthropological and psychocultural research on Chinese childhood for a long time (for a critical review, see Xu Forthcoming; Xu 2017: 149–53). The paradigm prioritizes vertical, parent–child ties in family relation and highlights Chinese family values such as filial piety, obedience, and parenting strategies such as shaming[22] and punishment. It aligns with long-lasting ideas about Chinese family and childhood, especially the emphasis on moral ideologies and adult teaching, nurturing, and transforming (*jiao hua*) in learning, although such ideas mostly derived from representations of elite families. Limited historical records of Chinese children's life, especially those from nonelite, working-class families, could partly explain why young children remain "the most blatant, intellectually innocent, and professionally overlooked among the unrepresented" in historiography (Hsiung 2005: 261). The invisibility of children's experience in earlier sinological ethnography, however, did not stem from lacking access to children's life. Instead, when anthropologists of the Wolfs' generation conducted village ethnographies, children were "roaming

---

[21] I use quotation marks for "the Chinese family" because the studies of culturally Chinese families have created an influential discourse in the body of sinological anthropology literature: Many foundational works in this field looked at Taiwan, Hong Kong, and elsewhere to study "the Chinese society" because anthropologists could not enter the PRC for fieldwork.

[22] Shaming is an enduring socialization technique in Chinese child socialization, as research in different time periods and regions demonstrates (Fung 1999; Xu 2017: 179–80).

Introduction

around, playing everywhere and anywhere" (Diamond 1969: 34).[23] But anthropologists have looked past children. The problem reflects a persistent behaviorist influence since the SCS project and the mainstream assumption in sociocultural anthropology, of children passively "assimilating" culture.

At that Golden Age of sinological ethnography, the "assimilating culture" assumption worked hand in hand with "the synchronic bias" that motivated ethnographic research in Taiwan (Harrell 1999): Many anthropologists, like the Wolfs, were looking past Taiwan to search for and recover "traditional Chinese society" (pre-1895, before the Japanese rule). They saw parents and the kinship community as the guardian of Chinese traditions, and they ignored schooling or other aspects of children's life that might have introduced different thoughts from parents' beliefs. That is why, in his draft manuscript, Wolf asserted this conviction (n.d.: 37): "while [Xia Xizhou] had already undergone substantial change by 1958, family life was not radically different than what it had been when the Japanese occupied Taiwan in 1895. What I recorded is therefore the closest we will ever come to a detailed account of children's lives in late traditional [imperial] China."

The "synchronic bias" on Chinese society and culture has largely disappeared in anthropology today, and social change has become the focus in our field, especially changes in family life[24] and moral values.[25] But this "assimilation" assumption about children still persists.

---

[23] In a recent interview, anthropologist James Watson said: "[I]f I look at the photographs from our research in the New Territories over the long term, they are littered with children, kids, everywhere. Every ritual, every family shot, there are waves of kids. If you look at the photos we have of village events, there are rafts of children of every age. Every family had multiple kids. And there are kids managing kids. 10 year old girls carrying their brothers around, all day long" (J. L. Watson, R. Watson, and Yan 2019).

[24] See recent edited volumes: Brandtstädter and Santos (2011); G. Santos and Harrell (2016); and Yan et al. (2021).

[25] Ethnographies on Chinese society have become a vital part of the new anthropology of morality and ethics (see a brief review in Laidlaw 2017).

Together with the entrenched idea of the "innocent child" in Chinese thought (Bai 2005; Kinney 2004; Xu 2020a), a simplistic view of human nature,[26] naïve assumptions about childhood learning have likely contributed to the paucity of research on child development in recent anthropological studies of Chinese family and morality (for a critique, see Stafford 2013).[27]

The Wolf Archive preserves systematic, ethnographic record of a historical world that no longer exists. It portrays the life of over 200 young children in a patrilineal village with an entrenched son preference, at a particular historical point in Taiwan, before massive transformations of family values took place in this patriarchal society: peak fertility, a hybrid school system built under Japanese colonial rule but incorporated into the Chinese authoritarian system, and on the verge of rapid economic growth and industrialization. My reanalysis brings "the invisible child" into the center stage to understand the socio-moral life of the so-called "traditional Chinese family." In contrast to the "child-training" paradigm in sinological anthropology that prioritizes parenting, my work centers on children's experience and highlights the role of peer interactions. I challenge popular discourses about children and childrearing, that is, obedience, passivity, and the "innocent child," to examine children's actual behaviors and thoughts that are far more complex and multifaceted than any childrearing precepts can encompass. To redress the "synchronic bias" underlying the Wolfs' works, I demonstrate how children's moral sensibilities about authority, punishment, and violence are influenced by schooling, policing, and gangsters in the historical context of Taiwan's Martial Law Era.

---

[26] The philosophical phrase, *ming ming de* (literally, "bringing the brilliant virtue to light"), is a pithy expression of Chinese thought that emphasizes the inborn goodness. This phrase is from a neo-Confucian classic, *da xue*, "The Great Learning." Some translated the phrase as "manifesting one's bright virtue," see www.acmuller.net/con-dao/greatlearning.html.

[27] My own work (Xu 2017) was among the few that focused on child development, but it focused on urban middle-class children.

Introduction

Rereading Fieldnotes with a New Methodology

The Wolf Archive is unprecedented. Ethnographic analyses on Chinese and Taiwanese childhood before and at his time were rare enough and mostly based on anecdotal reflections.[28] The systematicity and richness of this archive, with its sheer volume and its interdisciplinary methods, also set up a standard that is hard to reach for ethnographers today. To honor Arthur Wolf's legacy of studying human behavior with scientific rigor, I took advantage of new computational methods and technological tools today to reanalyze this archive. Anchored in ethnographic "close reading" of texts, the book ventures into new territory by integrating results from computational "distant reading," including NLP (natural-language-processing) methods, social network analysis, and fine-grained behavioral coding. Extending my effort to advocate methodological pluralism in anthropology (Xu 2019), this new approach of text reading also reaffirms the inherently humanistic nature of ethnography. The humanistic nature manifests in the intersubjective experience that made the texts (fieldnotes) possible, in the human expertise essential for constructing and interpreting "machine-reading" patterns and numbers, and in the layers of human biases in knowledge production.

An Extraordinary Archive

When Arthur Wolf first arrived at Xia Xizhou in 1958, the village was home to more than 600 people, including over 200 young children (ages below twelve). Most villagers descended from southern Fujian Chinese migrants who had settled in the area during the eighteenth and nineteenth centuries. The majority of villagers were connected through kinship ties. The village also included some recent immigrants, one new

---

[28] Mostly anecdotal ethnographic reflections, for example, Ward (1985): 173–200; and Skinner (2017): 74–76.

family from Jinmen (Quemoy) and a couple of mainlanders' (*waishengren*) households. In terms of economic prospects, most families were still poor by Taiwan's standards at that time, with a mixture of farming and factory work income. From this ordinary site, the Wolf's team collected extraordinary records, the most systematic archive of Chinese and Taiwanese children's everyday life. My reanalysis focused on the following types of data:[29]

(1) Naturalistic observations of children's social interactions at home, inside the village, and at the elementary school outside the village, consisting of three types: Spontaneous Child Observation (CO) includes 1,678 episodes of timed observations, average 250 words, and 2.5 minutes per episode); and situation-elicited observation (SO) includes 173 episodes of children's interactions in focal situations (not timed, average ninety-five words per episode).[30] Both types of observations, following the SCS field guide, were supposed to focus on a focal group of children (ages 3–11), but with a much larger sample ($n = 64$) than the individual site in the SCS ($n = 24$). In addition to these two, Wolf added a new method beyond the SCS guide, Mother Observation (MO, 160), 160 episodes of mother–child interactions interspersed with researcher–mother dialogue (MO).

(2) Interviews with children and mothers: Child interview (CI, seventy-nine children) about hypothetical scenarios of social interactions; mother interview (MI, forty-three mothers) about their child-rearing beliefs and practices. These two interviews used standardized protocols from the SCS. In addition, there is a collection of

---

[29] The book also uses a few episodes from fieldnotes indexed by letter G ("general"), as they are mentioned in the Wolfs' previous publications. These "G" data are general observations of the village life focused on adults. They are still in Wolf's private library, but I did not scan them or analyze them as part of this project.

[30] According to Wolf's draft manuscript (n.d.: 14), his team had recorded over 2,000 SO episodes, but I did not see that many SO fieldnotes when I visited the Wolf library.

Introduction

nonstandardized, spontaneous interviews (SI) with children and mothers, eighty-three episodes in total.

(3) Projective tests adapted to local context, to elicit children's spontaneous storytelling: One is the Thematic Apperception Test (TAT, ninety-two children), with a set of nine pictures portraying ambiguous social interactions; the other is Doll Play (DP, forty-six children), with a set of dolls representing family figures. Wolf designed these new stimuli distinct from the SCS project.

(4) Demographic and household information for all community residents. Each individual was assigned a unique number by Wolfs' team, a participant's ID. In each episode of fieldnote, individual names were replaced by these IDs, and these IDs are consistent across all fieldnotes. In addition to participant IDs, each episode of fieldnotes is also indexed by the event information (date, time, and location).

Arthur Wolf's capable research assistants made great contribution to such efficient data collection within two years of fieldwork. Under Wolf's supervision, two Taiwanese research assistants, MC and MS, collected the bulk of observational and interview data. In their late adolescence, these two women lived with the Wolfs, spoke Hokkien, and became children's trusted friends. Seen as "Older Sister Chen" by children and a confidant of village mothers, MC's role was especially crucial, which I will discuss in more detail in Chapter 1. She collected most of the timed COs, a core part of this archive. Given MC's good relations with children's mothers, Wolf designed a new task for her, to conduct MO, and he was quite pleased to see that mothers' words (in MI) largely matched their behaviors (in MO), thanks to MC's excellent work as an ethnographer. Margery Wolf served the role of "administer and scribe" (M. Wolf 1990a: 344), typing observations and interviews up into fieldnotes. These English texts constitute the bulk of the Wolf Archive. A male research assistant Mr. Huang Chieh-Shan, at that time a college

Rereading Fieldnotes with a New Methodology

student from the nearby town Shulin, worked with Arthur Wolf from 1959 to 1960 on weekends and during the summer.[31] He was in charge of the two projective tests, Doll Play and TAT, and these transcripts were the only Chinese documents preserved in the archive.

Transcription and Coding

The demand of processing this massive data archive at a time of limited computing capacity was one reason Arthur Wolf delayed his analysis. That is also why Margery Wolf's work on women and childrearing used only a tiny portion of these data, presented sporadically (1972, 1978). My team digitized all the above types of fieldnotes using OCR software and built a database through the Python programming language to organize the notes. This database allows for flexibly referencing across and linking different types of fieldnotes, that is, indexing by person ID, fieldnote ID,[32] fieldnote type (see List of Abbreviations), and fieldnote date.

My reanalysis of this archive respects the SCS/Wolf mixed-methods approach but also explores new ground. Although I integrate different types of fieldnotes to write this book, I approach CO, timed observations of children's interactions, as the core basis. Such systematic, naturalistic observation remains the SCS's most enduring legacy (LeVine 2010: 520). The data collection approach of Wolf's research assistants made the CO in his archive even richer and rarer. According to the SCS field guide, CO should focus on a predefined set of social situations and the target child in a selected sample. Wolf's RAs reported "everything the subject [target child] did and said and most of what the other people present did

---

[31] According to my phone interview with Mr. Huang in May 2021, Mr. Huang later became an important collaborator in Wolf's famous "Taiwanese household registers" project and the coauthor of the book *Marriage and Adoption in China, 1845–1945*.

[32] Under a given type of fieldnotes, each entry was assigned a unique ID in Python environment, starting from #0.

Introduction

and said" the moment they saw the target child without waiting for a specific situation to occur (Wolf n.d.: 13). Also, while the SCS field guide designed CO as "short excerpts of behavior rather than extended interaction sequences," Wolf's RAs did much better than that, by violating the instructions and recording extended behavioral sequences faithfully (Wolf n.d.: 13). Therefore, in contrast to situation-elicited short observations and standardized interviews based on a set of a priori themes, the content of CO, children's spontaneous social life, recorded in striking detail, lends itself to examining new themes and developing new conceptual interests.

Wolf's analysis of CO[33] followed the original SCS protocol, which focused on these behavioral domains: succorance, nurturance, responsibility, self-reliance, achievement, obedience, dominance, and sociability. It used a behaviorist "antecedent–consequent" coding scheme and focused on the target sample of sixty-four children (3–11 years) (J. Whiting 1966). I broadened the analytical scope and coded all children's (0–11 years) behavior recorded in CO, as every episode included behavioral details of all the present people, rather than merely focused on a particular target child. I also designed a new behavioral grading system that includes over thirty behaviors in everyday cooperation and conflict. Some of these categories are similar to the SCS themes, but I took into account behavioral intention, for example, distinguishing "leading," a cooperative act, from "dominating," a coercive act, and "playful teasing," a cooperative act, from "aggressive teasing." For each behavior between a specific pair of people in a given episode, I coded the behavioral theme, people's IDs, and their respective role (initiator or recipient). I assigned a score according to a binary (0.5 and 1) or tripartite (0, 0.5, and 1) grading standard that evaluates behavioral intensity.[34]

---

[33] He explained this protocol in his draft introductory chapter (n.d.: 35), but he did not get a chance to write up the actual analysis and result.

[34] A majority of themes were graded according to a binary system, for example, dominating: A score of "0.5" means mild dominating, a score of "1" means severe

I developed this system through the convergence of deductive, top-down and inductive, bottom-up qualitative coding processes: I combined well-established concepts in current scholarship, for example, typical prosocial behaviors such as resource sharing, helping, and comforting (Dunfield 2014) and salient topics in the corpus and local context, for example, tattling, sibling care, and "dirty looks." I identified over 12,000 behavioral interactions among more than 200 children in CO episodes. Such granular-level behavioral coding provided the foundation for quantitative analysis of each behavior and for comparing or aggregating different behaviors. It also facilitated triangulation with demographic and other data, for example, comparing actual behavior with children's answers to interviews and constructing a personality database for all the children. The book focuses on a subset of all behaviors I coded from CO. Statistical analyses of these behavioral and demographic data were run in R programming language.

I also approached projective tests differently from my predecessors, making what I consider better use of those data. First of all, Wolf adapted the projective tests to suit the local context, so these tests yielded more and better data than what the SCS produced. General projective tests at that time, invented in Western psychology, were designed to elicit fantasy and assess personalities, and were used by anthropologists when the "Culture and Personality School" was still popular.[35] But Wolf hired local artists to design culturally appropriate prompts that the child participants would find more familiar: They used a series of nine drawings for TAT, each drawing a sketch of children interacting with other children

or repeated dominating. A few themes that have a reactive dimension were graded according to a tripartite system, for example, sharing: A score of "0" means no sharing despite being asked to, a score of "0.5" means mild sharing or sharing with some hesitation, and a score of "1" means generous or repeated sharing.

[35] For a historical account, see Lemov (2011). The movement certainly influenced sinological anthropologists at that time: For example, G. W. Skinner brought projective tests to his fieldwork in Sichuan as part of the plan to study Chinese social personality but had no opportunity to use them (Skinner 2017: vii).

Introduction

and/or adults; for DP, they used a set of eight dolls representing family figures in a farmhouse setting.[36] But Wolf's team did not translate TAT and DP transcripts into English and did not consider these data very important, because he thought these materials were too realistic, reflecting children's actual life instead of disclosing their fantasies. However, I found children's narratives fascinating, illuminating their rich emotional and moral experience and imaginations. I coded these transcripts based on a few themes, such as child fighting, sibling conflict, family relations, authority, and punishment. These story-telling data provide a rare opportunity to see the local world through children's eyes.

NLP and Social Network Analysis

I used natural-language-processing (NLP) methods, especially computational and machine-learning approaches to textual data, and social network analysis (SNA), which studies patterns of relationships between individuals through a network approach, to analyze CO.[37] This section provides an overview of these methods and the detailed procedures and content will appear in individual chapters. In NLP framework,[38] my team treated one entry of fieldnote, an observational episode, as one document and the entire CO texts as a corpus. We transformed the CO corpus into "clean" texts after common preprocessing steps.[39] I then explored patterns of common words and their clusters, through word

---

[36] The Wolf Archive preserved an incomplete copy of the TAT stimuli, with four out of nine drawings missing. None of the dolls were preserved.

[37] All the NLP analyses were performed in Python environment. Social Network Analyses were performed in a mixture of Python and R environment.

[38] For more details on how to apply NLP methods in social science research, consult Grimmer, Roberts, and Stewart (2022).

[39] These "preprocessing" steps include transforming all words to lowercase; removing punctuation, numbers, and special symbols; excluding common stopwords such as "the," "a," and "an"; and reducing a word to its lemma form. "Lemmatizing" a corpus means grouping together inflected forms of a word as a single item, for example, replacing "gone," "goes," and "went" with "go."

frequency and word co-occurrence analyses. Going beyond such surface features, I used topic modeling, a popular form of unsupervised machine-learning technique, to explore latent topics and their patterns of distribution in the corpus (see Appendix). In collaboration with a data scientist, I also used BERT (Bidirectional Encoder Representations from Transformers), a type of large language models (LLM) developed by Google and based on deep learning methods, to quantify this corpus according to the topics I was interested in. In addition to NLP methods, I conducted two types of social network analysis on CO data, treating each person as a node and defining a certain connection between two persons (nodes) as an edge: The simpler one is co-occurrence network, based on which people were present in a given observation as well as demographic information. The more complex one is behavioral network that integrated behavioral coding results – theme, score, people, and direction (initiator and recipient) – with demographic data.

I used this human–machine hybrid approach for multiple purposes:

(1) Conceptual insights: Computational analysis guided by my human expertise revealed systematic patterns of children's social life that would have been difficult to detect through the human eye, for example, peer social network structures, demographic influence on behavior, and latent topics in the texts.
(2) Epistemological reflections: Comparing machine versus human intelligence, I found that the limits of computer algorithms illustrate the subtlety and complexity of children's moral psychology, inspiring me to reflect on the nature of ethnographic knowledge.
(3) Methodological dialogues: Social network analysis is increasingly popular in child development research (Neal 2020), but these fieldnotes provide rare, naturalistic materials in a non-Western, historical context to analyze children's networks and interpret them in light of ethnography. Similarly, with the rising "text-as-data" trend of computational text analysis across social and cognitive sciences

Introduction

(Grimmer, Roberts, and Stewart 2022; Jackson et al. 2021), my book offers critical insights into the benefits and limitations of using this "big-data" approach to interpret ethnographic fieldnotes.

Taken together, computational and quantitative analysis can complement ethnographic interpretation to generate multiple levels of insights from this corpus. For me, without first-person fieldwork experience, these textual, network, and behavioral patterns are helpful to reconstruct the lives of children through texts. But above all, from the original data collection to my reanalysis and writing, this journey involves several layers of transcription, translation, and interpretation. Reconstructing this ethnography involved comparing and integrating different types of fieldnotes and incorporating all other available data sources, such as the Wolfs' previous works,[40] ethnographies in the larger Haishan area,[41] and oral history interviews.[42] It involved discerning and reassembling the perspectives and voices of various actors: the anthropologists, or "foreigners" in children's words, the research assistants, and the children and adults. Moreover, I infused my own voice into this assemblage, my decade-long experience of studying children, and my personal memories of becoming a Chinese daughter and mother.

Book Outline

I arrange the content chapters in the following order: Chapter 1 portrays the unusual journey of reconstructing an ethnography, establishes my own voice, and sets the tone for subsequent chapters. Each of Chapters 2 to 5 weaves together interview, observation, and projective tests materials, and combines "close reading" with patterns from computational

---

[40] Including Arthur's draft introductory chapters and other documents.
[41] These ethnographies were produced by the Wolfs' students and associates.
[42] Formal or informal interviews with Stevan Harrell, Myron Cohen, and Huang Chieh-Shan.

analysis. Chapter 2 deconstructs the myths of "parenting" from children's perspective. Chapter 3 shifts to the world of peer play. Chapter 4 highlights how gender shapes children's moral experience. Chapter 5 presents an important case study of a brother–sister dyad to examine sibling relationships. Through examining different aspects and factors of children's moral life, these four chapters together establish the thesis of "'unruly' children."

Chapter 1 presents my "alternative fieldwork," how I make sense of my predecessors' fieldwork and fieldnotes. I introduce Xia Xizhou in its historical–cultural context, including its colonial history and changing kinship, economy, and schooling system. I contextualize the multiple boundaries, identities, and relationships between the researched and the researchers. I recover the experience of native research assistants, not just as mediators between anthropologists and children, but as lively characters participating in children's moral development journey. I expose the challenges of reconstructing this ethnography and the puzzles I encountered. I reveal the inherent ethical dimension of actions and interactions that made ethnographic knowledge possible. I also draw from my own experience and expertise to discern the voices, silences, and voids in this archive.

Chapter 2 reflects on a key assumption about the "traditional Chinese family," the "child-training" paradigm that emphasizes parenting and overlooks children. The chapter draws from interview and observational data with mothers and children to contrast an important local cultural model of parenting, preventing children's fighting, with the reality of prevalent fighting and conflict among children. It uncovers the experiences of "disobedient children" departing from the parental ideal of training obedience. After debunking the myths of Chinese parenting, I explain the inefficacy of parental punishment through the lens of children's socio-moral cognition. These findings remind anthropologists to pay more attention to the ethical experience and reflections of young children, the punished.

Introduction

Departing from parent–child relation, Chapter 3 delves into the world of peer interactions. I present general patterns of children's social networks and behavioral directions, highlighting the importance of child-to-child ties. A close look at children's peer interactions illustrates the common scenarios and key features of this humorous, playful world and examine how peer play facilitates children's moral learning. In peer play children are developing what I call "the spectrum of moral sensibilities": They are learning about and engaging in cooperation and care, conflict and dominance, and creating gray areas in between. This poses a stark contrast to the imagery of "the innocent child" permeating in historical and philosophical views of Chinese childhood that fixate on the brighter side of human nature in moral cultivation. Moreover, through deciphering children's pretend play, I illuminate "reality-based fantasies" and argue that these nonelite children, often relegated to history's silent margins, have a much richer inner life than my predecessors assumed. Lastly, while computational techniques uncovered latent patterns of children's social life, young learners' sensibilities in discerning layered intentions and moral sentiments defeat AI algorithms. This sheds light on the mystery of human sense-making and inspires reflections on ethnographic epistemology.

Turning to the issue of gender, Chapter 4 tells stories of mischievous, naughty, and fierce boys and girls. Systematic behavioral analyses reveal gendered patterns in children's moral experience, for example, boys initiate dominance, verbal and physical aggression more than girls, but girls assert themselves in more subtle ways, such as through tattling and scolding. I further explore how children's learning of authority, aggression, boyhood, and violence is shaped by their family life as well as the larger historical trends. The chapter also examines how young girls understand their own situations and defend themselves. Despite the entrenched son preference in this community, girls are far from passive or submissive. To honor Arthur Wolf's legacy on marriage and adoption and offer new insights on young girls' emotional experience, which was not addressed in Wolf's previous works, I present the case of an adopted daughter: An "unruly" girl who defies parental commands, asserts her own will, and negotiates love–hate relationships with different family members.

Chapter 5 presents an untold tale of an older brother and his younger sister. While their mother was the protagonist in Margery Wolf's classic ethnography, *A Thrice-Told Tale*, the story of these children was obscured. Childhood sibling relation in "the Chinese family" was rarely studied by anthropology, yet it is an important relation that shapes children's moral development. I delineate systematic patterns of this sibling dyad's social network positioning, uncover their distinct personalities, and trace their nuanced dynamics of care, rivalry, and coalitional maneuvers. This chapter is a unique narrative: In addition to illuminating childhood sibling relation, it simultaneously rediscovers the voices of these two children from ethnographic omissions and silences. Therefore, this case study echoes the dual themes of the entire book, children learning morality and anthropologists reconstructing an ethnography.

To sum up, my book traces how children learn morality in a patriarchal rural Taiwanese community during Taiwan's Martial Law Era. Through analyzing a historically significant fieldnotes archive, this book creates new linkages between anthropology, psychology, and Chinese studies, and incorporates computational approaches into ethnographic interpretation. The book contributes to understanding "becoming moral," humanity's key puzzle that has inspired recent interdisciplinary synergy, by highlighting the role of peer learning beyond parent–child transmission. From a cognitive anthropology approach, this book centers on children's complex experience and offers a revisionist account of "the traditional Chinese family" and "Chinese childhood," therefore challenges the entrenched moral values these popular imageries embody. Moreover, fusing different epistemological and methodological perspectives, the book draws from children's socio-moral sensibilities to reflect on anthropological knowledge itself. Children can teach anthropologists about ethnographic epistemology. Their minds hold the key to understanding human sense-making.

ONE

Fieldwork beyond Fieldwork

Reconstructing an Ethnography of Children through Historical Fieldnotes

Children "Playing Anthropologist"

All grown-ups were once children, and many do remember it. Decades later, the once "subjects" of Arthur Wolf's research in Xia Xizhou had a chance to talk – to the anthropologist – about their experience in his 1958–60 fieldwork. Arthur Wolf revisited his first fieldsite in the 1990s, introducing an American graduate student, Maria Duryea, to conduct her dissertation research on social change and childrearing in this community. Arthur Wolf and Maria Duryea spoke to some participants in Wolf's original research, children who had become adults. Although having no idea what "anthropology" or "fieldwork" was at that time, these grown-ups did remember Wolf's team and the strange things the researchers were doing.

They recalled Older Sister Chen (MC) following them around with her notebook. In fact, Chen's responsible and meticulous observations of children's social life constituted the most important and systematic records I could use to reconstruct their stories. They recalled Wolf's incessant typing (A. Wolf n.d.: 32) – they probably walked straight into the courtyard and gathered at the window to watch the "foreigners" doing their work.[1] In *The House of Lim*, Margery Wolf recorded a

---

[1] In my personal communication with Stevan Harrell in 2021, he recalled similar scenarios in his fieldwork in another Taiwanese village in the early 1970s, that kids

snapshot of this common scenario – being watched by the very "subjects" they were studying: "One afternoon he [the youngest boy in the Lim family] spent half an hour constructing a precarious pile of junk under our office window to provide a comfortable platform from which to observe us" (M. Wolf 1968: 96).

When the anthropologists were studying children, the children were studying anthropologists too. They even invented a game called "Di di da da" (A. Wolf n.d.: 32). They were, essentially, "playing anthropologist": "To this day [1990s], people tell stories of the children sitting out in the courtyard 'playing anthropologist', ticking away at an imaginary typewriter and shuffling an imaginary carriage back and forth, but the stories never mentioned the children asking endless, redundant questions" (Duryea 1997: 13).

Browsing the Wolf Archive, comparing what was stored in the archive – "the raw data" – and what was recalled, synthesized, and written later in all sorts of voices related to this research, I kept coming back to this scenario: Children observing, making sense of, and even mimicking what the anthropologists were doing. This scenario speaks to the fundamentally dialogic, intersubjective, and somewhat messy nature of fieldwork. It also echoes back to a central question motivating my rereading of the Wolf Archive: What children are and how they learn. Fieldwork, and the anthropological knowledge it produces, always builds from and through relationships between multiple actors. Different actors bring their own experience, curiosity, and positionality into ethnographic encounters. Such encounters always have some contingent elements and tend to leave puzzles.

> used to gather at his window and watch him typing at his desk: "And his [Arthur's] room probably had a window facing the courtyard, because (1) that's the way most windows faced; very few faced the back, and (2) the light from the 15W bulbs was not very good, and although we were young when we did that fieldwork so we could still see, it would be better to take advantage of the natural light (also saved on landlord's electricity bills)."

In particular, children bring quite surprising social dramas of ethnographic encounters, in interesting or annoying ways. Children, due to their social positioning, warn us the extent to which adult researchers' fieldwork can be immersive, both pragmatically and ethically (Allerton 2016): "Children not only share their experiences with anthropologists, but they also speak back to them, alternately suspicious and trusting, transgressive of social boundaries, critical of and cooperative with the researcher" (Borneman 2016: ix). At the epistemological level, children are the world's most exceptional social learners. They are natural observers with a keen eye for social knowledge. Therefore, ethnography with and of children poses some unique challenges and opportunities for anthropological knowledge production.

Notably, reconstructing this ethnography of children is rendered more challenging and interesting because of the various intermediate actors in the original fieldwork. Recovering the voices of these intermediaries and highlighting the collaborative nature of anthropological knowledge-making has become an important concern in our discipline's reckoning with the past (Gupta and Stoolman 2022). The intermediate actors in Arthur Wolf's fieldwork, his research assistants with local background, played a critical role in producing the fieldnotes. Not only serving as interpreters, more importantly, they were the ones, for the most part, directly and constantly engaged with the village children. Arthur Wolf was the team leader who designed the study protocols and supervised the entire fieldwork, while research assistants dutifully observed or interviewed children and their mothers, took notes in Chinese, and then reported to the Wolfs verbally, most often in English but sometimes in Mandarin; Margery Wolf was, in her own words, "administrator and scribe, spending long hours typing [in English] … verbatim accounts of observations as they were brought in by the field staff [the research assistants' dictation]" (M. Wolf 1990: 344). This unique set of fieldnotes originated from various types of labor, wove together different voices, and reflects layers of translation.

Children "Playing Anthropologist"

Moreover, a different anthropologist later coming to reanalyze these fieldnotes would add "yet another level of complexity in our search for meaning," as Margery Wolf foresaw in her reflections on this fieldwork (1990: 353). A stranger to these children and their researchers, my work inevitably complicates the already massive, polyvocal ethnographic project. Reading through these fieldnotes and related records time and again, I wish I had been there to witness the lively moments of fieldwork, to know these children in person. I fantasized about sci-fi time-travel scenarios. I had dreams about the village and its children. This project became an existential challenge for me as an anthropologist, as I lacked the kind of first-person experience, or "presence" in the fieldwork. I asked myself a million times: Is my attempt to reconstruct an ethnography of Xia Xizhou children doomed to fail?

But I was encouraged by my predecessor's own vision about the fate of these fieldnotes:

However flawed, fieldnotes are not ephemeral but documents that record one mind's attempt to come to understand the behavior of fellow beings. One day – fly specks, bacterial infection, and all – they must be part of the public record so that species should survive or be followed by some other postnuclear being cursed with curiosity, the fieldnotes can be reexamined for what they are: our feeble attempts at communication with one another. (M. Wolf 1990: 354)

With children as a special kind of interlocutors, this project therefore prompts me to rethink the nature of fieldnotes, ethnography and what it means by "knowing." Since ethnography is always approaching some partial truth, let me take a step back and reframe my question: What sort of agency can I exert and what affordances of this archive can I utilize to make sense of these historical texts? The bottom line is, although written without first-hand fieldwork, this book does emerge from my experience of rediscovering the Wolf Archive. It emerges from overlaying my own vision onto what my predecessors wanted to see and what the research assistants saw, from blending my own voice with the multiple voices recorded and/or obscured in those layered texts, and from piecing together one puzzle after another. This chapter presents an account of one mind's journey of meeting and attempting to communicate with other minds: my unconventional "fieldwork" about my predecessors' original fieldwork; my efforts, through different epistemological lenses and methodological tools, to give new life to old fieldnotes.

Tracing My Predecessors' Footsteps: The Village and Its Children

During my special "fieldwork," I kept a journal to document important moments of confusion and revelation, my various attempts at time travel or bits of detective work, in the process of figuring out what had happened in my predecessors' fieldwork. On January 20, 2021, I added this entry about what I dreamt the night before, me visiting a village that no longer existed.

Don't know why I had such a dream with an absurd plot (an emoji of embarrassment). I finally got to see this village that I had scrutinized on Google Maps to locate the river and the elementary school. A village whose houses, big and small, I had imagined for many times. I walked on the path towards the village and saw the largest house at the entrance, "the House of Lim", but somehow I did not find the big Banyan tree next to that house. Not far away I saw the village temple (*tudigong*), but it was burned down, and what remained was some kind of relic. There were people still living in the largest house. I started chatting with them. One moment it was "oral history", me talking to adults about their childhood. The next moment the adults became children and I was interviewing them! One child told me: "Our ancestors came from Hunan [a province in China, where I grew up]." That perplexed me: "Wait a second. Weren't they from Anxi, Fujian province?" And that thought woke me up from the dream (another emoji of embarrassment).

I was obsessed with the village map those days, trying to recreate an image on my computer from a pencil-drawn map Arthur created and

Tracing My Predecessors' Footsteps

preserved in the archive. The house-number system Arthur used was completely different from the one on the village map in Margery Wolf's "Women and Family in Rural Taiwan" (M. Wolf 1972: 44). But I also had to rely on Margery's books to figure out which household had what general stories and double-check some details as part of my detective work, because Arthur himself did not write a village ethnography. I managed to produce an e-version of Arthur's village map (Figure 1.1), imagining children playing in the various yards or gardens. My dream about revisiting the village, as absurd as it was, is a reminder that one inevitably inserts oneself into the story, consciously or not, while tracing other people's footsteps.

On June 15, 1958, Arthur Wolf, then an anthropology graduate student from Cornell University, arrived at his fieldsite. He first hopped on a train from Taipei to a town called Shulin – the pseudonym of which was "Ta-pu" in Margery Wolf's works. From the train station, along the east side of the town center square, he walked to a busy commercial street, then along an irrigation canal constructed by the Japanese colonial regime, down an alley on the right, then across a small bridge at the edge of the town, and finally, on a path into the countryside. As he remembered, "all this (buzzing town-style) activity gave way, abruptly, to a quiet rural landscape. The stained red brick and tile of the town was replaced by the bright green, of paddy fields, vegetable gardens, bamboo grooves, and great spreading banyan trees" (A. Wolf n.d.: 6). Walking another quarter mile down the path, he arrived at the Shalun Elementary School – where children in the village ahead studied. The village, Xia Xizhou, appeared a quarter mile ahead, along the path and beyond the school (Figures 1.2 and 1.3).

Decades later, Arthur recalled his first sight of the farmhouse he lived in for over two years: "Here, on the left-hand side of the path, stood the great banyan tree pictured on the cover of Margery Wolf's *The House of Lim*, and, on the right-hand side of the path, the home of the Lim family, the largest and finest in the village" (A. Wolf n.d.: 6). The real

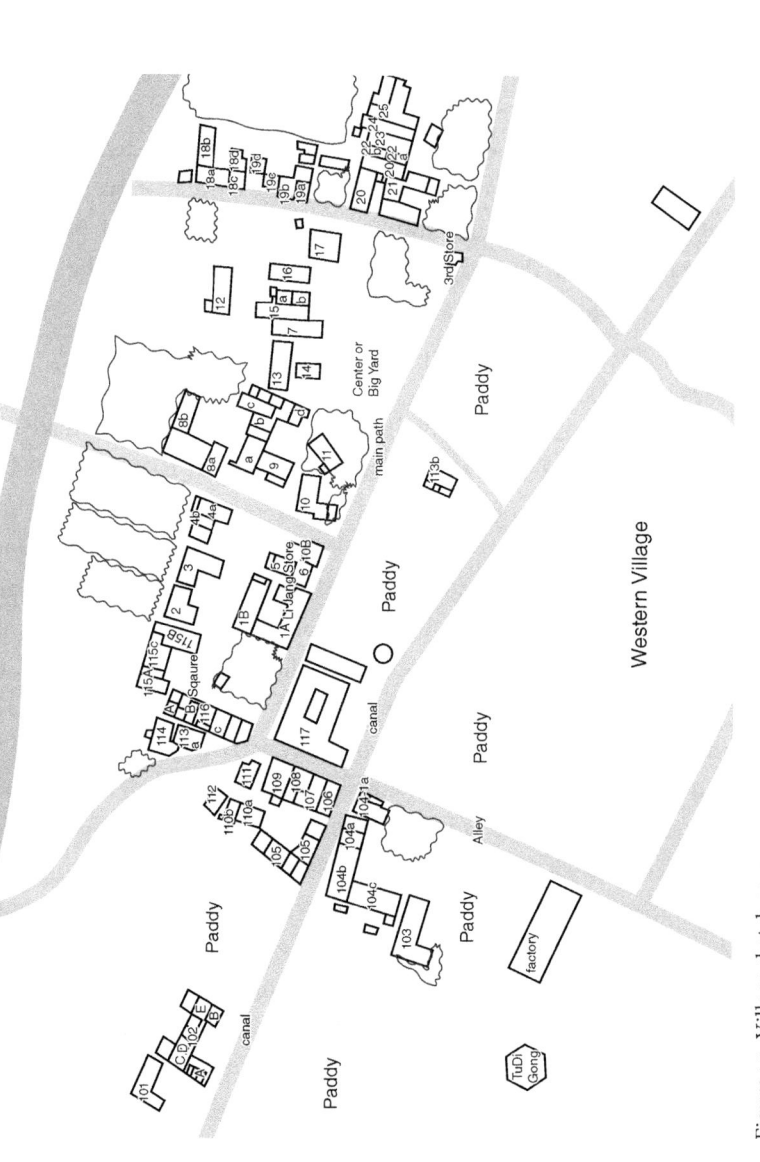

Figure 1.1 Village sketch map
Source: Adapted from a pencil-drawn map by Arthur Wolf.

Tracing My Predecessors' Footsteps

Figure 1.2 Children playing at the irrigation canal in Shulin
Source: Photo by Arthur Wolf.

Figure 1.3 Village houses and paddy fields
Source: Photo by Arthur Wolf.

surname of this Lim (Lin) family is Wang, and the Wang lineage is the main one in the village. Arthur rented some space in this Wang house, joined by Margery Wolf later that year. Arthur lived with this Wang family until late 1960, in a house with fourteen regular members and another fifteen who were in and out of it every day (M. Wolf 1990: 346). They witnessed all kinds of Wang family dramas and even frequently attempted to mediate the quarrels (*quan jia*) (Chou 2011). Once settled in the village, Arthur Wolf's first task was to reconstruct its history. He gained in-depth knowledge about this area from two key informants who were connected to this village but living in the nearby Shulin town: Wang Shiqing[2] and his mother Ms. Lai. One day an old gentleman in the village was exasperated by the anthropologist's questions about history. He suggested that Arthur go talk to a member of the Wang lineage, a man who "knows all about such things" (A. Wolf n.d.: 40). That's how Arthur came to know Mr. Wang, who later became a very well-known historian of Taiwan. Arthur often walked to Shulin town to meet with Wang, and he appreciated that Mr. Wang had taught him "what amounted to a year-long course on Taiwanese customs and the history of Taiwanese society" (p. 41). From this fieldwork, they two established a life-long friendship. Wang visited Stanford (1970–71) and taught Arthur and his research collaborator Huang Jieshan (Chieh-Shan) how to use the Japanese colonial household and land registers.[3]

On a hot and humid day in late September 2023, guided by Mr. Wong Min-Liang, Wang Shiqing's son, I visited Xia Xizhou for the first time, on the same exact route that Arthur took. We took the train from Taipei to Shulin town, walked along a bustling old street, amid newer streets later built during the industrialization era. The irrigation canal was long

---

[2] I use Pinyin instead of Wade-Giles system in accordance with the conventional spelling of Wang's name as it appears in academic publications.

[3] From these materials Arthur established his important findings about marriage, kinship, and incest avoidance (A. Wolf and Huang 1980). Mr. Huang met Wolf during his Xia Xizhou fieldwork and became his translator and research assistant.

Village History, Kinship and Economy

Figure 1.4 The Wang family house that Arthur Wolf lived in. The small section connected to the main house was the cement bag factory that belonged to the Wang family, where village children often came to play
Source: Photo by Jing Xu.

covered by concrete surface, the bridge marking the boundary between Shulin and Xizhou was replaced by a new street sign, and the big Banyan tree at the entrance to the village was gone. Most of the old houses were replaced by new ones and villagers had long moved into apartment buildings. But the Wang house that the Wolfs once lived was still intact, inviting me to imagine the naughty boy from this family climbing up the window to peek into the strange anthropologists' room (Figure 1.4).

Village History, Kinship and Economy

Kinship was an important element of this community's history, and Wang Shiqing's mother, Ms. Lai, became a key informant on these subjects. Her deep knowledge about the village households helped Arthur reconstruct accurate genealogies for a community with a high rate of adoption and other complications to its kinship structures. The founding ancestors of the Wang lineage came to Taiwan as immigrants from the mountainous interior of Anxi, a county in Quanzhou Prefecture in southern Fujian, during the Qianlong years in the eighteenth century. Although Ms. Lai was adopted into Wang's grandfather as a *sim-pu-a* (little daughter-in-law) at a young age, she was still called a *Chiang-chiu-a* by the villagers, because her biological family descended from Zhangzhou immigrants (Chou 2011: 79). According to the colonial household registers, in 1905, 65.7 percent of the male population bore the surname Wang. The Huang lineage also claimed to be among the earliest settlers here, with 8 percent of the male population bearing that surname in 1905 records.

The dominance of Wang lineage persisted. Even in the late 1950s, people living in Shulin town addressed Arthur as Mr. Wang, seeing him going in and out from Xia Xizhou and assuming he had to be a Wang (A. Wolf n.d.: 43). According to the census compiled by Arthur during this fieldwork, the village had a total population of 586 in 1958, including more than 200 children. Among the seventy-five families in this village, thirty families had the surname Wang, and six had the name Huang. Between 1905 and 1958, the village witnessed striking changes in kinship structures, the increase of stem families, and the decline of both joint families and elementary families (A. Wolf n.d.: 69). This means that, at the time of the Wolfs' fieldwork, grandparents were important caregivers of Xia Xizhou children and cousins were likely common playmates.

Despite the typical landscape of a farming village with plenty of paddy fields and some water buffalo, Xia Xizhou was never purely an agricultural community in its modern history. It was located on the Dahan River (Ta-k'e-k'en was its old name), the upper branch of Tamsui River, and midway between two towns, Shulin and Tucheng, while administratively in Banqiao township. The village was an excellent port in the Taipei Basin water transportation system during the late Qing and early Japanese colonial rule. At this bustling port, cargo ships transported tea and rice wine, while ferries and small boats carried goods and people to Taipei. After the Taoyuan irrigation dam was built, the river port gradually declined in Xia

Xizhou. By 1958, the only clues to its past were "three rotting boats in the bamboo groves" by the river (A. Wolf n.d.: 49).

From a child's point of view, the river was an attractive yet dangerous place. Adults told children tales of river ghosts. Children were not allowed to play near the river due to the risk of drowning. In many episodes, however, I have read about children having fun there, swimming in the river, holding parties on the riverbank, or hanging out on the tree nearby. But danger did lurk, and on one occasion, a research assistant happened to be there observing the children and she interfered in time. As Arthur recalled: "Good fortune had it that one day when a small boy fell in the river Chen Suhua (MC) was following him to make an observation. She called a farmer from a nearby field and the child was saved with the result that she became more popular than ever. I also benefitted as the person responsible for her presence" (A. Wolf n.d.: 59).

In 1958, male household heads in this village included coal miners, wage laborers, small business (factory or store) owners, vegetable or peanut farmers, and others. Married women made money through picking rocks for construction companies, washing clothes, and doing other menial labor. Some were supported by their daughters working as prostitutes in towns or in the city (M. Wolf 1972). Young men and women joined the labor force early, working in factories or doing apprenticeships in shops. For example, Wang Shih-ting, the head of "the House of Lim," ran a cement bag factory, using a shed attached to his house, and hired his relatives among other villagers. The great majority of families were still poor by local standards, even with a mixture of farming and other income: Average daily earnings were 20–30 yuan (NT) for men (the exchange rate was 1 USD = 40 NT), 15–20 for young men, and 7–10 for women (A. Wolf n.d.: 51). They were not equally poor though. The "House of Lim" family had the highest standing, distinguished by the largest house with all-brick walls and concrete floors (two rooms even with terrazzo floors), while others had smaller houses with brick walls or mud brick walls.

Under these circumstances, "mothers were reluctant to give a child fifty cents for a new eraser or two yuan for a pencil set" (A. Wolf n.d.: 51). For a typical family with three or four children, "the ten-cents children demanded several times a day added up to substantial expenditure," and daughters-in-law had reason to be angry at their lenient in-laws who indulged grandchildren with money to buy candy (A. Wolf n.d.: 52). But children did often succeed in wheedling pocket money from their mothers or grandparents, often as a bargaining strategy. There were three small stores in the village, selling a variety of goods, but as Arthur remembered, children were the most profitable customers (A. Wolf n.d.: 59). In fact, shopping, including running errands for adults, buying snacks, and even just mentioning the stores, appeared so much in the observational notes that I decided to create an entire category of it and feed the category to machine learning algorithms to sort out the texts.

The Question of Schooling

While shopping was always a source of excitement to these children, schooling was a mixture of bitterness and fun. Many children had fun playing outside class time, chasing around inside the classroom, in the hallway, or more enjoyably, playing in the schoolyard with swings, seesaw, and spaces for hopscotch, marbles, shooting rubber bands, and other games. The bitterness documented in observational fieldnotes – children's tears and fears – was largely induced by teachers' harsh discipline. Yelling and corporal punishment toward students who did not read or write well was so common that children played "school" and mimicked teacher–student dynamics during their leisure time at home. Some kindergarteners and first graders had an especially tough time, because they were still confused by school routines, and they were learning Mandarin from scratch as part of their compulsory education. At the height of ROC's Martial Law Era, students were not allowed to speak Taiwanese. At school, children were reported by each other when they

The Question of Schooling

lapsed into Taiwanese and offenders would be punished. They were vigilant at school. But at home they'd rather be called their Taiwanese nicknames, instead of official Mandarin surnames and given names. This leads into a brief explanation of the context and history of schooling in Xia Xizhou as it matters to children's developing sense of identity.

When the Japanese arrived in 1895, Wang Shiqing's great grandfather was the only fully literate resident of the village. Shalun Elementary School, a public school located between the village and Shulin town, was built and developed from the 1910s to 1920s under Japanese rule. At its founding, the school had quite a few teachers who were Japanese and had received training in Japan. As part of the colonial government's modernization project, the school saw a steady increase in Xia Xizhou children's enrollment in the 1930s and 1940s. This modernization project also included encouraging families to send their adopted daughters to school. In the postwar context, Mandarin was a new language to the village. Most adults grew up speaking a mixture of Japanese and Taiwanese Hokkien,[4] except a few mainlanders who moved here around 1949 – one of whom was teaching at this school. Most school-age children were educated at Shalun, and by third to fourth grade, they spoke fluent Mandarin.[5]

After the KMT took over Taiwan, education in the late 1950s, from policy to practice, focused on the principle of "Sinicization" (*zuguohua*), with the purpose of making Taiwanese children Chinese and cultivating their loyalty to the ROC party-state (Chang 2015: 155–204). Prioritizing two subjects, *guowen* (Chinese language and literature) and *shidi* (Chinese history and geography), elementary education aimed to improve children's understanding of China and cultivate a sense of affection for the Chinese homeland (Chang 2015: 156). Nonetheless, as pioneers in the golden age of "China" ethnography, the Wolfs went to Taiwan to examine patterns

---

[4] A branch of Minnan language.
[5] That's why Arthur and his assistant Mr. Huang Chieh-Shan decided to administer their "School Questionnaire" only to third-graders and older children, in a larger school at Shulin Town.

Fieldwork beyond Fieldwork

of "traditional Chinese" society. They were not particularly concerned about the effects of schooling on identity or social change (Harrell 1999). Therefore, among the observations at the local school or interviews about schooling, very few records touched upon the question of identity education, for example, what sorts of topics were taught to children in class, what stories were used, or how parents and children reacted to the content of teaching. Arthur Wolf and his assistant Mr. Huang Chieh-Shan even collected hundreds of what they called "School Questionnaires,"[6] but the focus was behavioral questions similar to the ones in Child Interview, without any related to identity or political socialization.

I did catch a glimpse of schooling's "identity molding" dimension, however, even in the very naming of classrooms. In one observation, for example, some children were bragging whose class was better, "loyalty classroom" (*Zhong-ban*) or "filial piety classroom" (*Xiao-ban*). These typical Confucianist terms were an integral part of ROC government's core doctrine, "Three Principles of the People" (*Sanminzhuyi*). Moreover, beyond school-related notes, bits of stories scattered across fieldnotes did shed light on children's own understandings and expressions of "insiders/outsiders." Exploring these stories and the puzzles behind them allowed me to peek into the different identities, boundaries, and relationships in this fieldwork.

The Making of Fieldnotes: Boundaries, Identities, and Relationships

"Adoga *(Big Nose) Is Coming!*"

Residents in Shulin town once frowned upon Arthur Wolf's choice of fieldsite. In their eyes, the village people in Xia Xizhou were too crude and had no culture. The village was home to hooligans and

---

[6] Unfortunately, these materials were not available at Wolf's private library.

gangsters – *lo-mua* in Hokkien (*liumang* in Mandarin) – who preyed on the town's merchants and were well-known in the Taipei basin area (M. Wolf 1968: 3, 46–49). As Arthur vividly remembered, the physical boundary between the town and the village was also a marker of social distinction and group identity, even for young children. The anthropologist found himself an outsider to these children when inside their village but an insider to them when outside their village (A. Wolf n.d.: 7–8):

Everyone knew exactly where the boundary was. For local officials and people who had to deal with them, it was important because it was the line between two townships; for people who felt a need for supernatural protection, it was important because it divided the realms of two gods; for gamblers and people who needed another kind of protection, it mattered because it was the passage between the territories of rival gangs; for men involved in local politics, it was significant because it divided communities that were and were not controlled by the Wang lineage; and for the children who are the subject of this study, it was significant because it was the outer edge of a safe world in which everyone was a neighbor if not a relative and beyond which everyone was a stranger and therefore dangerous. Meeting me on their side of the boundary, these children shouted, "Ah-tok-a, ah-tok-a," this being the most common of the many rude ways Taiwanese refer to Caucasians. But meeting me on the other side of the boundary, these same children addressed me using my Chinese surname and often walked the rest of the way home holding my hand. An outsider on one side of the boundary was an insider on the other.

Reading this scenario, I found myself amused by children's clear and flexible understanding of identity and their shrewdness in navigating social dramas. Boundary and identity are always relative, contingent upon the concrete situation. Xia Xizhou children would gang up against children from the neighboring Western village, not to mention against those from Shulin town. They would throw stones at newcomers to their territory, a few children who recently moved from Jinmen (Quemoy).[7]

---

[7] Such migration probably happened in the aftermath of the 1958 Taiwan Strait Crisis.

Fieldwork beyond Fieldwork

But within the village, the "foreigners" – or in their words, "Big Nose" ("Ah-tou-ka" or "Adoga" in Hokkien) – were the most visible outsiders to them. Children had an ambivalent attitude toward them: A little boy was scared of going to the store when he saw Margery Wolf there. An older boy felt embarrassed when he saw Margery observing him joking around. A father teased his little girl about giving her away to "the foreigner" as an adopted daughter, describing all the places she would get to visit by air. The girl grinned but insisted that she did not want to go.[8]

Most of the time, children were teasing the anthropologist behind his back, using this derogatory term to mock each other, or bringing the presence of "Adoga" to scare other children. On a hot summer day, two boys were climbing up a wall to catch bugs. One urged: "Give me some bugs!" The other refused. A third boy shouted: "Ahtogah is coming!" [To warn them because climbing the wall would be frowned up by adults] The boy holding the bugs was not deterred at all: "It doesn't matter. I won't stop." He even started grinning at the others – including research assistant MC who was observing this episode. He looked at them and sang: "Oh, Ahtogah please don't come, etc."[9] "American/foreigner/Big Nose" even became a convenient phrase for children to irritate others. Two siblings, seven-year-old Huang Shu-ting and six-year-old Shu-song got into a fight, simply because the little brother kept poking his older sister and pulling her nose: "You are an American. You are a foreigner. You have a big nose."[10]

Arthur sometimes followed his research assistant MC to observe children at school. One day, Wang Chen-jin, a seven-year-old boy who really hated studying, was fidgeting and jiggling the desk. Two classmates came over, jokingly warning him: "Big Nose. Big Nose!" Chen-jin turned around: "Where is the Big Nose?" One of those two naughty classmates smiled: "No, it's Sister Chen (MC)." Chen-jin ran up and

---

[8] SI #10, 07/07/1959.
[9] CO #22, 07/30/1959.
[10] SO #109, 08/15/1959.

grabbed him: "It's Sister Chen. Who told you it was Big Nose?" The other classmate went on with his chant, "Big Nose, Big Nose," while Chen-jin walked up to make a threatening motion to him. Chen-jin must have felt relieved to see MC, the children's trusted "older sister," but at the same time annoyed or embarrassed to be tricked by his classmates.[11]

"Why Do You Live with Foreigners?"

Children were quite curious about the relationship between the foreigners and their Taiwanese research assistants. They also felt a little confused about the status of these assistants. They would tease MC about her association with "foreigners." For example, a four-year-old boy Wang Jun-hsian saw his observer MC and told his older sister Wang Shu-yu: "Hit that Big Nose!" Shu-yu was embarrassed and scolded him: "I'll hit you instead of her! That isn't a Big Nose!"[12]

Although in somewhat naïve manners, children probed into the abstract categories beneath the surface features, just like ethnographers reflecting on the question of positionality. The following conversation,[13] between a seven-year-old girl Chen Yu-li, research assistant MS (whom children called "Teacher Ma"), and Yu-li's ten-year-old sister Chen Yu-chin, epitomizes children's understanding about identities in the larger context of the Cold War era.

YU-LI asked MS:	"Are you American?"
MS:	"Look at my nose and my skin. Isn't it the same as yours?"
YU-LI:	"Yes."
MS:	"Do you think I'm American?"
YU-LI:	"Then why do you live with the foreigners?"
MS:	"We are friends."

[11] CO #1253, 04/14/1960.
[12] CO #834, 02/21/1960.
[13] SI #32, 08/04/1959.

Fieldwork beyond Fieldwork

YU-LI to MS: "Who do you think will win, the Chinese or the Communists?"
YU-CHIN [Yuli's older sister]: "Of course the Chinese."
YU-LI: "Why don't we ask the Americans to fight the Communists?"
MS: "Why ask them to help us?"
YU-LI: "Because Americans have lots of money."
YU-LI "Do you think the Americans or the Chinese will win?"
MS: "We aren't fighting with Americans."
YU-LI: "Oh!"

Yu-li was clearly perplexed why MS was living with the Wolfs. She was also a bit confused by the relationship between the United States and Taiwan at that time. American presence in Taiwan increased a lot by the late 1950s, in response to the Second Taiwan Strait Crisis, bringing in soldiers, military support, and popular culture.[14] The May 24 incident in Taipei, 1957, marked the culmination of tensions in U.S.-Taiwan relations: An angry crowd of Taiwanese stormed the U.S. Embassy to protest the acquittal of American Sergeant Robert G. Reynolds who killed a ROC government employee Liu Tzu-jan (Teow and Pang 2015). Even in this relatively peaceful village, children saw KMT soldiers camping in their elementary school grounds or doing military exercises along the river bank. They probably heard about American soldiers or even saw some when they got a chance to visit Taipei streets. In a Child Observation (CO) episode, two boys were holding sticks as machine guns and "shooting" at each other, one pretending to be Sun Yat-sen and the other George Washington.[15]

Confusion about military activities aside, children's perception that "Americans have lots of money" was not an overstatement. Living

---

[14] For military presence and controversy, see www.thinkchina.sg/us-china-and-taiwan-complicated-triangular-relationship-1950s. For the influence of American popular culture among youths in Taiwan, amid the political tensions and military atmosphere of that time, Edward Yang's movie "A Brighter Summer Day" is a vivid illustration.

[15] CO #965, 03/06/1960.

among the villagers, the anthropology graduate student and his wife hired a cook, a translator, and research assistants. They lived in the finest house by the village's standard. Yu-li's way of thinking, the Chinese versus the Communists, also reflects the political atmosphere at that time. Framed in the ROC-PRC-USA triangle relation, they saw themselves as "Chinese," those in mainland as "Communists." But within the village, they saw themselves as Taiwanese, different from the few mainlander-immigrants in the village.[16] Children saw the research assistants as "insiders," quite different from how they saw the foreign anthropologists.

Moreover, it was not the Wolfs, but their Taiwanese research assistants – especially MC – who directly interacted with children the most and collected the great majority of the observational and interview data. They were intermediaries between the anthropologists and the research participants, and eyewitnesses to what was recorded in the fieldnotes. The close relationship between children and MC, and to a lesser extent, between children and MS, is worthy of exploration in detail.

Research assistant MS, shorthand for Ms. Sheng, a married young woman, was just completing a teacher training program at National Taiwan Normal University when she met Arthur Wolf. Her main role was to collect observational data centered on specific situations – "situation-based observations" (SO). In addition, she also participated in miscellaneous spontaneous interviews (SI), together with MC and Margery Wolf. Instead of following village adults and addressing her as "Ms. Sheng" (her maiden name), children mostly called her "Teacher Ma" – "Ma" as in her last name. This indicates a certain degree of power differential, as children saw her as an adult, and "teacher" was a respected category. In the example discussed earlier, right before asking the blunt question "Are you American?," little girl Yu-li was chatting with MS about teaching and studying. She first asked MS to show her how to write her (MS's) name.

---

[16] Mainlanders were also referred to in the diminutive, as *Gua-sieng-a*.

MS wrote it in the dirt. Then their conversation spun into an interesting direction:[17]

YU-LI: "Would you teach me next year?"
MS: "I am a very mean teacher."
YU-LI: "Then I would get to be first name [first place]."
A little later YU-LI asked MS: "Would you give me first name in the class?"
Her two older siblings and another child present all laughed at her. They said (to YU-LIN): "Aren't you ashamed? You ask her to give you first name!"
YU-LIN looked embarrassed and said: "No! No! My meaning was, if I studied very well I could get first name."
She looked at MS and said: "Isn't that true?"
MS agreed.

Although Teacher Ma was an authority figure, she was not really these children's teacher. Therefore, they were not afraid of her. They got used to her presence, her taking notes while they were playing, although parents tended to remind them to treat MS politely. A naughty toddler girl once took MS's notebook and looked through it. Her mom immediately scolded: "Your hands are too busy!"[18] But when parents were not around, the observed were quite comfortable teasing the observer MS. For example, when several girls were "playing house," pretending to make a meal with flowers and grass, they jokingly invited Teacher Ma to eat their cooked "cai" (vegetables) and had a great laugh about it.[19]

These episodes of children teasing MS or asking her funny questions immediately reminded me of my own fieldwork in a Shanghai preschool during the early 2010s: Children addressed me respectfully as "Teacher Xu." But unlike their real teachers, most of the time I just sat in a corner of their classroom to observe them or chat with them when they were playing during recess. I did not need to discipline them. Instead, they

[17] SI #32, 08/04/1959.
[18] SO #11, 07/20/1959
[19] SO #4, 07/20/1959.

happily anticipated me to bring them candy or other small treats, their reward for participating in certain research tasks during my fieldwork (Xu 2017: 16–19). Being a special kind of teacher, an alternative to the typical schoolteacher, between merely an authority figure and a relatable person, was a common experience for ethnographers who study children. This liminal role, when played well, can stimulate creative engagements with children (Allerton 2016: 34).

"Everyone's Confidante": MC and Children

Compared to MS whom children still saw as an adult and a special kind of teacher, the younger research assistant MC (shorthand for "Miss Chen") was perhaps as close to her young interlocutors as a researcher could ever be. Within a week or two of her arrival in the village children already began to call her "Older sister[20] Chen" (A. Wolf n.d.: 16). Within the first year of fieldwork Chen had become "everyone's confidante, everyone's friend" (M. Wolf 1990: 422). She often spent her free time gossiping in the village mothers' kitchens. These adult women would disclose their grievances to her (see M. Wolf 1990). They praised her for being kind to all of the children (M. Wolf 1990: 421). Some even thought that she would make a good daughter-in-law (A. Wolf n.d.: 16).

Several personal traits of Chen, not just her Taiwanese identity, helped explain why she could build such extraordinary rapport with her interlocuters and gather so much data with extraordinary quality: Child Observations, Mother Observation, Mother Interview, Child Interview, and miscellaneous data. According to Mr. Huang, MC was an experienced maid employed by an American family when she first met Arthur Wolf, at the age of about sixteen or seventeen.[21] She was intelligent,

---

[20] "Tan Tua-chi" in Taiwanese.
[21] It was quite common for American people in Taiwan at that time, including scholars and graduate students, to hire a local cook and amah. According to my interview with Mr. Huang Chieh-Shan in 2021, Chen spoke fluent colloquial

Fieldwork beyond Fieldwork

Figure 1.5 MC with a girl
Source: Photo by Arthur Wolf.

lively, and only a few years older – and only a little taller – than several of the children included in the study (A. Wolf n.d.: 16) (Figures 1.5 and 1.6).

The Wolfs spoke highly of MC's work. In the field, they soon discovered that MC could observe up to four minutes of timed interactions among children and repeat every word of it an hour later, with the aid of some notes (M. Wolf 1990: 344). The American anthropologists attributed this exceptional skill to Chinese schools' rigorous training of memorization. Moreover, Arthur confidently concluded that MC's rapport with children allowed her to "move freely in and out of the children's play groups without affecting their behavior .... Chen was sometimes drawn into the children's activities and then appear as an actor in her

English despite her limited education – equivalent to tenth-grade education (M. Wolf 1992: 9) – and low social status, because she had plenty of experience working for Americans.

The Making of Fieldnotes

Figure 1.6 MC with young children
Source: Photo by Arthur Wolf.

observation, but she is always there as Older Sister Chen, not as an observer and certainly not as a foreigner" (A. Wolf n.d.: 18).

True, MC was not just an observer to these children. Children were used to the presence of this "Older Sister." They would tease her as they teased each other. They wanted to involve her in their games. Rereading MC's observations, however, I found that she made a great effort to act as a detached observer instead of an involved participant. After all, she was a dutiful research assistant following her supervisor's command, that is, to study children's natural behavior.[22] But sometimes her close relationship with interlocutors posed a challenge to fulfilling her duty.

In some sidenotes within MC's observational texts, she complained how her emotional bonding with children could be a problem. For

---

[22] According to Mr. Huang Chieh-Shan, Arthur always told them to document or elicit children's natural behavior and speech (interview with Mr. Huang, May 2021).

example, when Cheng Shi-lin noticed MC, she ran up and threw her arms around her, ending the observation. MC expressed her frustration at the end of this episode: "She ruins many observations this way!"[23] This five-year-old girl was quite naughty. Once when MC was quietly observing a play session, Shi-lin teased her: "I am going to make some rice balls for Sister Chen!" MC added that she was furious, because Shi-lin always spots her before the other kids do.[24]

Feelings can be mutual though. Jokingly or seriously, children might get irritated at MC's performing a detached observer's role, because she was playing with them as a friend on other occasions outside her designated research time. During a fun, "playing house" observation,[25] Tsai Su-ying reached her playmate Cheng Shu-ching and said indignantly: "This Sister Chen! She won't play with us but she always stays around when we are playing." Shu-ching replied: "That's right." She threw MC an accusing look.

MC tried to cope with these situations through self-effacing tactics, but these tactics did not always work. She pretended to be doing something else on the side instead of observing children, for example, drawing on some tiles near the observed children, looking busy, but a child saw her, grabbed her tile, and started imitating her drawing.[26] Or, she tried not to respond when children cued her, assuming or inviting her as a participant in their play. At a hide-and-seek session, two three-year-old girls wanted to play with MC and kept saying boo at her. They were only interested in MC, despite another child trying hard to boo back and engage them. But MC just looked off into the distance and kept doing so until those two girls lost interest due to her lack of cooperation.[27] Because of her special bonding with children, even MC's

[23] CO #933, 03/03/1960.
[24] CO #1101, 03/23/1960.
[25] CO #1465, 05/11/1960.
[26] CO #1159, 03/30/1960.
[27] CO #1420, 05/06/1960.

action of "detachment" sometimes conveyed a message to the observed, however unintended it was. For example, during a Five-Sticks game, to settle repeated disagreements with another child, a girl turned to MC for support. MC simply ignored it and the girl felt embarrassed.[28] Despite trying so hard, however, there were moments when MC could not or did not detach herself from the observed situation. Many of these ambiguous situations lead to, or manifest as, moral entanglements.

Ethical Entanglement, Ethnographic Epistemology, and Learning Morality

Moments of dilemmas, ironies and ethical entanglements sprinkled across MC's observations could, according to her own mindset, raise concerns about compromising her research quality. However, from today's vantage point, we understand ethnographic encounters as inherently intersubjective, contingent, and messy. These moments make her notes more realistic and her testimonies more believable, especially in this research, where children were her main interlocutors. After all, immersive fieldwork entails the risk of exposing oneself, and MC, for sure, put herself in the thick of it. Her experience bears witness to "the often threatening, sometimes embarrassing, but always potentially insight-bearing situations of fieldwork" (Borneman 2016: x). MC cannot directly tell us what kind of insights her fieldwork experience, crucial for the making of these fieldnotes, might offer to her anthropologist-supervisors at that time. I only know that she parted ways with research afterwards and I was not able to get hold of her. However, when I reread these notes, MC's ethical entanglements become particularly meaningful not only to understanding how ethnographic knowledge was formed. These entanglements also shed light on how children learn morality, the central question that motivated this book.

[28] CO #574, 01/13/1960.

Fieldwork beyond Fieldwork

Some of these moments tell us about norms of courtesy and propriety central to the moral fabric of the local society. In a Mother Observation episode,[29] a young mother Wang Fei-yi punished her daughter in front of MC. The naughty eight-year-old girl Wang Lin-fang kept evading her responsibility, defying her mother's discipline, and even making fun of her mother. The mother became really angry, pinching Lin-fang until she began to cry. But the mother then apologized to MC for having punished her daughter when MC was present, explaining that she just couldn't help doing that because the girl was too naughty and annoying. Why did the mother have to explain herself to MC? A naïve reader might interpret this as the mom trying to save her own face for losing her temper in front of an outsider.

But the mother actually said: "I'm not punishing her because I don't like you." Right after this sentence, MC inserted an insider's explanation, as a supplementary note in parentheses: (There is a proverb to the effect, "You point at the chicken and scold the monkey."[30] Some people feel that if a person scolds a child in their presence, it is to show that they don't like them.) This short exchange captured layers of intentionality: First, MC was an insider, which is why the mother assumed that MC would understand this custom encapsulated in the Chinese proverb *Sha ji jing hou*. Second, precisely because the mother saw MC as an insider, she worried that MC would misunderstand the mom's real intention and thought that she scolded her daughter in order to express her dislike of MC. She worried that MC would feel bad. Third, the very fact that the mother bothered to explain herself shows that she actually cared about MC and her relationship with MC, which, again, testifies to MC's popularity and likability in the village.

This encounter well illustrates the richness of ethnographic intersubjectivity, the foundation for MC's knowledge and my reinterpretation.

---

[29] MO #112, 04/10/1960.
[30] In the original fieldnote it was "dog" instead of "monkey," which might have been an error of translation.

Moreover, this episode also leads me to the question of children's learning itself. Given that the daughter was present during the conversation between her mother and MC, I couldn't help but wondering about the child's experience at that moment: Wasn't it a moment of education to her, to learn about the custom of *Sha Ji Jing Hou*? She might also learn the multiple moral messages adults were trying to convey when punishing a child in front of other people – beyond simply showing a child that she would bear the consequences of her bad behavior. Meanwhile, she might learn about the meta-properties of communication itself, of detecting the speaker's intentions and the relevance to the audience (Sperber and Wilson 1996), which would be essential in her daily interaction with other people.

MC's ethical entanglements offer a window into children's colorful moral world itself. MC was not just a witness to children's stories. She even became, to some extent, a character in their very journey of learning morality. Some children cared about reputation. Inside the classroom, a six-year-old boy, a class leader, suddenly stopped his dueling game with another child, when he noticed MC, in order to project a "model student" image.[31] Other children loosened up more with her. They played "mambo dance," mimicking what they saw in popular culture at that time and addressing MC as "Miss, Miss."[32] They played "engagement" ritual and invited MC as an important guest.[33] They tried to enlist MC's support during disputes or asked for her help when they met difficulties. Some defended MC when other children tried to tease her. Some showed clear favoritism toward MC, sharing things with her but not with other children.

Adults and older siblings also seized the opportunity to teach a moral lesson to their youngsters in front of MC. When a naughty three-year-boy kept asking MC for pocket money, his older brother scolded him

[31] CO #348, 11/30/1959.
[32] CO #140, 08/26/1959.
[33] CO #250, 09/16/1959.

for being rude.[34] When two sisters fought during a meal, their mother teased them: "Aren't you afraid Sister Chen will laugh at you?"[35] In another occasion, the same girl who was teased by her mom assumed the role of moral authority: She scolded her younger siblings for having no manners because they just let MC stand while observing, and she quickly offered MC a stool.[36]

The presence of distant foreigners and familiarized local research assistants, and their engagements with children, all stimulated children to think about identities in their historical context. Their daily interactions with research assistants, and especially with MC, not only were shaped by local social norms, but also became part of their own moral experience, of managing reputation, navigating cooperation and conflict, and learning propriety. Examining the relationships and encounters behind the fieldnotes helped me to better understand the making of ethnographic knowledge and to reinterpret these fieldnotes through the new lens of learning morality. My reinterpretation, however, involves more than listening to the different voices present in or behind the notes. I also had to discern silences, deal with voids, and inevitably, draw on my own experiences to make sense of these texts.

Reinterpreting Fieldnotes

Voices, Silences, and Voids

Sometimes the conversations they [research assistants MS and MC] memorized and repeated to us made no sense even to them, but often the pages I typed from their dictation recorded material that we as foreigners would have found difficult to elicit – not because it was particularly private but because it was pithier, more judgmental, less considered.

– M. Wolf (1990: 345)

---

[34] CO #1072, 03/18/1960.
[35] CO #698, 02/08/1960.
[36] CO #1669, 09/04/1960.

Reflecting on these fieldnotes, Margery Wolf deemed her research assistants' voices as "more judgmental, less-considered," compared to what she or Arthur would have written. She was referring to some of the sidenotes MC and MS inserted into their dictation of what they observed. The research assistants often used these sidenotes to add explanations or assert their own comments about a situation, a cultural idiom, or a person. As I examined in the previous section, some of these sidenotes, however, turned out quite important for understanding local customs or individual personalities. These pithy notes disclosed the research assistants' personal opinions and impressions at the scene of observation, thus were helpful to remedy my problem of lacking first-person fieldwork experience. Such direct voices from the research assistants, however small in volume, added valuable, eyewitnesses' accounts to enrich the observational record.

The only male research assistant, Mr. Huang Chieh-Shan, whose straightforward voices, together with children's silences, taught me a different lesson of reinterpretation, that is, of reading between the lines. Huang was a college student who grew up in the nearby Shulin town. He worked for the Wolfs during his summer break and some weekends at the later stage of their fieldwork (1960), in charge of conducting two projective tests with children, Thematic Apperception Test (TAT) and Doll Play. These psychological tests, using a standardized set of pictures (TAT) and dolls (Doll Play) adapted to the local context to elicit children's imaginative storytelling, were consigned to a more peripheral, less important place. Some of the Mandarin transcripts of the original audiotapes were not even translated into English until the time of my re-analysis. Arthur Wolf (n.d.: 23) gave the following explanation, attributing the dissatisfying results of these tests to the instruments and to children's lack of imagination: "Very few of the children were willing or able to respond to either test with a spontaneous story. Huang had to ask again and again …, 'What is the father doing now? ….' In many cases the 'story' elicited was little more than a recitation of the child's family's daily routine." To me, however, these materials offer precious insights into the issue of studying children. Children's silences indeed scattered across the transcripts, and Huang indeed had to repeat his questions again and again. Huang's personal comments about the participants, inserted at the end of each transcript, also confirmed this awkward atmosphere: The child's attitude was unnatural, the child's voice was so small that even his breathing could be heard, the child was nervous, and so forth. In several transcripts, Huang mentioned that the child in question seemed really frightened, as if talking to a judge in an interrogation room. When I first read these comments from Mr. Huang, I wrote in my journal: "It must have been an awful experience feeling like trapped in an interrogation room, during the White Terror era in Taiwan[37]!" But what might have led to such silences and fear?

These interactions were not just affected by the pictures and dolls, or by children's personalities. After all, many of the same children also participated in Child Interview, but in that context the children were quite willing to answer MC's questions about hypothetical scenarios. The awkwardness had to do with the research setting and the researcher-child relationship as well. Huang went around to find the specific child assigned by Arthur Wolf, explaining that Prof. Wolf wanted the child to tell a story. Then the child was brought into a small room within the Wang house, which the Wolfs rented as their "testing room." According to my phone interview with Huang on April 20, 2022, many children were scared or reluctant to enter the room. "The children would have been even more scared if Arthur were to administer these tests himself, because he was a foreigner and he did not speak the children's native tongue," said Huang. But being a cultural and linguistic insider doesn't necessarily guarantee smooth communication or trust, especially when it comes to studying children. In this community, adult men, for example, father figures, were more distant to children than women (M. Wolf

---

[37] 1949–92, see www.nhrm.gov.tw/w/nhrmEN/White_Terror_Period.

1978). In this research setting, an isolated testing room in the house that the Wolfs lived in, Huang, a male adult with an abrupt personality, someone who had not spent much time with these children, could have triggered some nervousness among them. As shown in the transcript, he tended to insert short, sharp questions and keep pivoting back to his own questions instead of accommodating to children's direction of speech. Without access to the original audiotapes of these tests, I could not retrieve the scenes or figure out what Mr. Huang's exact tone and manner were like when talking to the children. But children indeed felt less comfortable talking to him than to MC. One observational episode confirmed my hypothesis, albeit in an indirect way: A mother was telling MC that her son, almost nine years old then, wouldn't go to the testing room to take the TAT with Mr. Huang, unless MC came to call him.[38]

Like spotting children bluntly chanting "Adoga/Big Nose" in observational texts, sensing their shyness in TAT transcripts was also a moment of revelation to me, not a setback. There are, however, voids in this archive that I cannot get around to and meanings I cannot recover. Arthur Wolf's draft introductory chapters were written in a narrative ethnography mode, from which I caught a glimpse into his first-person experience in the field. But besides those, he did not leave behind any personal diaries or reflective writings about that fieldwork. I got to know how children saw "the foreigners," but not how he thought about those children. This is not surprising. It was common at that time for male anthropologists not to write ethnographies in a personal narrative voice. Women anthropologists – or to be more accurate in the perceptive framework at that time, male anthropologists' wives – tend to write in a more personal voice (Tedlock 1996).

Margery Wolf did write a journal during that fieldtrip: "My journal recorded my irritation with village life, some wild hypotheses of causation, an ongoing analysis of the Chinese personality structure, various

---

[38] CO #1649, 07/21/1960.

lascivious thoughts, diatribes against injustices observed, and so forth" (1990: 345). Imagine what kind of vivid stories in the village that journal must have recorded! But that was not part of the Wolf Archive that I have access to. As Margery stated, she "would have been outraged had any of my coworkers attempted to read it" (1990: 345). At the time of fieldwork, as a wife, a scribe and an aspiring novelist, Margery did not consider her journal as part of "fieldnotes." In fact, many anthropologists at that time were taught to separate personal journals from serious fieldnotes.[39] It was not until later, when she carefully looked through different types of fieldnotes and her journal, that Margery Wolf began to piece together a fuller picture of the village and the personalities of its individuals. And that's how her ethnographies came into being, including her meta-reflections on ethnographic epistemology itself, *A Thrice-told Tale*. Perhaps every ethnographer, however much "first-person" experience they can hold on to, when looking back to past fieldwork, will always end up in a situation where they have to reconstruct meanings out of voices, silences and voids. Some of the challenges I face are common to all ethnographers, others unique to this project.

"It Serves You Right!": The Nature of Sensemaking

I read "It serves you right!" or "Serve you right!" in Child Observation episodes, one child scolding or teasing another. Then Wandou [my son, eleven years old] came into my office, shouting mischievously: "It serves you right!," for some trouble I complained about earlier. Well, Wandou can definitely help me to understand these children whom I've never met.
– My journal, 05/13/2021

Making sense of these fieldnotes seemed like an impossible mission. Getting the words correct, the numbers right, and the names matching the numbers, back and forth. Learning computer programming, forgetting,

---

[39] Personal communication with Stevan Harrell, October 2022.

and re-learning. Meticulously coding every CO episode, sentence by sentence, into behavioral categories and scores. Sometimes the work was so tedious that I felt I was losing my sense of purpose. But many sparkling moments, moments when I was amazed or amused by children, like the one I captured in this journal entry, gave new meaning to my journey. Sensemaking always involves using one's own experience as a resource or reference. My predecessors never addressed or got a chance to address the issue of children's developing minds, but I have long been fascinated by cognitive development, especially in the socio-moral domain. This distinct interest provides a vantage point for my ethnographic reinterpretation.

Children are very smart at reading social cues and learning about their social environment, as numerous studies in developmental psychology have shown. Yet children also pose unique risks for ethnographers. They cross boundaries that adults might cautiously observe, they make "total immersion" – a predominant model of village fieldwork – nearly impossible, and they make ethnographic encounters more or less difficult depending on the people and the situation (Allerton 2016: 1, 8–9). Therefore, I paid particular attention to how children engaged with different researchers, the contexts of such engagement, and why they were assertive in one occasion but timid in another. Children's various relationships, with the distant "foreigners" – distant in children's eyes, the familiar "Teacher Ma," the dear "Older Sister Chen," and Mr. Huang – who was native but perhaps a bit intimidating, form a full spectrum. I closely examined scenarios of children's emotional and moral entanglements with researchers. These encounters blur the boundary between "participant" and "observer," highlight the paradoxical nature of "participant-observation" at the core of the ethnographic method, and equally important, illuminate various moral lessons children were learning.

Morality and ethics have recently become a focus in anthropological theories, and fieldwork experience itself provides an important site for us to reflect on the intrinsic ethical dimension of human action (Lambek 2010b). Social theories tend to formulate human action "too automatically, too strategically, too self-consciously, or too self-interestedly," therefore flatten or obscure the ethical texture of social encounters (Lambek 2010b: 40). But most anthropologists who study the ethical nature of social life are talking about the adult world. Taking childhood learning as a central focus, I have shown that young children anthropologists encountered *in the field* drew from their rich moral sensibilities to make sense of human speech and action. Moreover, due to the nature of early childhood, a significant phase of acquiring social knowledge and ethical dispositions, the ethnographers even became interesting characters in these young actors' journey of learning morality.

Immersed in these fieldnotes, I often felt a sense of awe. It is an unusual archive, its volume and systematicity far beyond my expectations. Its quality probably exceeds that of many other fieldnotes-archive preserved privately or in public databases. Any first-person ethnographic fieldwork is necessarily incomplete (Carsten 2012: 29), but the repertoire of experiences documented in this rare archive exceeded what I could have ever gained if I were to have done solo, first-person fieldwork. These vicarious experiences in all the richness, layering with my own experience of studying children and raising a child, together helped me to make sense of Xia Xizhou childhood through texts.

Besides the special interlocutors and various intermediaries, the Wolfs' fieldwork distinguished itself from many village ethnographies back then in another crucial aspect, its mixed methods design that involved systematic, precise observations and standardized interviews and projective tests. This feature made it possible for me to incorporate quantitative, programmatic analysis of texts, behaviors, and social networks into ethnography. Contrary to the actual fieldwork that was a continuous, natural flow of experiences, these fieldnotes only captured discrete, "snapshot" units of data. Various types of computational analyses provide a new way to, in mathematical terms, connect the dots into lines, planes and multidimensional vector space, and reveal aggregative patterns. As the following chapters will show, machine "distant-reading" and my close reading together

Reinterpreting Fieldnotes

enabled me to transform individual participants from index numbers into embodied personalities and discover social relationships in bits and pieces of events. I was able to connect the dots, figuratively.

But above all, the foundation for sensemaking in this unique project was my effort to stay faithful to materials. The anthropologist Robert Smith, once a colleague of the Wolfs at Cornell University, reconstructed an ethnography out of another scholar Ella Lury Wiswell's fieldnotes, about women in a Japanese village Suye Mura. What he said illustrates this sensemaking process (Smith 1990: 363–64)[40]:

> For weeks I spent most of every day retyping the marked passages verbatim, beginning with the first entry. Before I was well into this stultifying task, I began to know the people in a new way. Some of the payoff was purely technical. For example, for the first time it became clear to me that XX, XXX, X [different names] were all the same woman …. When I was finally done, I had learned enough to spot continuities and inconsistencies, resolve most of the occasional ambiguities, and see how passages that had appeared to be unrelated (or unrelatable) to anything or anyone did in fact connect with what had gone before or came after …. So I am led to make the audacious claim that the voices of the women of Suye could be heard more clearly once I had interposed myself between them and their ethnographer.

I do not dare to say that the voices of Xia Xizhou children would be heard more clearly once I had interposed myself between them and their original researchers. I still wish that I had known those children in person rather than reading bits and pieces of their lives in texts. But if at the end of the day fieldnotes are nothing but anthropologists' "feeble attempts at communication with one another" (M. Wolf 1990: 354), I hope this chapter has made it clear that, although complicated by all the problems of reinterpreting other people's fieldnotes, my feeble attempts are worthy.

---

[40] Margery Wolf (1990: 346, footnote 2) had this interesting response to Robert Smith's reflections: "There is a similarity in the methods we employed to free the voices in our fieldnotes, but the barriers against which we were struggling were different. Or were they?"

TWO

Crime and Punishment

Parenting and the Disobedient Child

Bringing Children Back into the Study of Childrearing

On a hot day in August 1959, two boys from different families got into a fight. The physical conflict started from some playful greeting and teasing with research assistant MC, "Older Sister Chen." Because of her intimate relation with these children, MC became a character in their moral development journey, over the two years of dutifully and meticulously documenting her observations. As this observation started, she greeted children in a common manner, asking them: "Have you eaten (*jia ba bue*)?"[1] One protagonist of this episode,[2] a nine-year-old boy named Wang Ching-Chi, meant to answer that he had eaten, but mispronounced the words and instead said "I ate *two halves* (*nng bua*)." Liang Wei-Lin, an eight-year-old boy from a neighbor's family, started teasing him, yelling his comments repeatedly. All the bystander kids started laughing at him too. Ching-Chi finally got angry, hit Wei-Lin lightly and requested him to stop those comments. Wei-Lin didn't stop though. Instead, his teasing escalated into a new version, a song that mocked Ching-Chi as "Big Forehead." Amid Wei-Lin's singing, Ching-Chi angrily chased him, threatened him, and then hit him with a slingshot.

---

[1] This is a common greeting in Taiwanese, which figuratively means "Hello/How are you?"
[2] CO #28, 08/03/1959.

Bringing Children Back into the Study of Childrearing

Wei-Lin ran home and Ching-Chi chased after him, hitting him with a stick. At this point, Ching-Chi's mother heard them fighting and intervened: "Are you two still fighting in there?" They both left the house, but resumed teasing, chasing, and hitting. Wei-Lin's grandmother Mei-Chin came out too. Ching-Chi tattled to Mei-Chin about her grandson teasing him. Mei-Chin scolded Wei-Lin. His mother called from the house: "Quit fighting." But Wei-Lin ignored her command.

MC's observation ended here. Reapproaching these fieldnotes more than six decades later, we do not know how exactly this incident ended, after the eight-year-old boy ignored his mother's command. We do know, however, from ethnographies on Taiwanese families in that region at that time, that parents took children's fights seriously (Xu Forthcoming). In other words, there was a widely shared cultural model of prohibiting children's fights in those communities: Preventing such fights was a central parental concern because fighting among children could lead to estranged relationship between adults and disrupt social harmony. Parents did not hesitate to punish children, and sometimes resorted to harsh means. But previous works rarely mentioned how children reacted to punishment. In the Wolf Archive, however, I encountered numerous episodes like this, where children easily got into physical conflicts, readily tattled to available adults, but also defied parental commands. Child fighting attracted attention not only from the ethnographers present at that time but also from me, the reinterpreter of these fieldnotes. Machine-learning algorithms, applied to the entire Child Observation (CO) corpus, also automatically identified it as a salient topic, even without any input from the human researcher. In fact, the opening vignette was part of an episode that algorithms calculated as "the most representative document" under this topic. Materials from this archive suggest that children understood the norm of no fighting. They knew that they would be punished for violating it. But their practice often contradicted this norm, and parental punishment did not seem to be particularly effective. Why? And what does it tell us about the nature of moral development, as well as the making and unmaking of "cultural models" in cultural transmission processes?

Prior research on Chinese childrearing tends to fixate on parenting, assume a simplistic, behaviorist reward–punishment mechanism, and rarely concern children's mental and social worlds (for a critique, see Xu 2022b). In particular, scholars in anthropology, psychology, and education have elaborated on the folk concept of *guan* – parental control and discipline – and established it as the dominant method of child training in the "traditional Chinese family" (Chao 1994; Fong 2004; Ho 1986; Tobin, Wu, and Davidson 1989; Wu 1996). Relatedly, training obedience was found to be the primary goal of traditional Chinese parenting (Wu 1996). These works told us a lot about what values were taught and how – by parents, educators, or caregivers. But from a cognitive anthropology perspective, this paradigm misses a crucial part of the story – the learners' perspective. What did children actually learn and how did they learn it (Stafford 1995: 11)? To address this problem, to understand the cultural models and realities of childrearing, we need to take a more critical look at parenting. We need to incorporate children's own complex social inferences and emotions. We need to look at how children's collective minds, including both intrapersonal processes and interpersonal communication, play a vital role in the transmission of moral norms in intergenerational dynamics. In other words, we need to bring children back into the study of childrearing.

Through the case of child fighting, I examine adult caregivers' cultural models and practices and contrast them with children's narratives and behavior. This case allows us to compare and integrate multiple types of textual data, such as Child Observation (CO), Child Interview (CI), Mother Interview (MI), Mother Observation (MO), and projective tests with children. I also triangulate different methods to make sense of such texts in a systematic manner, including ethnographic "close-reading," NLP (natural language processing) techniques and quantitative behavioral analysis. Such systematic analyses reveal how children's attitudes and practices departed from the most important parental cultural model in their community and deviated from the parental ideal of training obedience. Moreover, I probe into parental discipline and its discontents, highlighting children's moral judgment, social knowledge, and emotional experience in the communicative process of punishment.

Against Children's Fighting: A Cultural Model of Parenting

Cultural models are generic mental representations or schemas, both factual and value-laden assumptions about the world, shared in a particular social group (D'Andrade and Strauss 1992; Strauss and Quinn 1997). Ethnographic records of Martial Law Era in Taiwan noticed a common priority in parenting among rural Han Taiwanese communities, that is, the prohibition of children's fighting. Parents in these communities took such fights seriously, and readily intervened if they witnessed these conflicts or were called upon to help. In this sense, the prohibition of children's fighting is a salient cultural model for regulating interpersonal relations. Scolding and beating children at home or in public was a frequent scene in several Hoklo villages across different regions of Taiwan: Norma Diamond, who did fieldwork in Southern Taiwan in the early 1960s, observed adults tying children up for a beating to punish children's aggressive misconduct (Diamond 1969: 33, 42). Emily Martin, during her 1969 fieldwork in a village not too far from her teacher Arthur Wolf's fieldsite, wrote vividly about scenes of little children being harshly punished. For example, two little boys, aged one-and-half and three, got into a fight with each other. Their grandfather ordered them to kneel down, scolded and hit them, with a crowd of adult and child spectators laughing and joining in the scolding (Martin 1973: 214). The Wolfs also noticed this cultural model of parenting in Xia Xizhou. Margery Wolf noted: "No matter what aspect of child training we discussed with mothers the conversation always turned to the control of aggression. ... When we asked a mother to describe a good child, the first characteristic was always 'one

Crime and Punishment

who does not get into fights'" (M. Wolf 1972: 74–75). Arthur Wolf gave a sociological explanation that prohibiting children's fighting was driven by Taiwanese villagers' concern for maintaining harmony with neighbors in a close-knit, interdependent community (A. Wolf n.d.):

> M[m]ost Taiwanese mothers … were extremely anxious about their children's getting into fights with their neighbors' children. Children were never encouraged to fight back. To the contrary, they were severely punished for fighting regardless of whether or not they had instigated the fight. The most likely explanation is Minturn and Lambert's suggestion (Minturn and Lambert 1964: 159) that "relative anxiety about peer group aggression is related to the intimacy of social and economic bonds among members in the community, and the degree to which children can disrupt these adult relationships."

Neighborly harmony, no doubt, is an all-encompassing meta-norm, or a higher-order cultural model, in a community like this. But in light of abundant observational and interview materials, I want to qualify Wolf's general statement in two directions, differences in the actual consequences of children's fights and variations in actual parental interventions: First, as many examples from Wolf's notes together illustrate, "the disruptive potential of child conflicts is far from uniform, suggesting that relatedness, relative affluence or influence all may be mediating factors in determining a situation's volatility" (Duryea 1999: 95).[3] In some cases two families could reach agreement in the situation of their children's fight so it did not spill over to affect the adult relationships in the long run.[4] But in other cases even sisters-in-law quarreled frequently after their children's (first cousins) squabbles and other women in their neighborhood group had to act as mediators.[5]

---

[3] Maria Duryea's dissertation, based on revising Wolf's original fieldsite, focused on social transformations of that community, including its drastic urbanization and economic development and the impacts of those changes on childrearing practices (Duryea 1999). She had access to Wolf's general observation notes of village life (data type "G") and drew from those notes to make this conclusion.

[4] For example, Wolf fieldnotes type G, page 900, see Duryea (1999: 95).

[5] See M. Wolf (1972): 46.

Against Children's Fighting

A related point is that, although parents shared the concern to prohibit children from fighting and were ready to intervene, actual interventions varied by person and were contingent upon the situation. Such variations, ironically, could contribute to negative sentiments between adults. For example, on a June day in 1959, while research assistant MC was asking a twenty-seven-year-old mother about her marriage, her four-year-old son got into a fight with a three-year-old girl, his second cousin living next door. The two children both wanted to sit on the same rock, but the boy got there first and sat down, leaving no room for the younger girl. The girl cried and said, "I want to sit down, too!" and hit him. He hit her back, and she cried harder than ever. At first the boy's mother just asked what the trouble was, and the girl said she wanted to sit down, and the boy would not let her. The boy insisted that he had gotten to the rock first. The boy's mother then told them to only sit on half the rock, but still the boy refused to let the girl sit down. The girl sat on the ground and cried until her grandmother came out of the house and asked what the trouble was. The boy's mother said, "Oh, nothing, they just wanted to sit on the same rock." The grandmother picked up the girl, hit her fairly hard on the face, and dragged her off, beating her on the way. As she did this, she scolded her granddaughter saying, "You always are wrangling with people for things!" The boy's mother laughed and said, "Go ahead and hit her, I don't care."

MC's comment was inserted in this fieldnote:

She [the grandmother] looked mad, probably because [the boy's mother] had not done anything about the fight. The meaning of the mother's last words is that the grandmother could go ahead and hit her granddaughter, but "I am not going to hit my child." The mother then turned to her son and said, "Next time she has something first, you better not take it away from her, understand?" Her son protested saying, "I didn't take it. I had it first." She just smiled and didn't say anything more to him, resuming her conversation with MC, albeit this time on the topic of parental interventions into children's conflicts.[6]

---

[6] June 1959, Wolf fieldnotes type G (pages 842–43), quoted from Duryea (1999: 93–94).

Crime and Punishment

The boy's mother, having witnessed how the entire drama evolved from its beginning, thought it was mainly the girl's fault because her son indeed got the spot first and the girl hit him first. The girl's grandmother, however, expected the other party to punish the boy perhaps as harshly as she had punished the girl. This sense of unfairness might reflect the grandmother's personal belief that one has to punish one's child no matter who started it. Or it might be a misunderstanding because she only saw what happened at the end of the conflict and wasn't aware of the cause.

Schematic cultural knowledge tends to have a network structure, consisting of interconnected concepts and/or precepts (Strauss and Quinn 1997). Systematic, standardized interview data allow us to discern what are the shared, core elements of the cultural model or schema, that is, the most strongly connected units, and what are the more varied, peripheral elements affected by situational factors. Wolf's team interviewed forty-three mothers (MI) in early 1959, and several interview questions tapped into parental attitudes and beliefs regarding children fighting. First, question 11a in MI asked: "How about when P [the interviewee's child] is playing with one of the other children in the neighborhood and there is a quarrel or a fight – how do you handle this?" Among the forty-three respondents, all of them said they would intervene, except for one who did not provide an answer. Some elaborated on their interventions and rationale, which give us information on the contingent and varied elements: Twenty-five mothers mentioned disciplining their children right away. Thirteen answered they would call them home, talk to them to figure out what had happened and whose fault it was. Four said they would call them home but did not mention further details in their responses. Interventions included scolding, hitting their own children, or when other kids were at fault, telling them not to play with those who hit them.

A few mothers said they would scold the other child or tell the child's mother, but several considered reporting to the other child's mother a bad solution, precisely out of the concern not to disturb neighborly

Against Children's Fighting

harmony. For example, Huang Lin Shu,[7] a twenty-eight-year-old mother of four answered:[8]

I call my children home and scold them. If the others are in the wrong, I tell my children not to play with them. [What if some other children hit your children and they come home crying?] I tell them not to cry. And when I see the other children again I tell them that if they hit my children again I will cut their hands off. I don't like to tell adults because there might be a misunderstanding and a long argument.

Additional fieldnotes provide further insights into Huang Lin Shu's parenting approach and her neighborly and kin relations. The following is an excerpt from an MO episode:[9]

MC:	"What would you do if someone came to you and told you that your children had been fighting?"
LIN SHU:	"No one would do this except those people in House 2. Everybody knows that there's nothing that you can do about that family."
MC:	"What would you do if you saw your children fighting with some other children?"
LIN SHU:	"Tell them to come back. Huang Shu-feng (a 5-year-old boy) fights more than the others [my other children]."

If parents or other adults handled children's fighting badly, it became a frequent topic in these village mothers' gossip. For example, in another MO episode, two mothers, Chang Chu-hui and Pai Wu Chan told MC about the problem with an old man Wang Chuang-yu of another household. This grandfather often bullied other families' children, instead of disciplining his troublemaker grandchild Wang Chia-fu. Pai Wu Chan told a story about her own daughter Pai Yan-yan once being chased home by the old man. Yan-yan had been scratched and was hurt very

---

[7] According to Hoklo Taiwanese naming custom, Lin is her maiden name. That's why I kept it separate from her first name Shu.
[8] MI #0, 05/01/1959.
[9] MO #0, 10/31/1960.

Crime and Punishment

badly. Chu-hui believed that when children got into a fight, each parent should take one's own children away from the fight. Below is Chu-hui's testimony:[10]

> Once Chia-fu and Ah-yin (my girl) had a fight. I was told of it so I went to find out what was really the matter. Chia-fu hit my girl hard, caught a hold of her front clothes and would not let go.
>
> I went over and pointed to Chia-fu's head, saying: "You, dirty boy. Get your hands off. Do you mean your grandpa will fight for you all the time?" Then I brought Ah-yin home.
>
> No sooner had I reached home than the old man Chuang-yu, Chia-fu's grandpa, walked towards me saying: "Come here, come out here."
>
> I said angrily, "What for?"
>
> He said, "I'll beat you for scolding my Chia-fu."
>
> I paid no attention. Fortunately his other grandchild (a teenager) came to take him home.

Besides the general consensus on intervening in a fight and managing one's own children, age difference is an important factor when calculating children's moral responsibility in a fight. An older child bullying a younger one was considered really bad. Margery Wolf noticed the principle that older children ought to yield to younger ones (M. Wolf 1978: 245). This concern emerged in MI questions and answers about children's wrongdoing. For example, question 12a asked: "Some parents have trouble keeping their child from being mean to smaller children and bullying them. How have you managed this with P?" Thirty-seven out of forty-three mothers (86 percent) explicitly disapproved this behavior: Among these, twenty-three mothers said they told their children not to bully smaller kids, using a normative, prohibitive tone such as "can't" and "shouldn't," eight mentioned they would beat their children up if this happened, and six mentioned scolding. Of the other six mothers, three said their children seldom bully younger ones, and three didn't

---

[10] MO #63, 08/03/1960.

answer. Question 12d asked: "What do you do when P (your child) hits or kicks another, younger child?" Among the thirty-four mothers who gave an answer, twenty-three said beating/hitting the child and ten said scolding the child. The only mother who did not mention "hit," "beat," or "scold" answered in a hypothetical manner: "My child seldom hits others. If this does happen, I tell her she can not hit others."

Third, like "Intervene when one's child gets into a fight" and "Older children bullying younger ones is particularly bad and deserves punishment," the prohibitive imperative "Do not fight back" is another core notion in this cultural model of parenting. Question 11c asked: "Do you ever encourage P to fight back?" Among the remaining thirty-nine mothers,[11] thirty-eight of them answered "No." And many of them used normative expressions, such as "I can't," "you can't," "you mustn't," or "parents can't," or absolute terms "I never" before the phrase "encourage children to fight back." Only one answered differently: "If the other child is the same age as my daughter, I tell her to fight back." That she considered age in assigning moral responsibility is consistent with her response to the previous question, how to handle it when one's child gets into a fight. This mother's rationale of handling a child's fight, after all, partly conforms to the precept against older children bullying the young: "It depends on who is right. If the other child is bigger and is in the wrong, I tell the other child's mother. If my child has done something wrong, I scold her."

Mothers' answers to the next question suggest that "Do not fight back" applies even if one's own child were the victim. To this question (11d), "What do you tell P to do when another child hits him?" only two mothers out of thirty-five who provided an answer said they would tell their children to fight back because they didn't want theirs to be bullied by bad children. Among those who did not want their children to fight back in this situation,

---

[11] Two respondents didn't give an answer, and one said something not directly informative. This one answered: "I am always worrying that he will fight with others. When he fights with others then he comes home crying" (MI-54, date unspecified).

their responses were one or a combination of the following: to call the child home, to tell the child not to play with the bully, to scold one's own child (i.e., "Why do you go out to play?"), to scold the other child, or to tell the other child's mother. Also, the concern of not letting children's fights cause bad feelings between adults reemerged in some answers.

Mothering practices largely converge with these interview responses. Compared with the responses elicited by MI, according to Arthur Wolf (n.d.: 19), "they [Mother Observation episodes] have a verisimilitude of the kind that distinguished great novels from popular romances. One need not worry that they reflect ideals rather than actual behavior." Research assistant MC was the key to ensure the quality of these observations and interviews with mothers, as she was liked and trusted by all. Interview and observational records illuminate this shared cultural model of parenting, that is, prohibition and disapproval of children's fights, with the underlying rationale to maintain neighborly harmony. To intervene promptly in children's fights, to prohibit children from bullying younger ones, and not to encourage children to fight back constitute the core elements of this cultural model, although the concrete intervention methods vary by situation and person.

To Fight or Not to Fight: Children's Narratives

While the cultural model against child fighting was well established and widely shared among mothers, children's own narratives pose a challenge to it: They understood the parental belief of no fighting, but only paid lip service. When presented with hypothetical scenarios of being hit by another child or when asked to interpret ambiguous pictures of two children, fighting back or fighting became children's default response.

First, just as MI analysis illuminates mothers' cultural model of parenting, results from standardized CI with seventy-nine children (ages 3–10) shed light on children's own attitudes. One question in CI used a first-person, hypothetical scenario to probe into children's reasoning

To Fight or Not to Fight: Children's Narratives

Table 2.1 *Answers to the physical assault scenario in Child Interview Question 8a*

Question	Revenge/intervention Coding	Number of children	Percentage (%)	Binomial test
8a	Yes	57	76	$p < 0.001$***,
	No	18	24	Cohen's g
	Total	75	100	$= 0.26$

"Yes" means the child would seek for revenge or intervention. "No" means no revenge or intervention. *** means $p < 0.001$.
Source: Adapted from Xu (2020b): Table 1.

about physical fights. The main prompt was: "Suppose another child (O) your age comes up and hits you: What would you do?" Out of seventy-nine children, only four did not give an answer, I excluded those four and coded the remaining seventy-five answers as a binary variable, whether or not P (the protagonist, the interviewee) seeks revenge/intervention (Yes/No), directly or indirectly. Specifically, "Yes" answers include two types: (1) direct revenge, such as "hit him," "fight with him," and "hit back" and (2) indirect revenge – for example, tattling and enlisting help from authority figures (parents and teachers) or older brothers to potentially scold or hit O. "No" answers mainly include avoidance ("Run back home") and ignoring ("It doesn't matter"). The results (see Table 2.1) reveal a general preference for revenge/intervention in the scenario of being hit. Among the fifty-seven "Yes" answers, thirty-seven were direct, tit-for-tat revenge, to fight back physically, and twenty were indirect revenge, to tattle. Children's audacious responses to questions about fighting stand in contrast to their mothers' insistence on no fighting and no fighting back.

While CI revealed children's actual attitude, what they *would* do, their narratives in another context showed that they knew what they *should* do: Children were not supposed to fight back. Based on CI, Arthur Wolf later made a written questionnaire to test more children in elementary schools. He and his assistant Mr. Huang Chieh-Shan brought the questionnaire to two schools, Shalun elementary where Xia Xizhou children attended and another school on the opposite side of Shulin town. In the classroom, Wolf asked the teacher to first wrote the categories on the board and then read the questions aloud, in Mandarin. For example, there were six responses categories for each of the aggressive questions: "hit him," "curse him," "tell my friends," "tell my mother," "tell his mother," and "do nothing." Although the original questionnaires are still yet to be found and I do not have the actual results, Wolf's own conclusion was quite clear: "[I]t was obvious that most of the children were not telling me what they would really do" (n.d.: 22):

In one class a boy sitting in the front row read aloud the responses to the aggression questions, "hit him, curse him," etc. shaking his fist as he read, but he always checked the last category, "do nothing." I asked the teachers in the Sha-lun school to leave the classroom and let me[12] administer the questionnaire, but this made no difference. Even when I diluted the response categories to "feel like I might hit him, feel like I might curse him," etc. the great majority of the children would not admit to responding to aggression in kind.

The contradiction between School Questionnaire and Child Interview results has to do with methodological differences. This contrast reflects, as I discussed in Chapter 1, children's sensitivity to communicative contexts, partners, and linguistic cues in fieldwork. The interviews were administered by children's trusted figure MC in a familiar, informal setting, and in Taiwanese, so children did not hesitate to say they would fight back. The questionnaires were administered by what they called "the foreigner" ("Big Nose") or by their teacher, both intimidating figures, in a formal classroom setting, and in Mandarin, actually the only language children were allowed to speak in that authoritarian context (Klöter 2004). So children were smart enough to merely give socially desirable answers, suggesting that they were aware of the prescribed norm.

---

[12] It remains unclear how exactly this was administered. In my phone interviews with Mr. Huang (spring 2021 and spring 2022), he proudly emphasized that he went along with Wolf and assisted with administering School Questionnaire.

Moreover, beyond the explicit attitude expressed in interviews, data from one projective test TAT shed light on children's implicit attitude on fighting. When encountering ambiguous scenarios about social interactions, or when speculating what the characters would do in these scenarios, "fighting" emerged as a dominant theme in children's narratives: Using NLP techniques to aggregate all ninety-two children's responses to all nine pictures, I found that the word "打架"/fighting ranked the 6th highest, appearing 694 times, only after the quantifier "一个"/one (1,239 times), a character's name "B1 (Boy #1)" (897 times), the nouns "孩子"/child (858 times) and "母亲"/mother (817 times), and the pronoun "他们"/they (701 times).[13] A closer look at these responses shows that "fighting" emerged either as an interpretation of what two or more child characters in the picture were doing, or as an antecedent of what the adult character was doing to the child character in the picture. In the latter case, children interpreted the adult–child interaction as punishment and automatically inferred that fighting was the reason. Bear in mind that children were nervous at the TAT testing scene, which has to do with the setting and the researcher Mr. Huang's personality, as I mentioned in Chapter 1. But because they were asked to tell stories about other people in the pictures, instead of about themselves, they did not have to suppress the intuitive idea of "fighting" that was against the social norm. Their interpretations demonstrate the saliency of "fighting" in their mental world, which leads us to examine this in their actual world.

The Reality of Child Fighting

Observational records provide rich information on the reality of fighting. Among over a hundred available episodes of "situation-based observations," children's disputes and fights were a focal topic, ranging from light hitting to more severe incidents, and immediate revenge

---

[13] I included these Chinese characters as they appeared in the original transcript.

Crime and Punishment

Figure 2.1 A boy in a fighting pose
Source: Photo by Arthur Wolf.

(e.g., hitting back) was quite common (Figure 2.1). Beyond these, CO data are especially suitable for a systematic evaluation. These observations were not guided by a set of focal topics but were designed to collect randomized snapshots of children's life as it spontaneously unfolded, including its most undramatic moments, for example, when a child idly looked at other children playing and felt bored. Therefore, I focused on CO texts, using both machine "distant reading" – NLP techniques – and "close reading" – granular-level behavioral analysis, to extract general patterns of children's fighting.

Natural language processing techniques work well to analyze linguistic patterns of these systematically collected texts. A machine-learning method called "topic modeling" can discern latent patterns of thematic structures in a corpus, based on word distribution probabilities. Topic modeling has become increasingly popular in digital humanities (Du 2019). In particular, I used unsupervised LDA (Latent Dirichlet

Allocation) (Blei 2012) to spontaneously identify a set of latent "topics" otherwise difficult to extract through manual coding. One caveat is that these statistical algorithms are agnostic to the actual meanings of tokens, words, sentences, or a document ("bag of words") (Fuller 2020). Therefore researchers need to infer the meanings of machine-generated "topics" – in the form of word clusters, and sometimes these "topics" don't make intuitive sense to the human eye. The LDA topic-modeling algorithms identified a total of fourteen topics in the CO corpus, some of which, fortunately, did make immediate sense in the context of children's life (see Appendix for more details).[14] One topic, ranked as the seventh salient, features these top ten keywords (in the order from the #1 highest probability to #10): "hit," "mother," "hard," "angry," "back," "head," "copulate," "laugh," "angrily," and "fight." This likely depicts scenarios of children's physical conflict (verbs like "hit" and "fight"), usually accompanied by some cursing ("Copulate[15] with your mother!") – very common among children, accentuated with the emotion of anger and interspersed with some laughing from the aggressors or spectators. The fact that this topic emerged from an unsupervised machine-learning exploration of CO corpus suggests the prevalence of children's fighting in their daily life.

Bear in mind that these results are all probabilistic estimations. What's more, naturalistic observations of young children are especially fuzzy and messy, and the boundary of an observation, or the beginning and ending of a text, was seldom demarcated by a single event. In the middle of an observation, children might be doing one thing at this moment, but switched to something else completely different. Or some incident suddenly happened at the next moment. They might be distracted by a noise, or called by their caregivers to run an errand, and ran away from

---

[14] I used Python's Gensim package to perform LDA topic modeling, implemented in Mallet tool.
[15] This is the standard word used in the English fieldnotes, although there might be other more suitable swear words.

the observer. Therefore, one episode of spontaneous observation, or one "document" in topic modeling terms, might contain several, sometimes unrelated "topics." Topic-modeling algorithms assigned each document a distribution of probabilistic "weights" of all topics, and the topic with the highest weight was selected as the "dominant topic" in this document.

These algorithms also identified what's called "the most representative document" under each topic, that is, the document with the highest percentage of contribution from this particular "dominant topic." I used an excerpt of this "most representative document" grouped under the topic of what I call "child fighting" as the opening vignette of this chapter. The dominant topic, "child fighting," contributed to 39.0 percent of this particular episode, a fairly high number.[16]

The algorithms then calculated the number of documents grouped under each "dominant topic." What I call "child fighting" was the dominant topic in 107 episodes, about 6.4 percent of the entire CO corpus. A good reference framework is the range of these numbers across all fourteen topics: minimum seventy-four episodes (4.4 percent of the entire CO corpus) and maximum 195 episodes (11.6 percent), so "child fighting" lies somewhere in the middle. In fact, children's fights might have appeared in many more episodes, but it was not the "dominant," or the most salient topic.

Beyond the probabilistic distributions generated by algorithms, I completed the granular-level, manual coding of the corpus, what I call "behavioral grading," to gain a more precise understanding of children's fights. Among all 1,678 CO episodes, I found that children's physical conflict happened in 324 episodes, about 20 percent of the entire corpus.[17] Furthermore, connecting behavioral grading of CO with demographic data, I found that 176 children were involved in physical conflict (in at least one episode), about 81 percent of all 218 children (ages 0–12) that appeared in CO texts.

---

[16] Across all fourteen topics, this statistic ranges from 31.3 percent to 50.1 percent.

[17] Physical conflict consists of two behavioral themes: physical aggression (scores 0.5 or 1) and dominating (score 1 only), and these two behaviors overlap in some instances but not all. For example, a child hit another child out of pure anger or as self-defense,

Parenting and Its Discontents: The Disobedient Child

Table 2.2 *Older children dominating younger children through coercion, according to behavioral grading of Child Observation texts*

Behavior	Type of instances	Number of instances	Percentage (%)	Chi-square test of independence
Dominance through physical coercion	An older child to a younger one	100	72.5	$X^2 = 36.535$, $p = 1.166\text{e-}08$***, Cohen's $W = 0.8348$
	A younger child to an older one	24	17.4	
	Two children of same age (by year)	14	10.1	

*** means $p < 0.001$.

Many scenarios that children described, when answering the hypothetical questions on physical assault in CI, indeed appeared in CO episodes. A few examples include: "Hit him with a bench," "Hit him with my fist," "Slap him," "Call older brother to hit him," "Take a rock and hit him," and "Hit him with a slingshot." Furthermore, many children's behavior violated the expectation of older children yielding to younger ones, an important doctrine in the local cultural model. In particular, when it comes to dominance through physical coercion, 100 out of all 138 instances (72 percent) involve an older child bullying a younger one (Table 2.2).

Parenting and Its Discontents: The Disobedient Child

Parents considered children's fighting as a major moral transgression and were ready to intervene and punish. However, not only did children's attitudes toward and actual practice of fighting defy the parental cultural model of no fighting, they did so *in spite of* parental discipline

> not for dominating purposes. Specifically, 167 children were in "physical aggression," 120 children involved in "score 1" dominating. A total of 176 children were observed in physical aggression or "score 1" dominating behavior. The behavior "physical aggression" was observed in 238 episodes and "score 1" dominating observed in 121 episodes. A total of 324 episodes had one of these behaviors or both.

Crime and Punishment

and punishment. In many families mothers were in charge of disciplining children when they misbehaved. Among the thirty-three mothers who responded to question 13g: "Who disciplines P when he is especially naughty," twenty-three of them said mother (self) was the one in charge (70 percent), five said the child's father (15 percent), three said multiple caregivers (9 percent), and two said it depended on who was present in that situation (6 percent). Corporal punishment was quite common, both for mothers and for fathers who were less involved in childrearing but whose beating could be frightening to children. When mothers hit their children, many of them tended to hit persistently. Thirty-eight mothers responded to question 14b: "Did you ever spank P?" Thirty-three said yes (87 percent), five said they seldom or never spanked their children (13 percent), but used other means, like scolding, making the child standstill, or slapping the child. Thirty-eight mothers responded to question 14o: "When you punish P, do you stop as soon as P begins to cry or do you punish P a definite amount whether P cries or not?" Thirty-four (89 percent) mothers said they would not stop when P began to cry. Many said they didn't care about the offender child's crying. They were so mad that they kept hitting P until the anger receded. The remaining four mothers (11 percent) said they seldom or never hit P.

One mother, across multiple questions in MI, insisted that she never hit her stepson, because being a stepmother put her in a difficult situation. "If he were my own child it wouldn't matter." The child's biological mother died when he was young. Unlike a biological mother, if a stepmother exerted too harsh punishment, people would cast doubt on her intentions toward the stepchildren. But her complaint tells us, again, that mothers in this village, in general, were expected to punish their children who got into fights:[18]

To be a stepmother is very difficult. I never hit P. I only scold him. Other people who don't have anything to do after they eat like that talk about me. If

[18] MI #4, 05/24/1959.

Parenting and Its Discontents: The Disobedient Child

P fights with other children the children's mother will say to me, "When his grandmother was here she punished him, but you don't care about it." I am very angry.

Children also anticipated that their parents would punish them if they got into a fight. CI question 9e asked: "What if your parents know about it (your misbehavior)? What would they do to you?" Among the sixty-three children who answered this question, fifty (79 percent) said their parents would punish them, through scolding, hitting, or both.[19] The older a child became, the more likely the child would expect parental punishment.[20]

But many children did not expect parental punishment to be really useful. Sixty-four children responded to CI question 10a: "What do you do when your mother scolds you for something you've done wrong?" I coded the answers into two broad categories, actively submitting to parental discipline or not, and found twenty-three "yes" (36 percent) versus forty-one "no" answers (64 percent), which means that children would not submit.[21] In the order from high to low frequency, "yes" answers include: changing their behavior, feeling bad for their wrongdoing, and even just superficially, crying to their mothers, pleading for forgiveness or promising they would not dare to make the same mistake again. The "no" answers are escaping/running away, ignoring (e.g., "Doesn't matter"), enduring but not doing anything (e.g., "Let her scold"), reasoning with mom (e.g., "arguing"), or scolding mom back.

Question 10c in CI, "What do you do when your mother spanks you for something you've done wrong?" elicited a similar pattern of responses, that spanking did not deter children. I coded according to a binary criterion of submitting to discipline or not and the result was twenty "yes" answers (32 percent) versus forty-three "no" answers

---

[19] Binomial test, $p < 0.001$, Cohen's $g = 0.29$.
[20] Binomial logistic regression, $p = 0.01$.
[21] Binomial test, $p = 0.03$, Cohen's $g = 0.14$.

Crime and Punishment

(38 percent).[22] Among the "yes" answers, compared to the scolding question, even fewer children said they would change their behavior. But some were smart enough to come up with a new solution, "Take care of the children for her," as a way to make amends and please their mothers. Among the "no" answers, some children upgraded their revenge from arguing, for example, "Ask my mother why she hits me," to hitting back, for example, "Ask my father to hit her." Some answers were particularly striking, for example: "Hit her. Not be afraid of her. If she used the broom to hit me, I would take it away from her and hit her back."

One might wonder, were these interview responses merely children's fantasy? Did they actually dare to disobey or rebel when being punished for fighting? Indeed, snapshots of children audaciously maneuvering against punishment spread over MO, systematic data on caregiver–child interactions. For example, naughty boy Wang Ching-fu often got into conflict with other children. His mother was quite annoyed by him and hit him a lot, sometimes using a big vine. In one incident, this seven-year-old and his neighbor's four-year-old boy Wu Chia-lin had a face-off, Ching-fu looking mad. An adult bystander reported to Ching-fu's mother. Mom yelled at him repeatedly. It started with scolding, "Stop it, you early death child!" Then she escalated, threatening to beat him up: "Do I have to beat you up again the way I beat you yesterday? Do you hear me?" That scolding and threatening, however, did not deter Ching-fu at all. He kept mumbling angrily and then hit Chia-Lin again.[23]

Besides disobeying their own parents, children also dared to argue back and scold other adults. A young mother Cheng Shi-lin was scolding an eleven-year-old boy Huang Chin-che for scaring her child Cheng Ling-lin and making the little boy cry. She complained: "This Huang Chin-che! Whenever there is no school or he gets out early, he always

---

[22] Binomial test, $p = 0.002$, Cohen's $g = 0.18$.
[23] MO #48, 9/2/1960.

Parenting and Its Discontents: The Disobedient Child

makes the children cry!" Chin-che kept arguing back. The woman got more agitated: "Whenever you say something to him, he always talks back." Chin-che countered: "It's my mouth! You can't stop me from talking."[24] I burst out laughing when I spotted this conversation, as if I heard my own eleven-year-old boy talking.

Some children even took advantage of the punishment situation and turned it into an opportunity for bargaining, especially over pocket money. One afternoon, old lady Wang Huang Yu was sitting on a dead limb in the yard, napping, and didn't pay any attention to young boy Cheng-jin's whining for some money. Another little boy Te-long was poking and teasing the observer MC, and Cheng-jin got into a conflict with him, bullying him. At this point, Te-long screamed and woke up the old lady. She scolded Cheng-jin, "You this child, how can you be so completely without good in you?" Cheng-jin paid no attention, and the old lady fell back napping. Then Cheng-jin took away Te-long's stick and they two started pinching and pushing each other, both of them very mad. Their noise woke up the old lady again. She yelled at them, commanding them to move away from each other. Cheng-jin did not obey at all. Instead he countered her: "Why don't you give me fifty cents then?"[25]

More generally, among all 215 scenarios of "obey" in CO, only in eight scenarios children fully complied to adults' commands or disciplinary measures (behavioral score = 1). In 124 scenarios children were hesitant or reluctant to comply (behavioral score = 0.5): In these scenarios, the adult had to repeat their commands or escalate their scolding or threats before the child in question finally listened. Moreover, in eighty-three scenarios children completely ignored adults' commands (behavioral score = 0). Training obedience, in order to achieve the ideal of filial piety, has long been considered the quintessential goal of traditional

---

[24] CO #355, 12/01/1959.
[25] MO #130, 9/4/60.

Crime and Punishment

Chinese childrearing (Wu 1996). These Xia Xizhou children's words and deeds, however, shed light on the rarely studied side, drawing our attention to the "disobedient child."

Punishment and Its Inefficacy

Why, then, wasn't parental punishment effective in deterring children from fighting? That strong parental punishment was not enough to change children's behavior points to the limit of a behaviorist, reward-reinforcement model of learning. The orthodox view is that punishment incentivizes people to adopt desired behavior through basic, negative-reinforcement mechanism of maximizing reward (desired behavior). Recent work in moral psychology, however, calls for appreciating the inferential and signaling processes of punishment that people respond to punishment as a communicative signal to be interpreted (Sarin et al. 2021).[26] I examine children's complex social cognition and the specific kinds of emotions children experience in the moment to understand what the punished actually learns from punishment. I argue that, in learning morality, young children, the target of parental punishment and (dis)-approval, bring in their own reasoning of and emotional experiences at the situation. They not only *interpret* the punisher's intentions, but also *evaluate* those intended messages and even judge the punisher's moral status.

First, let us look at parents' folk theory of punishment. Mothers saw punishment as necessary and beneficial for raising a good child – a child who listens to parents and obeys their commands. Thirty-eight mothers answered this question (14p) in MI: "What is your attitude towards punishing children?" Twenty-one (50 percent) said it always good to punish, mostly using normative expressions, for example, "Children should

---

[26] New research suggests that people in the context of receiving help also evaluate the sender's moral status (Yu, Zhou, and Nussberger 2022).

be punished," "You have to hit children," and "You must punish a bad child." Eleven mothers (29 percent) said it was good to punish sometimes, for example, in the right context – when a child misbehaved, or punish to the right degree – not too often, otherwise the child wouldn't be afraid and the punishment would lose its deterring power. Only six mothers (16 percent) did not think punishment necessary or good at all, stating that their children were quite well behaved thus did not need punishment.

Notably, this folk view by default understands "punishment" as physical – hitting children, and it can be quite harsh. As one mother said, "when I hit them [my children] I don't worry about whether they die or not." Many mothers pitted hitting – inflicting a cost – against what they called "teaching" – communicating with children to explain why certain behavior was bad. As part of "parental ethnotheories" (Harkness et al. 2015), this view of punishment reflects adults' naïve imaginations about children. They believed that hitting was necessary especially when children were young because (1) young children didn't have the ability to reason or understand much (see also M. Wolf 1978) and (2) hitting could induce fear in a child and thereby ensure *guan* (control), an important Chinese concept of socialization (for a critical review, see Xu 2017: 149–53). If children were trained this way at a young age, when they grew older, they would not need harsh punishment, and parents could reason with them.

Not only did many parents assume that young children lacked reasoning, they also thought little about young children's emotional reactions (Ward 1985: 195). Take anger as an example. Question 11e in MI asked: "Sometimes, children get angry at their parents when they are being criticized or scolded. How do you handle this with P?" Thirty-eight mothers responded, but only one mother said she would explain to her children why they had to be punished, so they understood and wouldn't get mad. Among the other respondents, twenty mothers would ignore P's anger, ten would punish P more (scold, or beat, or make P stand up), and eight said P wouldn't get angry.

Crime and Punishment

Contrary to these mothers' naïve assumptions, their young children had a more complex mental world: They were able to reason about right and wrong, and their rich emotional experience – although only partially documented in ethnographic notes – astonished me as I plowed through these notes. Ethnographies across cultures have identified emotional arousal as a universal method in childrearing (Quinn 2005). But we still need to closely examine the specific emotions aroused in children and what children learn from those embodied emotional experiences.

Arthur Wolf left this comment about projective tests (n.d.: 24): "A few of the stories reveal emotions that are not apparent in either the child observations or the child observations. Shown a picture of a child dropping a bowl one girl burst into tears, crying, 'Her mother will beat her! Her mother will beat her hard!'" Indeed, in TAT children were presented with several ambiguous scenarios about adult–child interactions and almost all of them interpreted them as parental punishment. Many children did express a sense of fear when narrating these punishment stories. However, instead of internalizing the conveyed doctrines or appreciating adults' righteousness, what children had inferred from these stories, or learned from similar situations in their real life, might have been adults' domineering status, coercive power, bad temper, or unfair treatment toward children.

Fear is not the only emotion aroused in punishment scenarios. Several mothers confessed that sometimes their punishment was more contingent upon *qi* – their anger or bad mood, than by children's misbehavior *per se*. Correspondingly, anger was another salient emotional reaction of children. For some children, such anger was out of a sense of injustice, directed toward the adult exerting punishment. For others it was directed toward the self, related to shame, an important emotional socialization goal and strategy in Taiwanese families (Fung 1999). Also, when a child witnessed another child being beaten by parents in public, a pained expression was documented in several episodes. In one episode, While MC was observing a four-year-old boy Wang Jun-hsian, a teenage girl nearby burst out screaming because her mother wanted to wash her hair. A crowd of children soon gathered, standing around watching the girl getting spanked for refusing to have her hair washed, and the girl screamed and cried louder. The bystander boy Jun-hsian looked very distressed. He might have been frightened. But as young children develop a sense of empathy and sympathy very early on,[27] the "distressed look" might also indicate the bystander's sympathy toward the punished. Children might have felt quite stressed in situation of severe punishment. In fact, during the last three months of Arthur Wolf's stay in Xia Xizhou, he managed to take the urine sample of children and safely transport it back to the U.S. Then his team found some positive correlation between mothers' harshness in punishment, according to the 1959 MI results, and boys' adrenaline level tested in 1960.[28]

Moreover, whatever signals the adult was communicating via punishment – power, righteousness, and/or a concrete moral norm, some young recipients rejected or perhaps even resented that signal. For example, instead of fear and/or compliance, children sometimes openly expressed their discontent with punishment and disagreement with adult-prescribed moral norms, asserting their own moral judgment of the situation. A seven-year-old boy Wang Yi-kun got into a fight with a younger boy. The boy's father Li Kuo-liang learned about this. He scolded Yi-kun for violating the moral norm of older children yielding to younger ones. He then cursed Yi-kun and threatened to beat him up. Yi-kun defiantly confronted him and articulated his own reasoning:[29]

---

[27] For a brief review of the emergence of empathy in early childhood and how it relates to their everyday life, see Xu (2017): 73–95.
[28] The details of this study were included in an unpublished mimeograph presented at the Seminar on Personality and Motivation in Chinese Society, Bermuda, January 1964, entitled "Aggression in a Hokkien Village: A Preliminary Description." Unfortunately, I didn't find it in Arthur's private library, therefore cannot make any valid judgment on the coding criteria and measurement of mother's harshness or the statistical procedures of the correlation analysis.
[29] MO #119, 08/11/1960.

Crime and Punishment

Li Kuo-liang scolded him loudly, "Kan.[30] Why did you hit a boy smaller than you? You should give way to a boy who is smaller than you. You should. Didn't you know it? You hit him so hard that you hurt him. I'll call the policemen and let them seize you."

Yi-kun held his head high up looking aimlessly around showing that he was not at all scared. Kuo-liang stopped to breathe and Yi-kun took the chance, saying, "He tried to take my thing away by force. He even pushed me down to eat the mud. Why shouldn't I beat him for it."

Kuo-liang cursed, "Kan. If you hit him again I'll surely beat you to death. Try it and see. Kan."

Then he walked away talking to Lin Liu-yan (a mother from another household), who happened to pass by, and telling the story angrily. This mother said, "He (Yi-kun) really is a bad boy."

What did the repeated scolding and cursing in the particular situation signal to Yi-kun? Instead of learning a moral lesson, Yi-kun might have interpreted the adult man's intention as selfish – to defend his own son and perhaps also to dominate Yi-kun, and Yi-kun did not like that communicated intention. Yi-kun thought he was righteously defending himself, because it was the other child who initiated the conflict and bullied him. He rejected the moral precept taught in this community that older children shouldn't hit younger ones. He defended another principle of reasoning, that hitting was justified when it was defensive and reciprocal. The emotion Yikun was experiencing in that situation was anger, rather than fear or guilt. Above all, that adult man probably failed to establish himself as a moral authority in the youngster's eyes.

Children also gossiped among themselves about adults. For example, a six-year-old girl Wang Su-chun, while playing with Wang Yi-kun, complained to him: "Bei-guang (her grandfather's older brother) is very mean. One day his grand-daughter Chang Ah-ying was just standing under the guava tree, Bei-guang came and hit her." Yi-kun extended his moral judgment and expressed his sympathy: "He shouldn't have

---

[30] A common swear word in Taiwanese.

hit her. She was just standing there. She didn't do anything." Su-chun agreed: "That's right. He's not supposed to hit her."[31] These children judged adults' behavior in clearly normative terms, with their own sense of justice and fairness.

"I Am Your Father!"

Ethnographic records of "the Chinese family" from past to present have said a lot about parental cultural models and disciplinary measures. Their analytical focus, nonetheless, was skewed toward adults – the punishers. This paradigm rarely focused on the feelings and reactions of the punished, and therefore underestimated the limits and limitations of "parenting." When I encountered scenarios of fighting and punishment in these fieldnotes, I couldn't help but wonder: What did these little ones think and feel about that, when they were disciplined by parents, or observed other children being scolded and shamed? When they pleaded to parents, did that deter them from misbehaving, or was that more of a negotiation strategy? When Wang Yi-kun rejected the adult man's accusation and defended himself for hitting that man's child, we are prompted to ask: How do children develop their own understanding of what is right and wrong, which might be at odds with what adults taught or demonstrated? How do they act, in concrete situations, against the prescribed cultural models?

During the past decades, although more and more anthropologists have made morality and ethics an explicit theoretical focus (for a comprehensive review, see Fassin 2012; Laidlaw 2017; Mattingly and Throop 2018), this new scholarship has rarely examined the perspective of learning, namely, how young children develop moral sensibilities.[32] On the other hand, psychological anthropologists have long emphasized the

---

[31] CO #69, 08/13/1959.
[32] See a similar critique in Xu (2019).

Crime and Punishment

role of early socialization in transmitting cultural models and moral values.[33] Parental approval/disapproval and emotional arousal are universal mechanisms in shaping children into competent members of their communities (Quinn 2005; Strauss and Quinn 1997: 104), although concrete strategies and processes vary across societies.[34] What many have overlooked, however, is the fact that the very efficacy of parental approval and disapproval hinges upon children's cognitive, emotional, and moral predispositions. For example, training obedience is a primary childrearing goal in many agrarian societies (LeVine and LeVine 2016), but not many ethnographers put children's own perspectives at the center of analysis. The Wolf Archive provides a rare window into children's actual experience. I highlight "the point of view of those who are punished" (Stafford 2010: 206) and examine the communicative dynamics of punishment. More broadly, this perspective opens up a new direction to understand a central question in anthropology, the intergenerational transmission of cultural models, as cultural transmission and human development are, to a large extent, mutually dependent.

A classic study that illustrates children's experience is Jean Briggs' ethnography of traditional Inuit society. Instead of scolding or physical punishment, adults playfully tease little ones, presenting them with interrogations and dramas about real-life dilemmas, in order to cause children to think about the world and themselves (Briggs 1999). As Briggs closely traces the "mindsteps" of a three-year-old girl Chubby Maata in her day-to-day experience, we get to understand how children process the messages and manage the emotions prompted in interactions with adults.

Parenting approaches vary greatly across cultures.[35] Standing in stark contrast to the Inuit people, mid-twentieth century Taiwanese parenting,

---

[33] For a review, see Chapin and Xu (Forthcoming).
[34] For example, Chapin (2014) provides a fine-grained ethnographic analysis of emotional and moral lessons through which children in Sri Lanka are trained to disavow their own desires and incorporated into local social hierarchy.
[35] For a recent synthesis on parenting in a variety of cultural contexts, see LeVine and LeVine (2016).

or more generally, parenting in those preindustrial societies with high levels of social stratification, was much harsher in general, for example, using corporal punishment (Ember and Ember 2005). Punishment has long been seen as a key mechanism for maintaining parental authority and training children's obedience in traditional Chinese societies (Wu 1981). Severe discipline was quite common in Martial Law Era Taiwan, that is, through a combination of corporal punishment and public shaming. Anthropologist David YH Wu, who grew up in Taiwan, had this observation: "In rural Taiwan it is not uncommon to see a boy running and crying aloud, pursued by his mother with a stick in hand, while bystanders watch with amusement" (Wu 1981: 156).

But just like Chubby Maata was encouraged to think about existential dramas in life, the feelings and reactions of Xia Xizhou children at moments of punishment must have, in some way, prompted them to think about their own situations. We have some records in this regard, but mainly in the form of adults' retrospection, when such punishment experience has become part of their childhood memory. For example, in the late 1970s, an adult Taiwanese woman remembered that at the age of nine, she had to kneel by the door facing the street so that passersby could see her. She remembered such humiliation, rather than the physical punishment itself, as causing most pain (Wu 1981: 156). While the audience watching the public beating and shaming felt a sense of pain and distress, probably a combination of fear and sympathy, the most unforgettable part for the child, the bearer of such punishment, was a sense of humiliation. This memory immediately resonates with me. Although I never had the same experience, having to kneel down and facing a crowd of spectators, I do remember, as a young girl, the feeling of humiliation and anger after punishment. Yes, humiliation and anger, more than fear. I never understood why I deserved certain punishment. Nor have I ever believed in the Chinese saying *gunbang zhixia chu xiaozi* (English counterpart "Spare the rod spoil the child"), a precept that my father, like many in his generation, kept preaching. I was

Crime and Punishment

always somewhat skeptical about "the obedient child" archetype, which is popular in Chinese discourse and integral to American stereotypes about Asian parenting.

Now that I have become a mother, my sympathy toward parental discipline grew tremendously. I understand that harsh punishment does not contradict deep love. Even though I never used physical punishment toward my own child, in countless occasions I was really tempted to spank him. I feel for those annoyed Xia Xizhou mothers, who had to juggle between caring for multiple children and working in and outside the house to make ends meet. But I also realize that, no matter what, children are going to have their own feelings and perspectives, which can turn out quite different from what parents have expected. Children's discontents toward parental authority will always be there, going hand in hand with the parental desire for control and obedience, and with, of course, mutual love and attachment. While this archive provided me a precious opportunity to peek into the actual experience of disobedient children, in the process of working on this project, I have also become more attuned to my own child's voices of discontents. One evening in 2021, when I was reading a research article on my computer, my eleven-year-old son entered my room, glanced at my computer screen, and started taunting me: "Haha! 'Punishment: One tool, many uses' [the title of the article]! What do you want? All that you think about is how to punish me, huh? You stinky mom!"

On another occasion, without any warning, he broke into my room and burst out: "Little Jing! I am your father!" This absurd statement channeled his discontents toward parental authority, perhaps a mixture of fear, anger, and perhaps also contempt, into humor, sarcasm, and amusement. It also echoes a particularly hilarious episode in this archive, where a group of defiant children were mocking parents in pretend play. Chapter 3, shifting from parent–child relation and dynamics to children's world, will begin with that episode and explore how children navigate cooperation and conflict and build their own moral world through playing with peers.

THREE

Playful Creatures

Learning Morality in Peer Play

Playing "Mom Spanking Children"

On a November afternoon, after children came back from school, MC spotted this elaborately coordinated pretend play:[1]

Chang Ah-yin [8-year-old, a leader figure in her play group] played "mother." She was running around "spanking" all the children. Three younger children, two siblings Wang Su-chun and Wang Ah-fa and another girl Wang Mei-yu were going back to Ah-yin. Ah-yin ran out and they all ran away yelling: "Mother is coming!"

They ran all the way to the center before they discovered Ah-yin wasn't chasing them. They came back. Among them, Mei-yu didn't go all the way and just as they got back she yelled: "Mother is coming!" Off they went again, laughing and yelling. They returned again. "Mother" (Ah-yin) wasn't in sight. Su-chun sneaked around trying to see her.

Suddenly Su-chun's little brother Ah-fa yelled: "Mother is coming!" And Su-chun jerked to a stop. This was repeated several times. Finally, Ah-yin called Su-chun to "come home." Su-chun walked over to her.

Two boys, Wang Yi-kun and Liang Wei-lin, were kneeling in front of Ah-yin, laughing and moaning: "Oh mother, I don't dare do it again. Please don't spank me."

Ah-yin was getting some rocks from under a basket. Su-chen picked up a stick and walked over to the kneeling children and pretended she

---

[1] CO #314, 11/20/1959.

was striking them, saying: "Oh, you dead child. What are you kneeling here for?"

Su-chen walked over to Wei-lin and repeated this. Wei-lin stood up (angrily) and said: "Why do you hit me?" He hit Su-chen back. Su-chen just smiled. Wei-lin knelt down again and took up his refrain of "Oh Mother, don't hit me."

Su-chen: "Oh, you dead child! What are you kneeling here for?"

They both turned around and said: "Well, it's your 'mother' that told us to." Ah-yin came back with two rocks on a "plate" and a stick in her hand. She lifted the stick as if to hit them and they jumped up and pulled on her and said: "Oh, please don't hit me." Then they each grabbed a rock and ran away. Su-chen stood laughing.

Ah-yin: "Oh, those two dead children!" She put away her "plate."

Yi-kun and Wei-lin came back with several children behind them, waving the stolen rods and saying: "We're here! We're here!" Ah-yin jumped at them and they all ran away.

Ah-yin to Su-chen and another girl: "Follow me! Let's go!" They ran off and MC stopped the observation as there were fifteen kids running in all directions (Figure 3.1).

Teeming with childish laughter and directive speech acts, this episode mimics everyday "crime-and-punishment" scenes. It shows us how children, the least powerful members of local society at that time, turned mocking parental authority and discipline into their own entertainment. In the meantime, this vignette points to the importance of peer groups in learning morality: Peer groups are a source of moral knowledge, an emotional community, and a crucial social space for rehearsing, negotiating, and creating moral norms. In this spontaneous episode, children creatively re-enacted what happened in their real life in dramatized ways, enriched their pretend play repertoire, merged reality and fantasy, blended performed emotions with actual feelings, and blurred the boundary between cooperation and conflict.

A systematic analysis of the world of peer play highlights the importance of child-to-child ties, revealing general patterns of children's social

Playing "Mom Spanking Children"

Figure 3.1 A group of children playing
Source: Photo by Arthur Wolf.

networks and behavioral directions. Examining children's playful world, both in ethnographic detail and with scientific rigor, can illustrate the common scenarios and key features of children's social world. In peer play, children are developing what I call "the spectrum of moral sensibilities." They are learning about and engaging in cooperation and care, conflict and dominance, and creating gray areas in between. Through a human–machine hybrid approach of "reading" texts, I take a close look at teasing behavior to compare human and artificial intelligence. While computational techniques can uncover latent patterns of children's social life, even state-of-the-art AI algorithms lost to young children in making sense of pretend play. Children's sensibilities in discerning layered intentions, sentiments, and meanings not only shed light on the nature of human morality but also inspire me to reflect on ethnographic epistemology.

Playful Creatures

Rediscovering Child-to-Child Ties via Social Network Analysis

Western notions of "peer groups" tend to emphasize same-age children who are not related to each other via kinship ties. But I adopt a broader, anthropological definition that includes both same-age peer groups and mixed-age groups, including siblings and cousins (Goodwin and Kyratzis 2012). In fact, in a close-knit community such as Xia Xizhou, most children were connected via kin relations, and many interacted in mixed-age play groups. To examine peer groups in Xia Xizhou children's social world, let us first take a look at their social network patterns, because these patterns will give us a systematic overview of who they were hanging out with in everyday life.

I focus on Child Observation (CO), the systematically and naturalistically collected fieldnotes on children's behavior, to perform social network analysis. Network analysis sheds valuable light on peer interaction in the following ways: A total of 436 people appeared in the CO corpus, including 260 children: Thirty-five adolescents between the ages of twelve and eighteen and 221 children younger than twelve. But among a total of 1,678 episodes in the CO corpus, nearly three quarters ($n = 1,231$) involve children exclusively (ages below 18), with no adults at all. Even among the remaining 447 episodes, oftentimes adults were merely present, not actually interacting with children. Contrary to the predominant focus on parent–child ties and parenting in Chinese studies, this pattern highlights the previously obscured part, child-to-child ties. Also, this rate of adult presence (about one quarter) is even lower than the average rate of mother presence in the equivalent CO data of the original Six Cultures Study (32–41 percent) (Weisner et al. 1977: 174).[2] This cross-cultural comparative perspective highlights the importance of peer relations in Xia Xizhou children's world, which prompts us to go beneath childrearing discourses and delve into children's actual social life.

---

[2] The only exception is Taira, Okinawa (mother present in only 9 percent of observations).

Rediscovering Child-to-Child Ties

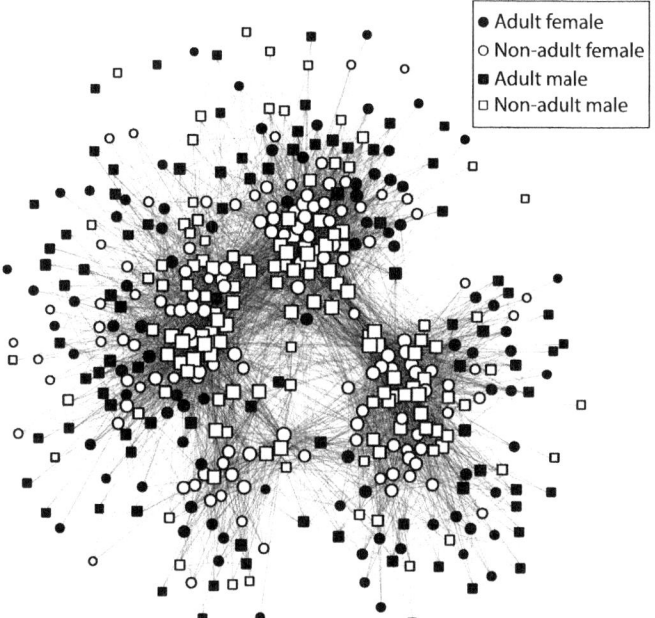

Figure 3.2 Child Observation co-occurrence network (including both children and adults)

Second, co-occurrence network analysis, based on first computing who appeared together in a given observation and then aggregating co-occurrence counts across all observations, confirms the primacy of child-to-child ties in this corpus.

Figure 3.2[3] portrays the entire CO network. Each node in the network represents a person, each edge (line) between two nodes represents the co-occurrence of these two people; the size of each node is calculated based on its "weighted degree centrality," that is, the node's direct connections weighted and aggregated, the weight assigned to each

---

[3] Analysis in Figures 3.2 was performed in R programming language (packages: igraph and qgraph) and visualized based on the Fruchterman–Reingold layout algorithm.

Playful Creatures

Table 3.1 *Number of behavioral-interaction entries grouped by age status and behavioral direction*

Age status	Behavioral role	Number of entries
Child	Initiator	10,800
Child	Recipient	10,988
Adolescent	Initiator	188
Adolescent	Recipient	156
Adult	Initiator	1,008
Adult	Recipient	752

connection (a pair of people) equal to the frequency of co-occurrence between that pair of people. Black nodes represent adults and white nodes represent children (below the age of eighteen). The nodes at the center are the ones with stronger connections in the network. This graph shows that children occupied a central position and that adults were at the periphery.

Zooming into the child-only co-occurrence network, modularity analysis shows that children formed four "cliques." I compared and contrasted the patterns of which children appeared together with those of the village women's groups detailed in Margery Wolf's book (1972: 42–52). The boundaries within these two types of groups diverge to a great extent. Children's groups, examined at a co-occurrence level, did not align with their mothers' groups, hence their social life manifests a certain degree of autonomy.

Moreover, in the CO corpus, beyond co-occurrence patterns, at a behavioral level, children interacted with peers a lot more than with adults. Analysis of the behavioral-interaction network shows that, among all behavioral-interaction entries ($N = 12,119$) coded from the CO corpus, children (ages <12) were the main actors, as both initiators and recipients, far outnumbering adults (eighteen years old and above) and adolescents (ages 12–18), see Table 3.1. The subsequent behavioral analysis in the rest of the book focuses on children below the age of twelve.

Last but not the least, family ties are an important factor in structuring peer networks. Homophily, the principle that nodes in a network, for example, people, tend to have links to other nodes with similar attributes, is a robust mechanism and an important parameter in social network analysis (McPherson, Smith-Lovin, and Cook 2001). In plain language, it means that birds of a feather flock together. Both in co-occurrence network and in behavioral-interaction network, household number is the strongest predictor of homophily among all demographic variables. This means that children who are from the same household, mainly siblings and sometimes cousins too, tend to be present together – in co-occurrence network,[4] and tend to actually interact together – in behavioral-interaction network, and this kinship/sibling effect is more pronounced than the effect of other demographic factors, such as gender.[5]

Playful Creatures

A hallmark of these children's peer world is playfulness. They climbed on the big banyan tree and shook its branches. They fought for the swing in the school playground, giggling. They enjoyed reading comics. They craved for snacks in the village shops and bargained with their mothers and grandparents for pocket money. They made cakes and dishes from mud. They stamped on lush green rice paddies. They were having fun and being creative even in the most mundane moments. They were children, the playful creatures.

---

[4] The probability for two people from the same household to have a tie in co-occurrence network is 0.886. The probability for two people from the same gender to have a tie is 0.240 (Exponential Random Graph Model).

[5] Correlation coefficient of assortativity score $r = 0.580$, meaning that 58 percent of the ties in the network are between children in the same household, a fairly high number (computed via iGraph in R); in contrast, the equivalent measure of the effect of gender is $r = 0.259$, meaning that 26 percent of the ties in the network are between children from the same gender.

Playful Creatures

This playful nature can also be examined quantitatively. I coded each episode in the entire CO corpus along the dimension of scenario type, including play, sibling care, housework, schoolwork, shopping/errands, and other work (e.g., helping with agricultural work). One episode can include multiple scenario types, and I found a total of forty-one combinations: for example, "play & sibling care" is one type of combination. Across all the episodes, "play" was the top scenario type, found in 1,602 episodes, including episodes that contain more than one scenario type. Within the contexts of spontaneous observation, children were always playing, even when they were also doing something else. The location data in the CO corpus, available in 1,672 episodes, offer useful insights on where children were hanging out with peers: They were most frequently observed near or inside someone's house (1,041 episodes), at or near school (221), and in village yards (123, including small yards in a house complex, big yards, and squares). They also gathered along various types of paths (79 episodes), inside or by the three village stores (74), by the irrigation ditch that runs from the main road through the village (40), by trees/gardens (35, including the big banyan tree, the guava tree, bamboo grooves, and vegetable gardens), by the river (24), by the temple near the village entrance (6), and at the paper factory of the big Wang house (2).

NLP analysis of CO texts sheds further light on children's playful world. In the cleaned and preprocessed CO corpus, the word "play" appeared over 4,000 times, as the third highest-frequency word, only next to "say" and "go."[6] Going beyond this superficial level of text-analysis, for example, word frequency counts, topic modeling efficiently reveals in-depth patterns of play: As described in Chapter 2, I used LDA topic-modeling algorithms to extract a set of latent "topics" that would otherwise have been difficult to quickly discern through manual coding. Inferring from the particular cluster of word distribution and

---

[6] Compared to the raw corpus, the cleaned and preprocessed corpus transformed all words to lowercase, removed punctuation, numbers and special symbols, excluded common stopwords and reduced a word to its lemma form.

representative texts automatically generated by the algorithms, one can see that quite a few topics among this list resemble particular types of games and interactions, or a mixture of different games and interactions (see Appendix).[7] I interpreted these "latent topics" as the following: playing hopscotch with tiles, playing card games with rubber bands as currencies, playing "marble" games using rocks, playing house, playing near water (ditches, pump) while washing clothes or vegetables, climbing trees, riding tricycles, jumping rope, playing ball, picking flowers, chasing one another or hide and seek, playing in the mud, and so forth. The underlying pattern of this machine-learning topic classification suggests that children's play is the most natural hallmark and overarching feature of these texts.

Manual classification and coding offers precise information on the kind of games children engaged themselves in: The most frequent type of game was hopscotch (161 times), followed by throwing rubber bands (109), ball games (96), card games, (79), playing house (75), playing with sticks (70), chasing/tag (65), playing in/around the trees (46), playing with cans or kick-the-can game (45), riding trikes or bikes (44), playing tops (37), playing in or with mud (37), marbles (32), hide and seek (31), jumping rope (30), maze-games (28), dueling games (28), fishing (26), picking flowers (24), and so forth. This list of play activities validates, to a considerable extent, the latent "topics" generated in topic modeling. Due to its naturalistic nature, each episode in CO usually contains multiple categories of games and scenarios, for example, "hopscotch, fighting, teasing." This pattern also aligns with topic-modeling results, that one latent "topic" might include several types of play settings or content. There are some differences between this manual coding and topic modeling though, "teasing" being one example, which I will discuss later in this chapter.

[7] Topic-modeling method won't generate an explicit name of any "latent topic," so the researcher still needs to interpret the meanings of such high-frequency word-collections, and sometimes such algorithm-generated "topics" are hard to interpret.

Playful Creatures

In general, three features characterize Xia Xizhou children's playful world: First, they played quite spontaneously, even in the middle of doing work, which means that, in their world, play and work were not distinctly separable. Second, play really mattered to children. Lastly, a good sense of humor saturates their play. The first point, spontaneity, suggests a certain degree of unpredictability in their social world. Children surprise you with their ingenious creativity. As an observer, you never knew which exact direction their peer interaction might be going, which became a great source of enjoyment for me while reading through CO. For example, children might be cleaning some chairs and wood boards, but all of a sudden they might invent a game of throwing the cleaning cloth around, with elaborate rules to compete over which child threw the cloth higher.[8]

Children took the matter of play very seriously. Sometimes they showed keener interest in play than in work (their assigned duties), even if the content of the game-play was quite similar to that of work assigned to them. The following episode of "playing house"[9] offers a glimpse into the special charm of play:

The children were playing house. Cheng Ling-li (a 6-year-old boy) came up with a pan of sand. He said to a 10-year-old girl Chang Chun-ling: "Here. Here is the sand." Chun-ling & Wang Shi-ling (a five-year-old girl) were cutting up vegetables. Chun-ling said: "Alright." Chun-ling's mom walked out just then and saw Chun-ling and said: "No wonder I couldn't find the pan! What? Did you go all the way to the river to get that sand? You stupid! When you are playing you will do whatever anyone tells you right away. If I asked you to do it, you wouldn't do it even if it were in front of the door!" Chun-ling smiled and looked a little guilty.

As MC noted at the end of this observation, Chun-ling's mom wasn't really mad, despite such moralistic scolding. Perhaps adults were amused by the seriousness of "playing-house" games. Children are indeed born to

---

[8] CO #567, 1/12/1960.
[9] CO #783, 02/14/1960.

find pleasure in play: They can transform every moment or occasion, however mundane it is, into entertainment. This playfulness permeated various kinds of everyday life scenarios, be it housework, sibling care, or school time. And it was often accentuated by humor, humoring themselves and others, as the following observation at a second-grade classroom[10] illustrates:

A girl (Chin-yen, 8-year-old) had a plastic bottle of tea in her hand. Another girl Peng Ah-lien said to her: "Give me a drink." Chin-yen countered: "No, I won't. I already have plums in it. How could I give it to you? (The school children put a certain type of plums in their water jugs to give the water a nice flavor. They relish this.)"

Ah-lien: "Well, then don't." She didn't look up from her work.

A boy named Wang Kuei-min lifted his head and said: "What? What did you say? Did you say you had plums in it?"

Chin-yen: "Yes, I have plums in it!"

Kuei-min started teasing her: "What? You say your grandmother is in it? (This is a play on the Taiwanese words from plum & grandmother.[11])" The children all laughed, including Chin-yen herself.

Chin-yen cursed Kuei-min: "Copulate with your mother."

Kuei-min kept teasing her: "You put your grandmother in it? What did you say? What?"

Chin-yen wouldn't pay any more attention to Kuei-min, but Kuei-min asked again a few times, laughing.

Lin Shu-hui (an eight-year-old boy) who sat next to Chin-yen smiled and said: "She said she put plums in it."

Kuei-min turned to laugh at him: "What? You put your grandmother in it?" They all laughed again and Shu-hui said it back to Kuei-min: "You put your grandmother in!" The two boys teasingly said this back and forth a few times and finally stopped and went back to their schoolwork.

This spontaneously playful world, punctuated by the spirit of humor, became an important space where children learned to navigate their social world and develop intimate moral understanding.

---

[10] CO #1241, 04/13/1960.
[11] *Mui* (plum) & *A-mah* (grandmother).

Playful Creatures

Drama and Ritual: Mimicking Adult Social Norms

We all have played games mimicking adult life when we were young, but we rarely wonder why. Like many Chinese girls, I used to dream of becoming a bus attendant. In the old days before automatic ticketing systems were invented, the bus attendant, usually a woman, carried a special purse, inside of which was a set of tickets neatly attached to a clipboard. When a passenger got onboard, she would pull out one paper-ticket, tear it into two halves, give the passenger one half, and save the other half as a receipt. Playing "bus-attendant" was my favorite game when I was five or six: At home I would put chairs in a row, carry a little red purse with a handful of well-organized paper-notes, and start yelling "Tickets! Tickets!" It turns out that, as documented in the fieldnotes, Taiwanese children shared a similar curiosity as the younger version of me.[12]

On an early autumn morning, three children were playing a bus-riding game. Pai Yanyan, a seven-year-old girl, played the driver, eight-year-old girl Chang Ah-ying played the bus attendant, and eight-year-old boy Wang Teng-kuo played the passenger. They all sat on a big tree branch that had fallen, the "driver" started the bus by shaking the tree, the "attendant" was saying "Beep! Beep!" and the "passenger" seemed quite content: "Oh, it bounces nicely." After a while, Wang Teng-kuo's little brother, five-year-old Teng-chih came up, holding a leaf and said: "I want to ride too. Here's a ticket." The "driver" did not want to let him in, but he insisted: "This is the station now." Eventually the "attendant" let him ride the "bus:" She broke his "ticket" (the leaf[13]) in half, gave half back to him, threw the other half away. Teng-chih sat next to his older brother.[14]

---

[12] In the late 1950s and early 1960s Taiwan, "bus-attendant" (*chezhang xiaojie*) was a popular profession for young women.
[13] Leaves were a very common "currency" in Xia Xizhou children's games.
[14] CO #200, 9/3/1959.

Drama and Ritual: Mimicking Adult Social Norms

This detail, breaking the "ticket" in half, brought back my memory of watching bus attendants in awe. There was some mysterious aura, an aura of authority and order, associated with the scene of bus-attendants issuing tickets. To my naïve eye, what they were doing seemed like a fun and elegant ritual. That might help explain why Xia Xizhou children also invented this bus-riding game with entertaining yet realistic features: They brought the most interesting or strange parts of the adult world into their own life. By mimicking those dramas in ritualistic ways, they got to experience, to a certain degree or through vicarious forms, the intriguing charm of those adult social norms that had fascinated them.

While playing "bus attendant" feels authoritative and cool, playing "police catching gamblers" – a realistic scene in Taiwanese society during the Martial Law Era, adds a layer of dangerous excitement in the fantasy of hierarchy, control, and punishment.

Wang Shi-ling (4-year-old boy), Wang Chin-yun (4-year-old girl), Chen Min-hua (4-year-old girl) and Wang Ah-chu (6-year-old girl) were playing a gambling game with cards. They were just pretending to gamble. There were some adults in the front room gambling.

Someone banged on the kitchen door and said: "Open the door."

Ah-chu walked over to the door and looked out the hole and asked: "Who is it?"

The child's voice repeated: "Open the door."

Shi-ling walked over and asked: "Who is it?"

Ah-chu said: "It is Chen Min-chin (Min-hua's older brother)."

Shi-ling: "Where is he?"

Ah-chu: "He has gone."

[This went back and forth for a while, that Min-chin naughtily knocked on the door and then ran away as soon as someone came to answer. A group of children came over to join this game. Eventually Wang Ah-chu's little brother opened the door and "policemen" broke in.]

Min-chin and another boy Wang Chao-min (Shi-ling's six-year-old big brother) came up and said: "I'm the policeman! Give me twenty dollars! Give me twenty dollars!" They held out their hands to all the "gamblers."

The girls all screamed and yelled: "No. No."

Playful Creatures

The two "policemen": "Alright! I'm going to catch people now."
[Some chasing and wrestling ensued. An adult called from another room, telling children not to fight. Children stopped for a moment but resumed the game soon.][15]

This episode not only juxtaposes "real gambling," adults in the front room, with "pretend gambling," children in the back room, but also embeds the gambling game within a larger game of "playing police." This snapshot of peer play tells us that children did not just keenly observe adults' social dramas. They also developed some understanding of adult moral norms. Gambling for money was quite common in the village, and some households even provided a formal venue, although gambling was illegal under the Criminal Code of the Republic of China at that time. Children probably knew that gambling was wrong and that those caught by police would be punished. For example, in a Doll Play session, a seven-year-old boy came up with this tragic story of gambling:[16]

Dad (doll) and mom (doll) were gambling for fun (not for money), but the police came and took them away anyway. They were put to jail because they did not have money to give to police. They didn't have food to eat. They were so hungry and so thin. When they came home, grandma (doll) cried. Police told them that if they gambled again, they would be sentenced to five years in prison.

In real life, children who were subjugated to adult surveillance and punishment also keenly rehearsed socio-moral dramas where the target of authority's gaze and normative regulation was themselves. In peer play they not only got to reverse that hierarchical positioning and experience what it was like to be the authority. They reenacted these humiliating scenarios in a comical manner. Besides mocking parental authority, as the vignette in the beginning of this chapter illustrated,

---

[15] CO #648, 02/02/1960.
[16] DP #508. This is a summary of the participant's answers, with the researcher's questions and prompts omitted.

Drama and Ritual: Mimicking Adult Social Norms

another common game that mimicked authority-child dynamics was playing "school." It was common for teachers to punish students, using a ruler to hit the students' hands, for example. In one of such play sessions, several children were playing the teacher ranking students and punishing the ones that did not get a good grade, with a strong-willed girl leader Pai Yan-yan (seven-year-old) as "Teacher."[17]

Wang Mei-yu (5-year-old girl) asked: "What grade did I get?" "Teacher" (Pai Yan-yan) didn't answer. The other children were all standing in a line, and "Teacher" walked away from them. They all followed her.

"Teacher": "All of you can't come and look." They all stopped.

"Teacher" knelt in front of House 116 and started to write grades on the ground. She wrote 4 grades.

[Then "Teacher" slowly announced the grades, calling each child out and having them stand in their respective "steps," according to the grades, A plus, A, etc. A 4-year-old boy Wang Ah-fa got A, Wang Mei-yu was told to stand next to Ah-fa, then Ah-fa's older sister, and 6-year-old Wang Su-chun on "the third step" next to Mei-yu. Finally Liang Chi-lan (5-year-old girl) was called, and she got A plus.]

They all stood in a line and Chi-lan asked: "Who is the best one? Who is the best one?"

"Teacher" told Chi-lan: "You can hit them." This implies that Chi-lan was the best.

Su-chen protested: "No."

"Teacher" re-affirmed: "She [Chi-lan] is A plus."

Chi-lan hit Mei-yu and Ah-fa.

"Teacher" corrected Chi-lan: "Ah-fa shouldn't be hit. He is the same as you."

[Ah-fa got A, Chi-lan got A plus, perhaps A was the cut-off point for punishment?]

Chi-lan asked: "Doesn't he have to be hit?" "Teacher" shook her head. Chi-lan turned back to Ah-fa and said: "Alright, I'll let you hit me back." Chi-lan put her hand out and Ah-fa hit it.

---

[17] CO #651, 2/2/1960.

Chi-lan hit Su-chen and Su-chen was a little angry and said: "Nah! Pai Yan-yan [the real name of "Teacher"]! I know you are smarter! [This is a sarcastic remark]"

"Teacher" ignored Su-chen: "Now, let's start over again. Come over here." "Teacher" walked a bit and sat down: "Now let us start." The children followed her. Su-chen kept repeating: "Nah! Pai Yan-yan! I know you are smarter." "Teacher" sat and drew something, ignoring Su-chen, but looking a little angry. (MC)

Another type of comical dramas, and a frequent genre of Xia Xizhou children's pretend play, is mimicking festive social events and religious rituals in the adult world, including banquets, weddings, and *bai-bai* – Taiwanese folk religious festivals, worshiping local gods and deities. Children must have found certain social norms in their community perplexing and absurd. They played those scenes out to entertain themselves. For example, how do young children make sense of adults' drinking and banqueting, so common and spectacular in the local scene? An ingenious drama is to "play drunk," mimicking what usually happened after banqueting. On a spring afternoon, a group of children staggered around the yard, pretending to be drunk, all laughing. Under a six-year-old girl's leadership, they managed to act out the most illuminating and laughable details, for example, drunk adults holding onto each other, one's arm around another's neck, pushing around.[18]

Xia Xizhou adults, like many in rural Han society, could go out of their way to show hospitality, for example, overtly competing to host the same guest. In a hilarious observation,[19] two little girls (both five-year-old) each had a hold of another girl's arms and were pulling her in different directions. One suggested to another: "Let's pretend she is a guest and we all want her to go to our own house." They two started acting and laughing: "Come on. Let's go to my house." This little drama immediately evoked my own memory, about one Chinese custom that

[18] CO #1455, 05/10/1960.
[19] CO #616, 01/22/1960.

Drama and Ritual: Mimicking Adult Social Norms

baffled me ever since I was young: During Lunar New Year and other festive occasions, my parents and their friends and relatives would give each other gifts, usually cash in red envelopes. Typically, this gift-giving action was the last step in a friendly visit, when the guest was about to leave: Saying goodbye at the door, the guest would suddenly pull out a red envelope and push it towards my mother's hand, and my mother would say no, start "fighting" to reject the gift, and the guest and her would go on back and forth for quite a few rounds. Till today I never doubted my mother's sincerity and humility, or the guests' good intention. But I still find it amusing – the overt action of "gift-giving and rejecting" as well as the underlying logic of creating or escaping indebtedness.

In their pretend play, young children showcased rich and precise knowledge about *bai-bai* rituals. One scenario of playing *bai-bai* involves "cooking" and preparing offerings for gods. This game was often mixed together with playing house. Children made altars. They used wood-sticks as makeshift incense sticks. They used new moon shaped mud-cakes as divining blocks – in real rituals a main tool for divination is a set of two half-moon-shaped wooden blocks.[20] They made rice cakes (with mud) and other food offerings. They even made clothes for different gods.[21]

An even funnier version of playing *bai-bai* is to mimic religious processions. To kill their boredom while on babysitting duties, children used their younger siblings as stage props for their *bai-bai* dramas. They improvised to use the baby carriage as the ride for their "gods processional." They carefully arranged chairs as the gods' sedan chairs and they remembered the exact positions of individual chairs. They put mud-cakes on top of the baby carriage as food offerings and tie the baby onto the chairs as a god in procession.[22]

---

[20] Such rituals with divining blocks were part of my own childhood experience. Growing up in Hunan, China, I used to accompany my mother to temples and got to know those divining procedures and devices well.
[21] CO #370, 12/03/1959.
[22] CO #1187, 4/6/1960.

Playful Creatures

In another observation,[23] three bored children, while making faces to each other, started mimicking "gods walking," a common scenario in local rituals:[24]

Wang Shih-huang (5-year-old) stood up and said: "I'm going to walk like a god." He walks stiff legged. Wang Chao-min (6-year-old) jumped down and walked funny too. Chao-min's little sister Shi-ling stood up and followed them. They marched in circles. Shih-huang had two sticks, one of which looks like a chicken leg. Shi-ling also has a stick.
Chao-min's grandmother came out and scolded him: "Sore Feet! (He has had bumps on his feet.) If you don't stop walking around like that either you or your sister is going to cry (e.g., get hurt)." They ignored her.
Grandmother: "Didn't you hear me? I don't care. If you won't stop playing now, don't cry loud later." Nobody paid any attention to her.
Grandmother: "I know who is going to cry first … Shi-ling! You are going to cry first and then Chao-min will be the second one. You are both crybabies." Nobody listens to her.
A three-year-old boy Wang Min-ho came up with a pan and asks Shih-huang: "Give me the chicken leg." Shih-huang probably didn't hear. He kept marching in the circle. Min-ho grabbed the stick from him. Shih-huang didn't say anything and kept marching. Then Min-ho started marching and banging the pan.

An important part of cultural transmission and learning is to develop knowledge and sensitivity about social norms in the local society. Like other games presented in this section, in this episode, children brought a local religious custom into their own world. They performed truthful details in this pretend play: strange motions of marching, loud noise to signal the gods' coming (banging the pan as if the pan were a gong). They blended humor and seriousness, and probably expressed a mixture of curiosity and mockery. To a child's eye, some norms and customs likely

---

[23] CO #61, 08/12/59.
[24] The most common gods seen as giant puppets in street parades were *Qiye* (Seventh Lord) and *Baye* (Eighth Lord), very popular in Taiwanese and Chinese folk religion. The former is very tall and played by a man on stilts, so he walks awkwardly (personal communication with Stevan Harrell, October 2022).

Cooperation, Conflict, and Coalition

seemed puzzling or awkward, others exciting and fascinating, and still others dangerous. Children must have carefully observed those scenes in local society, that's why they could enact all of them vividly. They then imitate, creatively reenact, and mock those norms and customs. These amusing moments highlight the crucial role of peer play in learning about the adult moral world.

Cooperation, Conflict, and Coalition: Constructing Peer Norms

Additionally, and often simultaneously, during peer play, children learn to navigate cooperation and conflict and construct their moral rules. In the same episode[25] presented earlier, the five-year-old boy Wang Shih-huang started bossing the others around, right after mimicking ritual processions. He invented a new game and made these rules: When Min-ho was banging the pan, Chao-min and his little sister Shi-ling should lie down on the floor. When Min-ho stopped, they should get up. But conflict emerged while they were playing this new game:

After Min-ho left, Shih-huang pointed his stick to the two, ordering them to get up, which they complied. Shih-huang continued to march in a circle, and commanded them to get up again. This time, the girl Shi-ling did not comply, despite Shih-huang repeatedly threatening: "Get up. If you don't get up, I'll cut your head off!" Shih-huang lowered his stick until it was really near Shi-ling's neck and then he jumped up. Shi-ling's brother Chao-min came and took the stick away. Shi-ling sat down and cried.

This short vignette encapsulates several general features of peer interactions in naturalistic settings: First, negotiating rules, a key part of collective action, was a common situation where children spontaneously organized to coordinate and cooperate. Second, cooperation could easily evolve into disagreement and conflict, and the direction was hard to predict. Third, because children often appeared in playgroups, multi-agent

---

[25] CO #61, 08/12/59.

Playful Creatures

Table 3.2 *A sample of high-frequency behaviors*

Behavior	Frequency	Behavior	Frequency	Behavior	Frequency
Leading	1,550	Dominating	718	*Scolding	856
Following	1,028	Submitting	365	Physical aggression	512
Not-following	432	Not-submitting	233	Verbal aggression	314

Note: *"Scolding" is different from pure verbal aggression as the former includes actual content of blame, accusation or teaching, while the latter is just an expression of anger and usually in the form of swearing.

dynamics was a frequent scene, in 548 out of all 1,678 episodes, which adds to the complexity and uncertainty of social interactions. In this vignette, for example, three-child cooperation – one boy leading and a brother-sister dyad following – quickly morphed into dominance, submission, and non-submission, which then escalated into brother protecting his sister against the aggressive playmate.

To situate this vignette within the entire CO corpus, let us look at some numbers (Table 3.2). Leading was the most frequent behavior in the corpus. It means one child making a noncoercive attempt to lead another child, for example, Shih-huang suggesting a new game rule to the other two children. Correspondingly, the target child could willingly follow or not follow. Dominating was also a frequent theme. It means attempting to change another's behavior through coercive means, including violence or threatening with violence. Shih-huang's later attitude towards Shi-ling is an apt example. The target child might submit to such coercion or not submit.[26] In situations of domination and conflict, scolding was the most frequent behavior, followed by physical aggression and verbal aggression (i.e., cursing).

---

[26] There might be other responses to dominating, for example, tattling.

Cooperation, Conflict, and Coalition

Besides establishing and negotiating game rules, cooperation and conflict also arose in the contexts of resource access, exchange and distribution. These experiences are ubiquitous across cultures and they facilitate the emergence of fairness in early childhood (Xu 2019). In contemporary urban middle-class communities parents and educators often make great effort to promote explicit teachings on resource sharing and link it to character development (Xu 2014), In contrast, Xia Xizhou children, in the context of multi-child families and communal spatial arrangements, often figured out the rules among themselves.

Sometimes the shrewd or domineering child gets a larger share. A group of children were collaborating around the fruit tree, one in the tree picking fruit and then throwing it down, the others waiting on the ground to pick it up. A thirteen-year-old boy Cheng Chen-yu told the other children to take turns picking up the fruit. After a while, the children forgot whose turn it was. Chen-yu ended up getting the most. He gave some to the children who asked for a share, but his pockets were full of the riper fruits.[27]

Playing favoritism was quite common, for example, in a card game, the dealer giving a thicker card to her sibling and a thinner card to a neighbor's child. But when a third-party witness was around, this child would try to act like a fair arbiter and side with the victim.[28] When disagreement occurred between two parties, the third-party child would improvise some "ostensive detachment" method (Boyer 2020) to show impartiality: Two children both wanted some seeds from a boy. The boy handled the situation smartly, taking some seeds out of his pocket and throwing them on the ground one after another.[29]

Children not only evoked principles of fairness to motivate resource sharing and exchange favors, they also relied on coalitional tactics. An

---

[27] CO #21, 7/30/1959.
[28] CO #792, 02/15/1960.
[29] CO #245, 9/14/1959.

Playful Creatures

indirect mechanism is gossip behind one's back. Gossip is an important strategy in facilitating reputation-based cooperation (Számadó et al. 2021). Stories of conflict frequently figured into children's gossip, through which they discerned the reputation of other social partners, both children and adults, and simultaneously constructed their own reputation. The following conversation[30] is one among many examples.

A boy Wang Chin-feng complained to another boy Yang Ching-min: "That Chen Min-chin is a real cheater. Every-time we play rubber bands with him he never will give them up when he loses. If you keep on asking for them he starts to cry. He only knows how to cry. Cry is his best method." Ching-min suggested: "Why don't you go tell his mother? If you go tell her, it doesn't do any good. She will just scold you."

More explicit coalitional dynamics abound in peer world. On a November afternoon, an eight-year-old boy Wu Chao-lai tried every means in order to ride four-year-old Wang Chin-yi's tricycle. After Chin-yi rejected him, Chao-lai walked over to Chin-yi's older brother Tian-yi, and an elaborate maneuver began:[31]

Chao-lai to Tian-yi (quietly): "You go tell your little brother to let's play on the bicycle and we'll give him this (a hoop). Alright?" Tian-yi went over to Chin-yi and suggested this.
Chin-yi: "No." Chao-lai looked unhappy. After a while he said to Tian-yi again: "Why don't you go tell him again and say if he'll let me I'll be his good friend." Tian-yi: "I don't know."
Finally, Chao-lai went up to Chin-yi and said (quietly): "If you'll let me play on your bike, I'll be your good friend." Chin-yi: "No!"
Chao-lai had 40 cents in his hand and showed it to Chin-yi, saying: "If you let me play I'm going to buy something later and I'll let you have some." Chin-yi: "No! I don't want it."
Chao-lai looked dejected and walked off, he called a five-year-old girl Li Mei-yi and said: "Would you go buy something for me?" Mei-yi agreed.

---

[30] CO #808, 02/16/1960.
[31] CO #307, 11/15/1959.

Cooperation, Conflict, and Coalition

Chao-lai gave her 20 cents and told her to buy some candied fruit. She ran off.

Chao-lai walked past Chin-yi and said: "See? I told Mei-yi to buy something for me and I'm not going to give you any." Chin-yi just looked at him.

Tian-yi was putting a brick on the rice rake to make it stand up. When he took the brick off it would fall down. Chao-lai called it a trap. Tian-yi's big brother, 9-year-old Chin-huang also had a rake and they were trying to trap unwary passersby.

Chao-lai to Chin-huang: "I'll play on your side." He ran over and sat down by Chin-huang. He showed Chin-huang how to put the brick on it using the rake. Just as Chin-yi came by on the trike they took the brick off and the rake came down on Chin-yi's head. Everyone laughed and Chin-yi just looked confused, not knowing exactly what happened. He rode on.

Tian-yi yelled: "Cut him off. Cut him off." Chao-lai: "Alright." He ran over and put the rake in front of Chin-yi. Chin-yi couldn't pedal over it, so he jumped off the bike, pulled it over the handle and rode on.

Mei-yi came back with Chao-lai's candy and gave it to him, saying: "It was 2 for 10 cents." The other kids ran up. Chao-lai gave one to Mei-yi and ate one himself.

Chin-yi: "I'll let you ride now." He ran over to Chao-lai repeating his offer. Chao-lai agreed and gave him a candy. Chao-lai got on the trike.

It is hard to tell why Chin-yi eventually changed his mind, just for the candy or also because of the concerted alliance against him. But the most striking part in Chao-lai's persistent attempts was the various strategies: from direct requests to indirect mobilization, his proposals from reciprocal favor exchange to friendship to material goods, and his manipulative efforts, from touting to helping others in order to isolate and pressure Chin-yi. This episode illustrates the broad spectrum of moral sensibilities children were developing in peer play. In everyday life, different sensibilities were often entangled together, for example, respect for fairness and promise of reciprocity wrapped under Machiavellian scheming, even just in a five-minute event.

Playful Creatures

Human versus Machine: Reading Moral Sensibilities and Layered Intentionality in Playful Teasing

Children not only spontaneously mixed together the brighter side of morality, often associated with cooperation, with the darker side, conflict and dominance. They even cleverly manipulated that boundary, creating a gray area that mixes aggressive and affiliative elements, therefore blending into the whole spectrum of moral sensibilities. Playful teasing is a particularly prevalent activity that blurs the boundary of cooperation and conflict. Playful teasing seems so natural to children, showcasing the rich social cognition abilities that are developing in a young age. Yet it is also challenging to accurately and thoroughly "read" children's playful teasing, especially the kind of ambiguous pretend-play that weaves reality into fantasy, due to the layered intentionality and complex moral sensibilities underneath the behavior. Therefore, playful teasing provides a unique angle to connect the two themes of this book, how children learn morality and how anthropologists (re-)interpret fieldnotes – or more broadly, how we interpret human behavior via text. I explore different methods to figure out their relative merits and limitations. I compare how children spontaneously "read" and enacted it, to how AI text-analysis algorithms stumbled over recognizing it, and how ethnographers interpreted it ("got" it) but with much effort. By doing so, I venture into methodological and epistemological experimentation to explore the nature of human learning and explain why children deserve more attention from anthropologists.

Teasing is a quintessential example of this gray-area behavior, a communicative process that mixes elements of aggression, humor, and ambiguity (Shapiro, Baumeister, and Kessler 1991). Teasing is ubiquitous in childhood across all cultures (Schieffelin and Ochs 1986), with deep evolutionary roots, that is, seen in nonhuman primates (Eckert, Winkler, and Cartmill 2020). Playful teasing is a really prominent theme in the CO corpus. It occurred 936 times, the third most frequent behavior, only next to "leading" and "following." Another type, "aggressive teasing," occurred 405 times. Aggressive teasing is easier to discern, as explicit cues of aggression are present[32] and the teaser's intention, that is, to dominate the target person rather than to have fun together, is obvious.[33] In contrast, playful teasing is much more ambiguous for the communicative partner to interpret: "For playful teasing to be successfully interpreted as affiliative rather than aggressive, the teaser, to some extent, has to understand the recipient's expectations and predict their likely reaction. Likewise, the recipient needs to draw accurate inferences and correctly identify the teaser's intent as affiliative, looking beyond any mildly abrasive behavioral elements" (Eckert et al. 2020). For example, in a Taiwanese fishing village in the 1980s, anthropologist Charles Stafford observed a group of sisters and cousins "hitting each other, quite hard, trying not to react amidst the laughter," a playful game with the purpose of learning how to "take punishment" (1995: 52). Imagine, a game like this could have evolved into a fight, had some of the participants failed to make the correct inferences about the purpose of the game and the intentions of the other participants.

Although playful teasing can become a challenge to the communicative partners, different types of evidence, not just the prevalence of this behavior itself, reveal that Xia Xizhou children understood its playfulness. In other words, they "got it."[34] In Child Interview, seventy-four children (ages 3–12) responded to this hypothetical question: "Suppose another boy (girl) your age makes fun of you, what would you do? What if he/she says you are stupid?" Forty-six children's answers indicated they would not take that seriously (62%),[35] including reactions such as

---

[32] For example, hitting a child hard while making fun of the child, in contrast to hitting lightly with a tree leave (playful teasing).
[33] I adopted a behavioral science classification according to Eckert et al. (2020).
[34] There were, of courses, exceptions to this general pattern, when children misunderstood or overreacted to benign teasing, or when children overdid their teasing, which then led to conflicts.
[35] Binomial test $p = 0.047$.

laughing back, ignoring, "not a big deal," and so forth, and only twenty-eight children (38 percent) said they would resort to aggressive means such as hitting, tattling to authority, social exclusion, and so forth. Their answers in the teasing scenario posed a contrast with those in physical aggression scenario, which they took as a much more serious offense and would therefore react more aggressively (see Chapter 2). They were able to discern the nature of such interactions in the spectrum from cooperation to conflict. They were sensitive to their social partners' intentions and they could react in a reciprocal manner.[36] Moreover, the various playful scenarios in CO texts, some of which I presented in this chapter, all show that children were able to detect each other's layered moral intentions in contexts and communicate effectively despite ambiguities in the meanings of speech and behavior. Behavioral analysis also supports this ethnographic insight: When a child initiates a playful teasing interaction, playful teasing is the most common reaction of the recipient, about 10 times more frequent than aggressive teasing, and much more frequent than other aggressive reactions.

While children could spontaneously and effectively understand playful teasing, when it comes to "reading" texts via Artificial Intelligence (AI) algorithms, the story is more complicated, which prompts us to ponder how humans learn about and make sense of the social world. On one hand, unsupervised topic-modeling method did generate quite a few "latent" textual-patterns that suggest ecologically valid topics, namely, topics that are largely consistent with the "scenario type" results from my manual coding of CO episodes: for example, child fighting, which was discussed in Chapter 2, and the various games children played, which I presented earlier in this chapter. On the other hand, none of the latent "topics" identified via topic-modeling algorithms looks like teasing, despite the actual prevalence of teasing in children's reality. High-ambiguity of playful teasing scenarios, due to features of human

---

[36] For more details see Xu (2020b).

psychology, that is, layered-intentionality, and human sociality, that is, complex coordination, might help explain why machine-learning techniques such as topic modeling failed to capture its saliency.

Beyond topic modeling, I collaborated with a data scientist to use a more advanced machine-learning technique called Bidirectional Encoder Representations from Transformers (BERT) to analyze CO texts. A popular large-language-model AI, BERT is built from massive language data as a training source, known for its ability to capture a deeper understanding of language context, and suitable for flexible, "supervised" text-analysis (González-Carvajal and Garrido-Merchán 2021). Recall that unsupervised topic modeling automatically classifies texts without prior data training, or in other words, researchers did not feed any structural information to the algorithms, regarding specific themes (word-clusters) the machine should search for. In contrast, we put together a list of core themes as well as keywords under each theme to "supervise" BERT algorithms. BERT then assigned weights/scores of each text under the different themes specified by us human researchers. Two of these themes are "cooperation" and "conflict," in line with the central questions of my ethnographic inquiry. Through evaluating similarity between texts (each CO episode as one text), our models performed well in general, successfully identifying the main themes and their respective saliency in each observation.[37] But it still mis-evaluated, or got "confused" by, a certain type of observations, that is, elaborate situations where children pretended to dominate or even assault others, but for the purpose of mutual entertainment.

A typical form of playful teasing, these pretend-play scenarios apparently looked like "conflicts" but the actual atmosphere was "cooperation." Such observational texts are complex enough to challenge AI techniques such as BERT. A revealing example is the vignette I presented in the beginning of this chapter, about a group of children playing

---

[37] For detailed methodology and results, see (Hernandez and Xu in prep).

"mom spanking her children."[38] While the algorithms calculated "conflict" as the most salient theme, more so than "cooperation," children clearly knew it was just a game, not real conflict. When documented in texts, the pretended scenes of hitting and spanking, accompanied by scolding/cursing "You dead child!" and pleading "Don't beat me, mom!", can confuse language AI algorithms. Yet children correctly interpreted each other's intentions and signals during this episode. They quickly responded and aptly cooperated to act out a complex game. They laughed out loud in that hilarious game. They injected ingenious creativity into peer play. These young minds beat the most sophisticated and trendy AI algorithms in many cognitive tasks, especially tasks that require innovatively acting upon the world (Gopnik 2022).

Another layer of this human–machine hybrid experiment is the comparison between the human interpreter and the AI algorithms to decode, or even decipher, the same materials. Third-party interpretation of playful teasing, especially the kind of pretend-play that involves multiple children and elaborate coordination, can be quite difficult. Text-analytics programs were much faster at processing large amounts of fieldnotes and automatically detecting patterns. Despite so, the human researcher's ethnographic expertise proved irreplaceable in deciding what kind of patterns to extract, and in actually comprehending the *meaning* of texts, especially those texts about ambiguous social interactions. Through manual coding at a document level (each episode as a unit), I coded ninety-six CO episodes in which teasing was a main scenario type, and it ranked as the third most frequent scenarios in the entire corpus.[39] At a more granular level, identifying one behavior typically within one sentence or across a few sentences, I was able to discover plenty of playful teasing behaviors distinct from actual aggression, as reported earlier.

---

[38] CO #314, 11/20/1959.
[39] The type of scenario that has the highest frequency is playing hopscotch, 161 episodes; the second highest is playing rubber bands, 109 episodes.

However, interpreting the layered intentions of children's pretend play through texts was not an easy task for me. I relied on the excellent work of MC, the first-hand ethnographer and participant observer. In other words, MC had keener insights about the meaning of behaviors than I was, because of her immersive experience. MC got to know these children well, had participated in many of their games, and therefore understood each child's idiosyncratic personality and the various formats and cues of their pretend play. Thanks to her faithful documentation, these observational texts contained a wealth of subtle details that helped me to "simulate" those scenarios, as if I were the present observer. I had to exercise my raw effort, spending much time to contemplate how exactly a linguistic or behavioral cue should be interpreted. I also drew from my scholarly expertise developed over years of training: my knowledge of child development and my sensitivity to meaning-interpretation in naturalistic social life. Last but not the least, I used my human commonsense that AI research has yet to fully decipher (Choi 2022), let alone to completely incorporate. I was once a child and had similar or relatable experience; I am a mother on a wondrous journey, witnessing the magic of child development, attuning myself to children's experience, and still trying to comprehend the child's enigmatic mind.

Taken together, I leaned on all these "sense-making" experiences, devices, and efforts to interpret the meaning of ambiguous behavior in its context and to develop knowledge – to *learn* – about the social world in question. After all, these CO texts were written *by* ethnographers, from MC to Margery and Arthur Wolf, and perhaps also mostly *for* ethnographers. Underlying such texts there is unstated but shared knowledge among ethnographers about human psychology in social contexts that language AI programs are still catching up with. In deciphering children's playful teasing, the ethnographic method, the slow and hard-to-standardized way of "close-reading" to gain *deep knowledge*, can "outperform," in some aspects, AI algorithms that are trained by 3.3 billion words and powered by *deep-learning* neural networks. And this leads us to the mystery of human learning, a final point I want to make from this human–machine comparison: Interpreting pretend-play teasing from texts was an effortful adventure to me and also posed challenges for some machine-learning algorithms. For children, however, detecting and creatively enacting such "playful teasing" seems so effortless. Why are children, despite their young age, so natural at it?

Playful teasing tends to require more "mind-reading" skills on the part of both parties in this communication (Eckert et al. 2020). Indeed, from infancy onward, human children develop a sophisticated and consistent "theory of mind" (ToM) by attributing their desires, beliefs, and emotions to themselves and to others (Wellman 2014).[40] These basic ToM abilities and foundations are present in early childhood across cultures, playing an important role in cultural transmission and social learning, that is, learning from other people (Barrett et al. 2013). Second, across many cultures and from an early age, children draw from perceptions and inferences of mental states in contexts to make moral judgments (Barrett and Saxe 2021). As we see in CO episodes, children attribute moral intentions and judgments to specific persons: Wang Chin-feng gossiped to his friend that another boy was a "cheater," not complying to game rules; Wang Yi-kun complaining that old man Bei-guang was mean – punishing his grand-daughter for no good reason. Moreover, children's socio-emotional intelligence and moral sensibilities are attuned to and shaped by the experience of living with other human beings: They learn from other people around them, and they learn effectively from the history of interacting with social partners. They are exceptionally good at extracting the right kind of patterns and inferring causal relations. They can bring in all that information, at the current

---

[40] The debates over exactly when and how children develop ToM have a long history and many crucial questions remain, especially concerning the domain-general versus domain-specific learning mechanisms. For a review see https://iep.utm.edu/theomind/.

moment of teasing, to help make inferences about a person's intention, and evaluate their social partners and situations. Not only so, they lean on those inferences to update their own expectations and predict others' behaviors: In cognitive science terms, as a new wave of research suggests, children are, naturally, Bayesian learners (Gopnik and Tenenbaum 2007; Ullman and Tenenbaum 2020).[41] Lastly, children actively explore the social world, and in this process construct new, surprising and even unpredictable "realities": like a scientist, the child thus creates a wider space of possible hypotheses to sample and test (Gopnik 2020: 8). The rich and sometimes hilarious pretend-play scenarios in Xia Xizhou are a good example, combining patterned interactions and unexpected "surprises," mixing randomness with creativity.[42] Cognitive scientists are amazed and intrigued by children's developing mind: "Children take the plethora of ambiguous information coming in through their senses and turn it into meaningful, abstract, structured representations" (Gopnik and Bonawitz 2015: 75). With the rising trend of making AI more human-like, computer scientists are turning to the question of child development, and together with psychologists, advancing the vision of teaching AI to learn like children (Frank 2023). With the fast development of language AI, discerning features of children's playful teasing might become easier for newer algorithms. But regardless, these algorithms still operate through extracting statistical patterns of natural language properties based on enormous amounts of training data and their impressive linguistic competence is still dissociated from social cognition (Mahowald et al. 2023). In comparison, detecting statistical regularities is just one of

---

[41] A definition of Bayesian learning: "current knowledge is represented as a set of hypotheses with a probability distribution (prior probabilities, or shortly priors). Learning consists in observing evidence and reestimating probability distribution of the hypotheses given the observed evidence (thus creating posterior probabilities)" (www.lancaster.ac.uk/fas/psych/glossary/bayesian_learning/).

[42] My interest in children's pretend-play is also inspired by the psychologist and philosopher Alison Gopnik's recent work: https://psychology.berkeley.edu/news/what-babies-tell-us-about-artificial-intelligence.

many tools for children: They learn in multiple and flexible ways about the social world, drawing upon limited amounts but various kinds of "training data," and innovatively act upon it (Yiu et al. 2023). We do not know the full details of children's learning algorithms yet, but we do know that studying children is the key for deciphering many mysteries of humanity.

Human children are the best learners of all beings. The kind of pretend-play teasing I presented is just one example showcasing how they learn. But this specific example can shed much valuable light on anthropological epistemology. The way children learn to discern layered intentions and moral sentiments is exactly the foundation for deep knowledge and "thick description" of social life – for the thing called "ethnography." Yet in ontological and epistemological reflections anthropologists rarely draw inspiration from children.[43] We look past them. If anthropologists truly want to understand human sensemaking, perhaps it is time for us, like those AI researchers, to take children's developing minds seriously.

What Is It in Play?

Everyday play facilitates children's emerging moral understanding, about normativity and about right and wrong (Wright and Bartsch 2008). In Xia Xizhou, the seemingly "unruly" children – in parents' eyes – learned various kinds of norms, including constructing their own moral rules, in everyday peer play. For example, they mimicked adult society dramas, they negotiated cooperation and conflict in gameplay, they enlisted third-party support to defend justice, and they gossiped to gauge other people's reputations and establish their own.

Xia Xizhou children's playful world opened my eyes to new questions concerning family, morality, cultural transmission, and learning: First,

---

[43] One anthropology colleague added this comment when reading a draft of this chapter: "Maybe they (anthropologists) don't want to admit how child-like they are in a cultural context not their own."

What Is It in Play?

children in many societies spend more than half of the time in each other's company with no adult present, for example, Mayan children in Guatemala and Aka children (ages 5–12) in Central Africa (Ellis, Rogoff, and Cromer 1981; Hewlett et al. 2011). However, studies of the so-called "traditional Chinese family" have long prioritized parent–child ties and parenting in transmitting values and shaping moral personhood. A systematic analysis of Xia Xizhou children's social networks and behavioral interactions highlights the importance of peer ties. This study also urges us to redress certain assumptions in the study of Han families and societies and look carefully into *who* children learn from and *how* and *what* they learn.

In a similar vein, recent studies of social learning and cultural evolution have highlighted the significance of peer learning, departing from the previous focus on vertical (adult–child) modes of knowledge transmission (Lew-Levy et al. 2023; Qiu and Moll 2022; Stengelin et al. 2023). Children not only learn from their peers, but create subcultures, new traditions, and moral norms (Morin 2015). The story of Xia Xizhou children thus contributes rare and systematic ethnographic evidence to this emerging, interdisciplinary conversation.

Moreover, in their playful world, Xia Xizhou children were developing a whole spectrum of moral sensibilities. Coordination easily evolved into conflicts, and shrewd manipulation and domination sometimes co-existed or even motivated cooperative behavior. How these complex inclinations were often entangled together in children's daily life calls into question the imagery of "the innocent child" that permeates Chinese moral discourses.[44] This insight also affirms the unique value of "close-reading" children's life in naturalistic contexts. Anthropologists have become increasingly focused on morality and ethics "as an intrinsic

---

[44] Historical representations of Chinese childhood tend to fixate on the "good" and "innocent" (see Hsiung 2005: xi; Bai 2005: 1–20), and Chinese views of childhood emphasize the bright side of human nature in moral cultivation (Bai 2005; Kinney 2004).

dimension to human activity and interpretation" that cannot be simply reduced to "interest, compulsion, obligation, competition, or imitation" (Lambek 2010b: 40). But few have looked carefully into children's world to interrogate the fundamental question: Where do such complex moral sensibilities come from? On the other hand, the booming psychological research of early moral development so far has predominantly relied on controlled experiments (c.f., Xu 2017). Ethnographic "close-reading" is much needed to illuminate how children use their rich social cognition to navigate the inherently ambiguous and unpredictable moral world.

Children's social cognition, including emotional and motivational processes, is the anchor point of this ethnography, where critical reflections on several different lines of scholarship meet and intersect. In sinological anthropology, classic works showed that adults saw small children as very passive, without much imagination, and anthropologists thought children would inevitably assimilate such adult attitude from early on (Ward 1985: 189, 195). Even Arthur Wolf himself expressed this impression that Xia Xizhou children had impoverished fantasy, because their responses to projective tests were repeating what had happened at home instead of more creative storytelling (n.d.: 34). But through carefully examining their peer play in observational texts, my reanalysis brought into light children's complex imaginations and emotions, especially in pretend-play. Although societies and communities vary in the kind and amount of opportunities for fostering children's pretend play (Edwards 2000; Lancy 1996: 92), Xia Xizhou children did enjoy many kinds of pretend play during their free time. Their pretend play often contained realistic elements, as real life has imposed constraints on young children's imagination in every society (Harris 2021). Notably, their "reality-based fantasy" was not simply copying what they observed, but creative reenactment and even deliberate mockery. These non-elite, rural children, often relegated to silent margins in history, had a much richer inner life than previous work once assumed.

I was fascinated by the kind of playful teasing scenarios that blend rich moral sentiments, because children seemed exceptionally good at it. This behavior contains important "meta-communicative" properties (Bateson 2000 [1972]: 185) and is predicated upon "shared intentionality" that underpins unique human sociality and culture (O'Madagain and Tomasello 2022; Tomasello and Carpenter 2007). Even infants before the age of two are able to process the complex social intentions in playful teasing, differentiate teasing from superficially similar but serious behavior, and they find teasing more fun (Colle et al. 2023). At a time when scientists are ambitiously striving to teach machines to read human situations and make moral judgments (Jiang et al. 2022), I wonder if machines can ever simulate a young child's mind to learn morality through playful teasing. Taking inspiration from children's developing socio-moral sensibilities, I combined and compared human and artificial intelligence to decipher such playful teasing and interrogate the nature of meaning-interpretation, ethnographic epistemology, and human knowledge.

Children's play indeed points to the deepest mysteries of human learning, and this chapter opens up more questions than it answers. In the next chapter I turn to another important aspect of children's moral life and peer learning, that is, gender. I explore boys' and girls' overlapping and differential moral worlds, worlds that are often taken for granted but easily overlooked.

FOUR

Gendered Morality

Fierce Girls and Naughty Boys

Rethinking Gendered Morality

Wan-iu: (a four-year-old girl) was sitting on a small stool near the well. A neighbor came out and said, "Wan-iu: let Thiam-hok (a two-and-a-half-year-old boy) sit on your stool so he won't get dirty." Wan-iu: pushed him away and said, "No, you can't have my stool. Get away." Wan-iu's mother shouted at her angrily, "You are a girl! Give him that stool. I'll beat you to death!" Wan-iu: looked unhappy but gave up the stool. This little girl had no brothers, or she probably would never have gotten into this kind of trouble. By age 5, most little girls have learned to step aside automatically for boys.
–M. Wolf (1972: 66–67)

This vignette, from Margery Wolf's classic ethnography, *Women and the Family in Rural Taiwan*, succinctly illustrates the gendered nature of certain moral expectations in Xia Xizhou childhood, for example, fairness in resource distribution means that little girls should yield to their brothers. Gender biases such as son preference and daughter discrimination have long become a central theme in the study of patrilineal, patriarchal Han Chinese families (Freedman 1966), and childhood experience is critical in shaping such gender biases (Croll 2000; Greenhalgh 1988). Despite such commonsense knowledge that features the perspective of adult socializers, however, there is a striking lack of systematic ethnography concerning young children' gendered moral experience.

Based on this particular Xia Xizhou fieldwork, *Women and the Family in Rural Taiwan* was a groundbreaking ethnography that placed women's perspectives at the center of understanding family relations, despite their structurally disadvantaged position in the traditional patriarchal and patrilineal Han Chinese family. Margery Wolf highlighted rural Taiwanese women's agency in pursuing their own goals: For example, as outsiders married into her husbands' households, women created "uterine families" through exerting power over her sons and grandchildren (1972: 36). That ethnography, focused on adult women, did include one chapter on childhood and drew our attention to young girls' unfortunate situation in comparison to boys: At preschool age, a Taiwanese girl already learned "her first subtle lessons about the second-class status of her sex": She was called a "worthless girl" since she could understand words; by school age she has had much more family responsibilities than a boy her age, for example, doing chores and taking care of younger siblings (M. Wolf 1972: 66).

But the materials Margery used only constitute a tiny portion of the Wolf Archive. Even if most little girls in Xia Xizhou had indeed "learned to step aside automatically for boys," as Margery concluded, we would still want to find out if those little girls had any sort of agency: Are they completely docile and passive? If not, what tactics they could use to maneuver against the prescribed norms, and how might they understand their own circumstances? Also, what does it mean to be a good or bad boy in that particular historical context? And what kind of moral experience shaped boys' selfhood?

For example, in contrast to the opening vignette, the following Child Observation episode[1] depicts a comically shocking scenario about young girls bullying two little boys. This story alludes to a much more complex moral world beyond the general impression of gender differences:

[1] CO #353, 12/1/59.

Gendered Morality

Lai Li-hsin (five-year-old girl) was with her little sister Li-lin (who was about to turn 3). Another five-year-old girl Liang Chi-lan came over and Li-hsin said to her: "Do you know there was a baby sleeping on the ground?"

Chi-lan: "Yes, it was this baby. Ha! Ah! Sleeping on the ground." (This was all said in a singsong accompanied with grimaces. It was mainly to tease the baby.)

Li-hsin walked up to that little boy Wang Lin-kuei (three-year-old) who was holding his baby brother. Li-hsin put her leg over Lin-kuei's head and yelled: "You won't grow up (this action and statement is a bad insult)."

Lin-kuei didn't say or do anything. Li-hsin's playmate Chi-lan came up and did the same thing. Li-lin did it, holding on to her big sister and then Wang Mei-yu did it too and hit Lin-kuei on the head. The girls repeated this several times, with a great deal of laughing. Li-hsin did it again and hit Lin-kuei (unintentionally).

Li-hsin led the girls to do the same thing toward Lin-kuei's baby brother, alternating between the two boys. The other girls went away but Li-hsin stayed. She upgraded her action by swinging a rope around the two little boys, the rope as an extension of/proxy for her leg. She even showed a passerby boy how to play this game of insult and humiliation. Then her aggressive teasing escalated: First, she looked around, made sure no adult was watching, and hit Lin-kuei really hard. Her little sister joined her to hit Lin-kuei's baby brother too. After that, Lin-hsin picked up a piece of dirty paper and stuck it on the baby's neck and said: "I'm giving you a bath." Throughout the entire observation that lasted four and half minutes, Lin-kuei occasionally protested, threatening with his fist, but he never said a single word.

The juxtaposition of these two stories prompts us to explore the question of gender in more depth and with greater systematicity. It leads us to closely examine children's actual behaviors, not just moral precepts. It also reminds us to look at children's own motivations, thoughts, and feelings. The first episode depicts a girl conforming to a moral norm and performing a prosocial act, but in the second episode young girls got quite aggressive and little boys were meek, which seems to contradict local expectations. But there is more to the comparison between the two episodes: In the first episode, the little girl did not want to give the stool to the boy; it was her mother's scolding that changed her mind. In contrast, no adult was present in the second episode, and at some point the girl Li-hsin even looked around to make sure no adults were watching before she hit the boy. Perhaps girls learn to be meek in the presence of authority but act more boldly when the authority is not immediately present? The reality is more complex and therefore more interesting than the ideals.

In what follows, I first provide an overview of gendered patterns in children's prosocial and aggressive behaviors. To contextualize these behavioral patterns, I look at how children's learning of aggression and violence is situated within the local community and also shaped by the larger political and historical context of Martial Law Taiwan, for example, gangsters and policing. As to the moral world of girls, countering the trope of gender stereotypes, I showcase how young girls understand their own situations, navigate the gender hierarchies, and defend themselves. Lastly, to honor Arthur Wolf's classic research on marriage and adoption and offer new insights on young girls' emotional experience, I tell the story about an adopted daughter: An "unruly" girl who defies parental commands, asserts her will, and negotiates love–hate relationships with different family members.

Gendered Patterns in Peer Cooperation and Conflict

Ethnographic observations in sinological anthropology have rarely examined the relationship between gender and children's prosocial and aggressive behavior in peer interactions.[2] Fine-grained behavioral analysis of Child Observation provides new insights into this question, which

---

[2] One exception, with a much smaller sample size and less behavioral categories though, is Jankowiak, Joiner, and Khatib (2011).

Gendered Morality

Table 4.1 *Total number of behaviors by gender and interactional direction*

Number of behaviors	As initiators	As recipients
Boys	4,955	4,982
Girls	4,244	4,217

also extends the SCS legacy and enriches cross-cultural comparative insights on gender differences in children's behavior (B. Whiting and Edwards 1973). While child development studies have predominantly focused on behavioral initiators, my analysis also included behavioral recipients. The numbers of boys and girls involved in child-to-child behavioral interactions are roughly equal (106 boys and 110 girls, ages below twelve).[3] But in general, boys initiated more and also received more behaviors, "received" in the sense of being a recipient/target of an observed behavior (Table 4.1).

To analyze patterns of specific behaviors, I calculated behavioral proportion scores through dividing the number of an observed behavior by the total number of all observed behaviors, not by the total number of boys or girls. There are inherent features of children's social life in a community, for example, some children are more active than others,[4] as well as contingent factors in naturalistic observations, for example, some children happened to appear in observations more than others. In other words, there are "outlier" children for every observed behavior, therefore calculating the average number of a certain behavior per person is not really informative. I then analyzed gender-specific behavioral preferences through comparing proportion scores of concrete behaviors by gender (Tables 4.2 and 4.3). The following two tables display only behavioral themes where gender differences reached statistical significance.

---

[3] In addition, there were four children whose gender information was missing.
[4] Social network analysis provides systematic evidence for this.

Table 4.2 *Gender differences in initiated behaviors, two-sample proportion test*, df = 1

Behavior	# of behavior initiated by girls	# of behavior initiated by boys	% of all behaviors initiated by girls	% of all behaviors initiated by boys
Scolding	315	259	7.42	5.23
Playful teasing	295	451	6.95	9.1
Dominating	258	367	6.08	7.41
Helping	177	164	4.17	3.31
Tattling	141	102	3.32	2.06
Physical aggression	141	280	3.32	5.65
Aggressive teasing	119	218	2.8	4.4
Granting access	80	65	1.89	1.31
Sibling care	75	23	1.77	0.46
Verbal aggression	71	190	1.67	3.83
Not granting access	60	47	1.41	0.95
Comforting	55	25	1.3	0.5
Throwing a dirty look	48	15	1.13	0.3

All of these behaviors showed a 95% confidence interval that did not include zero.

Overall, gender differences were more widespread in initiated behaviors rather than received behaviors.

Several noteworthy findings from CO shed light on how gender intersects with children's conflict and cooperation: First of all, this large sample of observational data confirmed a well-established pattern in child development research, that is, boys initiated direct, physical aggression more often than girls. This is a consistent pattern discovered across different cultures and age groups, via different methods, and in meta-analysis reports.[5] Observational research on singleton children in urban

---

[5] There is a growing literature on this topic in psychology, see, for example, Archer (2004); Hyde (1984); Loeber, Capaldi, and Costello (2013); and Endendijk et al. (2017).

Gendered Morality

Table 4.3 *Gender differences in received behaviors, two-sample proportion test, df = 1*

Behavioral theme	# of behavior received by girls	# of behavior received by boys	% of all behaviors received by girls	% of all behaviors received by boys
Physical aggression	148	273	3.51	5.48
Request for access	144	126	3.41	2.53
Submitting	117	203	2.77	4.07
Verbal aggression	92	169	2.18	3.39
Sibling care	70	28	1.66	0.65
Comforting	53	27	1.26	0.54

All of these behaviors showed a 95% confidence interval that did not include zero.

China also found that boys displayed more physical aggression than girls during play time (Jankowiak et al. 2011). A novel discovery from these fieldnotes is that boys also received proportionally more physical aggression than girls in this sample.

Other forms of direct aggression showed mixed results: Girls initiated proportionally more instances of scolding, that is, criticizing somebody for specific reasons and more "dirty looks," but boys initiated more verbal aggression, such as swearing and cursing, merely expressions of anger without resorting to substantial reasoning. Even two and three year olds were observed bursting out all kinds of swear words when getting annoyed by others, which of course reflects culturally specific features of language and moral socialization. Symmetrically, boys were also more likely to be the target of verbal aggression. Boys attempted to dominate others more than girls, that is, demanding another person to do things against that person's own preference. In correspondence with their domineering tendency, boys received proportionally more submission than girls. Also, boys displayed proportionally more aggressive teasing than girls as initiators, but not as recipients. Finally, "throwing a dirty look," a subtle nonverbal form of aggression, was rarely examined in prior quantitative research, and especially nonfeasible in self-report or survey research. But it emerged in many scenes of Child Observation, and girls initiated this more than boys.

Regarding indirect forms of aggression, girls proportionally tattled more, reporting someone's misbehavior to an authority. Girls also proportionally initiated more social exclusion through refusing to allow other children to join group games ("not granting access"). Prior meta-analysis or cross-cultural studies did not find consistent gender difference in indirect aggression (Card et al. 2008; Lansford et al. 2010). But other researchers have argued that such inconsistency might have to do with methodological differences, especially problems with self-reports, and multiple observational studies found that girls displayed more indirect aggression (Björkqvist 2018; Österman et al. 1998). My analysis lends support to the pattern identified in these observational studies that girls are associated more with indirect aggression. It also sheds light on children's culture in Xia Xizhou: For example, tattling to authority was an important strategy of indirect retaliation. Also, girls were more involved in certain popular group games, such as hopscotch, jumping rope, and playing house, and they were more likely positioned to control access to these games – in fact, this was confirmed in the result of girls as recipients of "request for access" more than boys.

Contrary to aggression, when it comes to prosocial behaviors, gender differences are much less clear. Experimental psychologists contend that the effects of gender vary for different types of prosocial behavior, such as helping and sharing (Fabes and Eisenberg 1998), and such effects also depend on the context of measurement (Eagly 2009). Evolutionary anthropologists, aiming to discover human universals and variability through cross-cultural economic games, found no evidence of strong universal gender difference in children's development of generosity and fairness (House, Silk, and McAuliffe 2023). In a patriarchal community like Xia Xizhou, with entrenched gendered division of labor and son preference, however, gendered patterns of prosocial development were identified in Child Observation. Expanding from what controlled experiments typically define as prosocial behavior, for example, instrumental helping, resource sharing, and emotional comfort (Dunfield and Kuhlmeier 2013), I analyzed a broader range of behaviors suitable to Xia Xizhou children's world, such as sibling care, and granting access to games/play groups. Moreover, results from my analysis need to be interpreted within the local context.

Overall, girls initiated proportionally more prosocial behaviors than boys did, but there were also exceptions in specific types of behavior. Girls were more often caretakers than boys, as shown in sibling care and comforting (in most situations it was an older sibling comforting a crying baby). Notably, girls, and in this case baby girls, also received proportionally more sibling care and comforting than boys. Compared to boys, girls also showed a mild preference for helping others, and for granting other children the access to certain group games. However, in some other prosocial behaviors, there was no gender preference as initiators, for example of resource sharing. In addition, boys initiated proportionally more playful teasing, in the ambiguous gray area between cooperation and conflict, but boys and girls were equally likely to become recipients of playful teasing. Some of these differences reflect local cultural norms, for example, girls as caretakers of younger siblings: It was a common scenario to see young girls carrying a baby on their backs. Other patterns might have to do with the particular types of games boys and girls were engaged in. For example, there was a lot of playful teasing in boys' pretend play games such as "dueling." Negotiation over permission and access to certain collaborative and cooperative group games such as playing house and hopscotch happened a lot to girls. As explained earlier, older girls were more likely to become leaders of these specific games.

Learning Aggression from Family Experience

On several occasions I have heard a three or four-year-old imperiously warn his mother to stop interfering with his (usually dangerous) activity lest he summon his father to beat her.

–M. Wolf (1978: 226)

When Arthur Wolf resumed his analysis and writing on Xia Xizhou children, his theoretical interest in approaching the SCS's behavioral systems, such as aggression, had shifted from behaviorist learning theories to examining inborn knowledge. He came to believe that human behavior was not very malleable. Many scientists indeed explain the robust gender difference in physical aggression through biological and evolutionary lenses, for example, sex-selection theory (Archer 2004). But regardless of what specific "inborn knowledge" children are equipped with, their actual lived experience is what the Wolf Archive can directly illuminate, and that experience really matters. Learning aggression from observing punishment inside the family, or one violence begetting another, is documented in many societies (e.g., Ember and Ember 2005). One source of such observational learning is adult members of the family. As Margery Wolf's observation about a defiant little boy suggests, even toddler children were keenly observing adult life. In this scenario, from previous experience witnessing how his father treated his mother, the boy not only learned to use violence as a threat. He also learned about gender hierarchy, men's authority and dominance over women, and therefore his own privilege.

Another type of experience that contributes to the robust gender difference in physical aggression is parental differential treatment of boys and girls (Endendijk et al. 2017). Parents in many cultures, especially patrilineal societies, tend to use more physical control toward boys than toward girls (Munroe et al. 2000). Transcripts of Doll Play sessions provide unique materials to examine children's emotions and thoughts about gender and corporeal punishment. The Doll Play test in the Wolf Archive used a set of eight dolls in a farmhouse with a table, chairs, and

Gendered Morality

Figure 4.1 Doll Play (DP) test materials
Source: Photo by Arthur Wolf.

a tatami bed.[6] The set of dolls (see Figure 4.1) resembles a typical family in the local community, including grandmother, father, mother, and five children (older brother, older sister, younger brother, younger sister, and a gender nonspecified baby).[7] This test features school-age children's spontaneous storytelling about family scenes. The Wolfs' team managed to collect Doll Play data with forty-six children, a gender-balanced sample, and some children were interviewed twice. Many children told stories that reflected truthful details of their own family life, such as their family's demographic composition and relationships, thus I call their storytelling as "reality-based fantasy."

---

[6] The Japanese introduced the tatami to Taiwan during their colonial rule and this material cultural influence was still seen in Xia Xizhou in the late 1950s.
[7] It is still a biased representation, however. For example, some grandfathers in this village also contributed to childcare, but Doll Play did not include a grandfather figure.

Learning Aggression from Family Experience

One prominent theme across these narratives is corporal punishment. Boy characters were mentioned more than girl characters in these punishment narratives. For example, a mischievous boy Huang Shu-feng, aged five at the time of Doll Play, had one older sister, one older brother, and a younger baby brother. He identified the baby in Doll Play as a boy, the older brother as a second grader and the older sister as a third grader, similar to his own family situation. Shu-feng told this punishment story:[8]

Q: What happened next? (Before this, Shu-feng mentioned that dad earned some money.)
A: The baby brother asked mom for pocket money. Mom said she had no money.... It was older brother who told the little brother to ask for money. Mom asked the baby who sent him to get money, and the baby said it was older brother. Mom went to hit older brother, using a rope. Older brother begs: "I dare not (to do that) anymore."
Q: What was mom's face like, when she hit older brother?
A: Red ... She was mad. Older brother said he dared not, and mom stopped hitting him.

This punishment scene, mother hitting older brother with a rope, emerged in Shu-feng's older sister, eight-year-old Shu-ting's Doll Play transcript too:[9]

Q: One day they two [older brother and older sister] were arguing. Sister went home and told mom. Mom said: "Ok. When he gets home, I'll hit him." Brother was scared to death and ran away, not daring to go home. Then dad came home after work, and brother followed him.
Q: Did dad know [about brother and sister arguing]?
A: Yes. He hit older brother's hand with bamboo. Brother hid underneath the table to sleep, and encircled the table with chairs. Mom was about to cook. She saw the chairs and put them away, then she saw older brother and started spanking him. Brother fled to the bedroom and

---

[8] DP #5, 09/27/1960. In Doll Play excerpts, "A" refers to the child's answer, and "Q" refers to the adult interviewer's question.
[9] DP #7, 09/28/1960.

Gendered Morality

closed the door. ... [the next day] They went to school, and brother hit sister again. Sister went to tell mom. Mom said "I'll hit him even more badly when he gets home." Sister was really happy. When brother came home, mom hit him with a rope. Brother fled outside, brought the chairs out, and [brought] the table out. He said: "I won't go home. I'll be my own family." He slept outside on the chair, and stole some food from home. He said he'd quit school. When mom got up the next morning, she said: "All the chairs are missing!" She couldn't find them. Brother was really happy. Mom sent sister to find the chairs. Sister saw them and reported to mom. Mom hit brother again, using a rope. Brother went crying and running, and he felt really mad.

In both Shu-feng and Shu-ting's narratives, it was the older brother who got hit by his mother, with a rope, which was probably a familiar scenario in their own life. But some other children's vivid description of cruel violence, in Doll Play and TAT, clearly reflects their impression or imagination about adult moral transgressions, about crime and punishment in the larger world. This connection was easy to miss, as the Wolfs never wrote about the projective tests results. Also, psychological and cross-cultural studies on gender difference in aggression tend to focus on children's immediate socialization experience and have rarely situated children's behavior in the larger historical and political context. But this sort of void and omission is what makes reexamining children's gendered moral knowledge more exciting.

"Bad Boys Become *Lo-mua*": Learning Violence from the Larger Society

[Wang Kuei-min (eight-year-old boy) looking at Drawing #4, see Figure 4.2]

Q: What do you see here?
A: One is crying, one is running, and two are fighting.
Q: Why are these two fighting?
A: They fight because they hit people on purpose.

"Bad Boys Become *Lo-mua*"

Q: Which one hits people on purpose?
A: That guy (points to the boy who is fighting with the girl).
Q: Are boys worse or girls worse?
A: Boys are worse.
Q: Why are boys worse?
A: He is a hooligan, so he is worse.
…
[Wang Kuei-min looking at Drawing #9[10]]
Q: What do you see here?
A: There is a kid bending over there and crying.
Q: Why is he crying?
A: … being hit by others so he is crying.
…
Q: Why does he fight with others?
A: … he likes to fight, so he uses bamboo to fight with others.
Q: What do you think he will become in the future?
A: Become a hooligan.
Q: What do hooligans do?
A: To take knifes and kill people.

–Excerpt of TAT transcript[11]

The most salient theme in children's storytelling about moral transgressions and violence in the adult society was that of hooligans or gangsters (*lo mua* in Hokkien). Xia Xizhou was known for its history of gangsters. The village was "the home of a gang that preyed on the town's merchants," and the passage between the township Shulin and the village marked the boundary between the territories of rival gangs. Margery Wolf's *The House of Lim* described the history of this village's gang: Lim Hue-lieng (pseudonym), the eldest son in the most prominent family, and the older brother of the Wolfs' landlord,[12] started out as the leader

---

[10] This drawing is missing in the Wolf Archive.
[11] TAT #54, summer 1960. In TAT excerpts, "A" refers to the child's answer, and "Q" refers to the adult interviewer's question.
[12] He died before the Wolfs moved to Xia Xizhou.

Gendered Morality

Figure 4.2 TAT Drawing #4
Source: The Wolf Archive.
Photo by Jing Xu.

of all gangsters in this village in the 1930s, then of all the other villages around here, and eventually of a large area of the Taipei basin. Although the village was looked down upon by some outsiders, such as merchants in Shulin who were exploited by the village's gangsters, according to Margery Wolf, the gangster activities in a way ensured the internal order and security of this village (M. Wolf 1968: 48):

He and the other *lo mua* from here used to fight a lot and they were so famous that even now no one dares to do anything to hurt this village. If someone made a comment about somebody's walking too close to one of our girls, they would fight them right away, or if someone said something in public they would set a time and fight with them later. And if they heard a man was coming to our village to visit a prostitute who lived here, they would wait for him on the path and beat him up. They did all of this to protect the good name of the village. … Even the peaceful, quiet men of the village who abhor the kind of life Lim Hue-lieng led are willing to admit that there is still an aura around the name of Peihotien that causes thieves to pass it by. American friends in the well-policed city of Taipei maintained elaborate systems of locks and watchmen, but were robbed repeatedly. We left expensive cameras, typewriters, and watches scattered about our unlocked rooms and never lost so much as a pencil.

In the late 1950s, the new generation's youths also participated in gangster activities (M. Wolf 1968: 48):

> The petty *lo mua* activities of today's young men are as disapproved by the older and more stable elements of the population as they were thirty years ago, and perhaps with more reason since there seems to be considerably more fighting and far less activity in support of the community and traditional morality. Peihotien's reputation provides the young men of the village with a high status among their peers, but it also demands that they maintain certain standards. They are less able than other youths to ignore a slight or an insult.

Without systematic evidence on this particular matter, it is hard to draw any conclusion on how exactly this local gangster culture might have shaped the younger children's life. But the story of Arthur Wolf's good friend, the Taiwanese historian Wang Shiqing who was born in Xia Xizhou, tells us that at least some parents worried about it: In 1941, after Wang finished elementary school (sixth grade), his mother Ms. Lai moved the family from Xia Xizhou to Shulin town, out of the concern that the home villagers' *lo-mua* culture was not good for his upbringing. This story became a celebrated tale in Wang's biography, and Ms. Lai became a local parallel to "Mencius' Mother," the virtuous mother figure in ancient China who relocated home three times to improve her son's education, that is, for her son to receive good influence from good neighbors (Chou 2011: 28).

Young children, keen observers of adult and adolescent social life, definitely had some idea about *lo-mua*. They were taught that bad boys who got into fights, stole from parents, or did not do well in school would eventually become *lo-mua*. They might have witnessed some *lo-mua* violence, or at least heard about it. In Child Observation, children sometimes accused their peers of being *lo-mua*.[13] In projective tests, especially TAT with a set

---

[13] For example, CO #120, 08/21/59.

Gendered Morality

of pictures that portrayed ambiguous scenes of children interacting with each other or with adults, many young participants spontaneously told stories of violent scenes associated with *lo-mua*. The excerpt of eight-year-old boy Wang Kuei-ming's transcript was just one among many examples in which children asserted that boys who liked to fight would end up as *lo-mua*. Asked how those misbehaving boys would feel, many answered that they would be afraid of becoming hooligans. Killing with a knife seemed to be *lo-mua*'s signature activity. A seven-year-old boy even associated parent–child fights, interpreted from one of the TAT pictures, with street violence: "[both the child and the mother would fight] with a knife. My mother told me, those (*lo-mua*) fighting on the streets were all fighting with a knife."[14]

Asked what he saw in the first drawing of TAT,[15] of a young boy looking at some round-shaped objects (see Figure 4.3), ten-year-old boy Cheng Ling-hui interpreted the objects as coins, a frequently evoked imagery in TAT responses. Ling-hui told a story about the boy in the drawing, who often came to steal his mother's money. In this story, the boy wanted to spend the money on gambling and prostitution, both of which were common pastimes for local adults. It would only make sense if a bad boy like this becomes a *lo-mua*. Indeed, Ling-hui went on talking about *lo-mua*, murders, and policemen:[16]

Q: Is he [the boy who steals his mother's money] a good kid or bad kid?
A: Bad kid.
Q: What will he become in the future?
A: He will become a *lo-mua*.
Q: What does a *lo-mua* do?
A: Steal other's money.
Q: What else?
A: Kill.

---

[14] TAT #62, summer 1960.
[15] This drawing is missing in the Wolf Archive.
[16] TAT #18, summer 1960.

Figure 4.3 TAT Drawing #1
Source: The Wolf Archive.
Photo by Jing Xu.

Q: Why does a *lo-mua* kill?
A: *Lo-mua* is a kid that nobody takes care of.
Q: How will a *lo-mua* feel when he is killing someone?
A: Afraid.
Q: How will a *lo-mua* feel?
A: He will be afraid when he kills for the first time. He won't be afraid anymore in the future.
Q: Why will he be afraid for the first time? Why won't he be afraid in the future?
A: He gets used to killing.
Q: Why will he be afraid for the first time?
A: He has never killed someone before.
Q: For the first time, what is he afraid of?
A: Afraid of the police.
Q: What will the police do?
A: Catch and sentence him to death.

Gendered Morality

In these children's young minds, *lo-mua* can be extremely violent, and it was only fair that bad guys eventually got caught by the omnipotent police. The scene of policeman punishing bad boys did not exist only in children's fantasy. It also existed in their reality, for example, in parents' threats toward them, especially boys. In the following observation,[17] a mother threatened her son of sending him to the police station, for the son would not admit his misbehavior, and the very naughty boy was scared:

MC observed Chen Hsia punish her eight-year-old son Chen Feng-chu for eating some rice cakes without permission. When she found the rice cakes missing, she asked to find out who had taken them. Feng-chu said that his little brother Feng-hui had eaten them. Feng-hui said that this was not true and seemed to know nothing about it. Feng-chu still denied eating the cakes, so mom said that she would take both boys and the remaining cakes to the police station and let them decide who had stolen the other cakes. She said that the police had a magnifying glass which they could use to find out who had taken the cakes. Feng-chu did not want to go to the police station.

Little brother said that he had seen Feng-chu eating the cakes: "Everytime he steals something he says that I did it." Little brother said that he would go to the police, but Feng-chu still refused to go, so mom told him that he had nothing to fear if he hadn't taken the cakes.

He still refused to go, and so mom took a stick and began to beat him: "Your mother was not in your debt when she bore you. ... Your kind of a child is useless. Go away. Go away." And with this she beat him out of the door.

A few minutes later older brother Feng-hsiang (10-year-old) came in and told mom that Feng-chu was outside cursing her. Mom then got him and tied him to the sofa, telling him that she was going to call the police. Feng-chu was really scared and promised mom that he would never do it again.

Mom said: "Your skin is too thick. You have said that you wouldn't do it again before. This is your last chance. Don't I give you money every day to buy things to eat? Why do you steal? Are you going to grow up to be a thief?

[17] SI #4, 1959/04/15.

[even] Feng-hui is too big to steal things to eat. He is even embarrassed to eat what we put on the table. Why do you always say that he was the one who did it?" Mom then untied him and made him kneel for a while on the floor.

Children in many societies fear or fantasize about police. Parents in many societies threaten misbehaving little ones with police punishment. For example, when I was doing fieldwork in Shanghai, my son was going through his "terrible-two" phase. Every night he kept throwing tantrums and refused to go to sleep. Among all the strategies I tried to make him go to bed, the only effective one was to threaten him that the police car was coming. On numerous nights, amid bustling city sounds, I had to hold the crying toddler and bring him to the balcony of our apartment: "Listen! The police car is right there, down in the yard of our compound, to catch babies who don't go to bed." My toddler boy at that time had very limited knowledge of the actual reality of police power: His understanding primarily came from reading picture books with all kinds of cars and trucks, including police cars. But the limited knowledge of toddler boys in Xia Xizhou was of a different kind: For example, they would be tricked, in the middle of playing a "gambling" game with cards, when older children warned them that policeman was coming to catch gamblers. Sometimes children saw policemen running errands in the village, and they looked at policemen with curiosity. Children must have passed by the police station near their village. Besides being threatened by parents about what police could do to the little ones, they might have overheard adult gossip about policemen's various duties and terrifying deeds. Xia Xizhou children's understanding or imagination of policing offers very specific insights into the political reality in the late 1950s rural Taiwan.

The Wolfs' fieldwork was conducted at the height of Taiwan's Martial Law Era, when police shouldered many local social surveillance and management responsibilities (Chen 2007). But built upon the foundation of Japanese colonial police system, policing during the early decades

Gendered Morality

of KMT authoritarian rule in Taiwan was also known for its culture of violence.[18] Efforts to reform the policing culture in the 1950s and make it more welcoming in local society did not seem effective (Chen 2007). It is hard to piece together a detailed picture of policing in this village from an adult perspective, as we lack systematic materials. But stories scattered across different types of data provide a rare glimpse into what policing was like in children's life and on their minds.

First, the miscellaneous local surveillance functions of policing in the historical context were visible in children's games and narratives. Crime drama like "play police" is a common children's game in many places where policing is an institutional reality.[19] But Xia Xizhou children's various "play police" games offer vivid details of local concerns: For example, police catching thieves who steal chicken and rice from village households, police catching gamblers, and police inspecting household cleaning every month. Their projective test transcripts also shed light on these local functions. For example, looking at one picture in TAT that features a child running and an adult watching (see Figure 4.4), a young girl told this story: A boy is looking at (another household's) roof; he wants to steal vegetables from that garden. Asked what the child would feel, she said: "Would be caught by the police." Again, this kind of "bad child" was, by default, a boy.

Besides everyday surveillance functions of policing, the culture of violence also emerged as a recurrent theme in children's spontaneous narratives: Minor offenses would lead to severe punishment, for example, being shot to death. Gambling appeared to be a big deal in these stories, and police would put occasional gamblers in jail for years. Several children told stories about their parents getting caught by police on the

---

[18] Taiwansheng linshi sheng yihui dierjie disici dahui zhuanji (xia) [Taiwan Provincial Interim Assembly, Second Session, Fourth Meeting Compilation (Volume 2)], (1956): 1728.

[19] For one vivid example, see Catherin Allerton's study of "thief-police" game among working-class Malaysian children (2016): 35.

"Bad Boys Become *Lo-mua*"

Figure 4.4 TAT Drawing #7
Source: The Wolf Archive.
Photo by Jing Xu.

train and brutally punished, for trivial reasons, that is, missing a station and overstaying on the train. Furthermore, in children's eyes, *lo-mua* and policing were intertwined in the loop of violence and punishment, clearly a realistic insight.

In all these "reality-based fantasies," children likely weaved together what they had observed or heard about, such as stealing, killing, and policing, into their fearful but vivid imaginations of violence.[20] The

---

[20] The prominence of violence, gangsters, and policing in children's narratives posed a contrast to anthropologists' experience in some other rural

Gendered Morality

Wolfs' team in theory had a unique opportunity to examine gender and political socialization of Taiwanese children in early and middle childhood. But how children felt the pulse of politics never figured into the Wolfs' research consciousness, and that void itself was a marker of intellectual history. Like the other studies in "the Golden Age" of sinological anthropology, the visions of their research reflect biases of that particular political and historical context: For them, political turbulences in Taiwan's Martial Law Era, like Japanese influence in an earlier period, were just insignificant noise compared to the lasting "Chinese" culture in the island province (Harrell 1999). The connections between childhood and Taiwan's politics, then, must have seemed even more trivial.[21] For example, American child psychiatrist Robert Coles, renowned for his studies of children's political life, was a contemporary of Arthur Wolf. But it took a long time for him to realize that there was a political dimension in children's experience. He only began to systematically examine this topic after many years of researching children (Coles 1986).[22]

Fortunately, existing fieldnotes allowed me to discover bits and pieces of political socialization process and how this bears on gendered moralities. Violence in that particular historical time had indeed left its mark on children's developing minds, shaping their understanding of what it means to be a bad child, or more accurately, a bad boy, and what prospects await him. Now let us turn to "bad" girls.

---

communities in a later era: For example, according to my personal communication with anthropologist Myron Cohen in 2021, he recalled that during his fieldwork in a Hakka village in the late 1960s, there weren't many fights among youths, nor strong tension with local police, which likely reflected its varying political atmosphere, less tight control at that time, and local context, joint families and no gangsters.

[21] Besides, in that authoritarian era, American anthropologists like Wolf might have avoided political questions in order to protect the research participants.

[22] Robert Coles saw his first young patient in Boston in 1956. Only until much later did he explicitly look into children's political life, and he delivered his first lecture on this topic in 1974.

"Iron Teeth" and "Sharp Mouth": "Unruly" Girls

A group of girls were picking up wood on a summer afternoon:[23]

Li Lan-mei (nine-year-old): "I'm going to hurry up and fill my basket so I can go home. It's too late."
[It was about 6 pm]
Wang Ah-yun (ten-year-old): "How late is it? Wang Li-chu said the sun was still very high and she wasn't going to go home until it went down."
Lan-mei: "Wasn't Li-chu's father scolding her when we left?
Ah-yun: "She's not afraid of her father. She is just like me. She has iron teeth."
Li-chu (nine-year-old): "I'm not afraid of my father. If he scolds me I'll say: 'Aren't I good to pick up the wood for you?'"

MC added a note in this observation, right next to the phrase "iron teeth": "She [Li-chu] is very stubborn and keeps arguing a lot." This short conversation exposes two interesting dimensions of girls' moral world, on one hand, moral expectations specific to girls, for example, helping with housework, and on the other hand, how girls assert themselves despite those normative expectations. In this case, Wang Li-chu was fulfilling her duty of picking up wood, yet she probably also wanted to enjoy more time with her friends outside. At home she probably argued with her parents a lot, given that she wasn't afraid of her father, even though in this community many children were frightened by the stern father figure, and she used her good work as her bargaining chip.

Not only did Li-chu and Ah-yun have "iron teeth," the other girl Lan-mei was not a meek character either. In one observation, an adult woman accused her of having "sharp mouth." While washing vegetables by the river, Lan-mei and a seven-year-old girl Wang Lin-fang got into a fight over territorial issues, when Lin-fang came to wash clothes – both dutifully doing housework. Lin-fang's mother came over and asked what

---

[23] CO #173, 8/30/1959.

Gendered Morality

had happened. Lin-fang kept saying that Lan-mei hit her. Lan-mei disagreed and started cursing, which made Lin-fang's mother very angry. She shouted to Lan-mei: "I didn't scold you when my daughter told me that. Why do you talk that way? You are a girl. Why is your mouth so sharp?" Then the mother scolded her daughter too: "What did I tell you at home? I told you not to fight with others. Why do you always fight with others? ... You are such a bad girl. You always like to fight others."[24]

What does it mean to be a good girl? In many villagers' eyes, first and foremost, good girls, or good children in general, should not get into fights.[25] A good girl is supposed to keep herself quiet.[26] She should not argue back or use coarse language. But the earlier conversations about "iron teeth" and "sharp mouth," the vignette in the beginning of this chapter, about a group of older girls bullying little boys, and many other episodes in the fieldnotes, all tell us that young girls were far from docile. The detailed quantitative analysis of children's behavior in this chapter also supports this conclusion: Although girls were less physically aggressive than boys, they resorted to a variety of other means – sometimes more frequently than boys – such as tattling, scolding, throwing a dirty look, and social exclusion, to defend themselves or control others.

For parents, a good girl is a good daughter and sister. She listens to adults, takes care of household chores, and sacrifices for her brothers. A fifty-year-old woman praised the girl of a new family who recently moved to Xia Xizhou from Jinmen: "The daughter is very polite. She buys candy to give to her little brother and doesn't eat any herself."[27] But this does not mean that the daughter has no understanding of the unequal situation, or that she has no desire for the same food. For example, two sisters, five-year-old Wang Ah-tao and eight-year-old Wang

---

[24] SO #85, 8/4/1959.
[25] To parents, the default criterion of a good child, for both sons and daughters, is "not getting into fights" (M. Wolf 1972: 75).
[26] In one observation, a mother even scolded her daughter for running around playing ball at school (SI #30, 3/28/1959.)
[27] SI #9, 4/13/1959.

Su-yeh gossiped about their little brother. Ah-tao saw that the little brother managed to get their grandpa to give him some pocket money and they were going to the store to buy melon seeds. Ah-tao and Su-yeh then hurried to the store to get a fair share for themselves too.[28]

A good girl should take care of younger siblings. Girls indeed shouldered sibling care duties more frequently than boys, as behavioral analysis demonstrated. But babysitting could be a very annoying duty for girls, so they found ways to evade their duties or enjoy themselves while half-heartedly performing their duty. As Margery Wolf observed: "Little girls who have younger siblings of either sex explored many techniques for fulfilling their responsibilities to parents, but still joining the village play groups" (1972: 66). Mothers can get very angry with their daughters for not doing a good job. The following scene of quarrel happened between two daughters and their mother: One daughter was the "iron teeth" girl Wang Li-chu, and her nine-year-old younger sister Li-lien was reluctantly getting ready for sibling care.[29]

Li-lien started to walk into the room and said to mom: "Do I have to get the blanket too?"

Mom (angrily): "Why not! The more you eat the stupider you get."

Li-lien smiled to herself (amused at her mother's choice of scolding) and walked into the other room to get the things to tie the baby on her back. When she came out mom was scolding Li-chu who had just come in and handed her jacket to her mother.

Mom: "… To raise this girl is like dying! It is worse than a boy. Somebody else's boy who is 8 years old knows how to cook, but you!"

[Li-chu continued to annoy her mom]

Mom: "You! Already over ten years old and don't know how to do anything but talk back!"

[After a while, Li-lien got the baby tied on her back and wanted to go outside. Perhaps she wanted to go play with other kids.]

---

[28] CO #1206, 4/7/1960.
[29] CO #940, 3/3/1960.

Gendered Morality

Mom yelled: "Now don't you take him out into a strong wind! If I see you with him in the wind again, I'm going to beat you to death!"

Besides punishment, some adults also used pocket money or other promises as incentives for girls to babysit. Margery Wolf observed this strategy (1972: 66) but she did not describe what the girls thought about it. Actually, girls cared about receiving fair reward and resented unfair treatment. Once MC had this hearty conversation with fellow girls:[30]

MC to Shih Mei-lin (seven-year-old): "I see you taking care of your baby brother all the time. Does your mother give you some money for taking care of him?"

Mei-lin (scornfully): "No, she always says that she's going to give me a dollar, but she never does. She always fools, she sweet talks, but never does give me a dollar."

Wang Ah-Mei (eleven-year-old) then told MC that an adult woman [unnamed] is always making the other children take care of the children in her family: "She always says that she is going to take us to a movie or buy us something, but she never does, and if we won't do it, she says, 'All right, all right, I'll remember, I'll remember'. Ah-Mei seemed to resent this treatment very much."

The young, female research assistants must have played a crucial role in getting the girls to talk about their feelings and opinions because the research assistants could empathically understand these girls' experience. Another important aspect of the village girls' moral life is schooling, which MC and MS identified with and captured in fieldnotes.

"It Is No Use for You to Go to School!"

Wang Chun-yu, the daughter of the wealthiest Wang family in the village, was finishing up fifth grade in summer 1959. She had been refusing

[30] MO #12, 2/9/1960.

"It Is No Use for You to Go to School!"

to go to school because of some tension with her strict teacher, who hit her hard for not doing homework.³¹ She stayed home but did not help around the house. Her mother got very angry and scolded her. But whenever her mother tried to hit her, Chun-yu ran away. Chun-yu even argued back, saying things like "I don't have to listen to you!" According to MC, Chun-yu often said dirty words to her mother. A relative of the family, a young prostitute, was staying in the house temporarily. MC heard this woman saying this to Chun-yu, in the presence of Chun-yu's mother: "It is no use for you go to school! You would just have to cook anyway and it wouldn't help you. ... You should work and then you would have money to buy clothes, etc."

During the pandemic years, I had spent a lot of time in the kitchen cooking for my family. I kept thinking about this episode, imagining how Chun-Yu thought about the young prostitute's comment on the fate of girls (see Figure 4.5). I also wondered what the observer MC might have felt at this scene. After all, MC went to school and later, allegedly, worked as a maid for Americans in Taiwan.³² While talking to these girls, MC had occasionally mentioned her own, similar experience or attitude, for example, about classroom antagonism between boys and girls, and about

Figure 4.5 A girl contemplating
Source: Photo by Arthur Wolf.

---

³¹ SI #15, 7/1/1959.
³² According to Mr. Huang Chieh-Shan's recollections (personal communication, April 2021).

165

Gendered Morality

exam-related anxiety. What a pity that in this episode MC did not leave any comments behind! But at least we got a glimpse into the kind of conversations young girls were exposed to, conversations that might have prompted them to think about what it means to be a woman.

Girls also had their own reflections about unfairness and gender discrimination at school, that boys bullied girls and that some teachers preferred boys. They confided in research assistant MS:[33]

MS: "Do girls and boys play together at school?"

Wang Li-kuan (ten-year-old): "When we were in the first and second grade we did, but not after the third grade. The boys and the girls cannot get along. The boys always bully the girls. Once a boy who was Class Disciplinarian hit the girls with a stick even though we weren't making any noise. So all of us girls hit the Class Master who was also a boy. He cried. The teacher came and scolded us, saying we shouldn't fight with one another. The Class Master represents the teacher."

MS: "Do you dare to hit the teacher?"

Li-kuan: "My teacher is a man and is very bad. He favors the boys. He says the girls like to talk."

On the same day, MS interviewed a group of younger girls who were playing together:[34]

MS: "Which of you wants to be Class Master?"
The four girls all shouted: "I want to. I want to."
MS: "Why do you want to be Class Master?"
GIRLS: "The Class Master gets to control (*guan*) the others."

Later, MS talked to one of these girls, Huang Su-yun (seven years old), knowing that she wanted to be Class Master: "Are you Class Master now?"

Su-yun: "Not yet. My teacher likes boys, and he also likes to let those whose grades aren't too good be Class Master. This makes me very angry. Why is it

---

[33] SI #0, 5/23/1959.
[34] Data Type 5, #1, 5/23/1959.

like this? I don't know. The work of the present Class Master [a boy] is not as good as mine. My homework is always 'Excellent'."³⁵

Once an old woman accused her granddaughter: "You are one of those girls that never do what people tell them."³⁶ That must have been an exaggeration though: None of the young girls could completely ignore what they were told to do. Their lives were constrained by various ethical obligations, and they were aware of those obligations. But contrary to purely miserable and submissive personalities, various stories of "unruly" girls emerged in these fieldnotes: They were perceptive of the inequalities imposed upon them. They tried to defend themselves and maneuvered to advance their own interests. They also wanted to be in power, to *guan* (control) others, like those "class master" boys. Even in the more extreme case of inferiority and insecurity, such as adopted daughters, young girls still found ways to negotiate cultural models and assert their agency.

A Fierce Adoptive Daughter

Sitting in front of House 7, we [Margery Wolf and MC] overheard Wang Tian-lai teasing his little girl Mei-yu by saying that he was going to give her to the foreigner as an adopted daughter. He told her of all the places she would get to in an airplane. The little girl grinned but insisted that she did not want to go.

–SI #10, 7/7/1959

The topic of adopted girls contributed to Arthur Wolf's most important discovery, that is, the common practice of "minor marriage" in this and neighboring Taiwanese villages: Many families adopted baby girls and raised them to become daughters-in-law. These "little daughters-in-law" are called *sim-pu-a* in local dialect. Wolf has written extensively about this marriage custom and its psychological consequences, such as

---

[35] Data Type 5, #2, 5/23/1959.
[36] CO #958, 3/06/1960.

Gendered Morality

incest avoidance formed in the process of childhood cohabitation.[37] He also wrote about maternal sentiments, for example, in an article entitled "Maternal Sentiments: How Strong Are They?" (A. Wolf 2003). While his conclusions were mostly based on statistical analyses of demographic data, I was more intrigued by a rarely addressed question, the "sentiments" of adopted girls: What was it like to be an adopted girl in that community? What kinds of emotions were salient to them? How did they make sense of their own situation?

By the late 1950s, the minor marriage custom had largely disappeared in Xia Xizhou,[38] but it was not uncommon to adopt daughters. Although these girls were not expected to marry their adopted brothers anymore, their emotional world, examined in ethnographic detail, can still shed valuable light on gendered moral experience. First of all, adoption still looms large in the village girls' life, as a realistic threat (A. Wolf n.d.: 73):

> In 1958 this Cinderella-like image of the *sim-pu-a* was still so vivid that threatening to give a child away as a *sim-pu-a* was the most effective threat a parent could make. Children who ignored scoldings and threats of physical punishment were reduced to tears when their mother, exasperated beyond bearing, threatened, "You remember that person who came here yesterday. She was looking for a *sim-pu-a*. You want me to give you to her?

Girls were adopted at a young age, therefore such a threat was also presented to daughters when they were little. For example, MC noted this: "Last year they [parents] threatened to give her [Chang Ali, 2-year-old girl] away whenever she dirtied herself. She would cry and scream: 'No. No. No'."[39] Wang Chui-ying, a *sim-pu-a* of an older generation, a

---

[37] A. Wolf (1966, 1968, 1970, 1995, 2014).
[38] Under Japanese colonial rule, Xia Xizhou's marriage customs changed radically. Minor marriages were the most popular form until the 1920s. After 1950, among the twenty-three women who married into Xia Xizhou, only five came as "little daughters-in-law," and the last minor marriage in the village was consummated in 1953 (A. Wolf n.d.: 72).
[39] Baby Survey #20, 11/06/1959.

mother in her late thirties at the time of the Wolfs' fieldwork, remembered the trauma of adoption:

I slept with my grandmother and she petted me each night until I went to sleep. It was the same until I married. No matter how late it was, I would wait for my grandmother before I would go to bed. I was afraid to go to sleep by myself. That was because they tricked my parents that way and adopted me so young. (M. Wolf 1968: 125)

Despite the emotional scars, the adopted girl found comfort in her (adoptive) grandmother's petting. This hints at the complexity of sentiments in young girls' world, of attachment and fear, of bonding and pain.

Among the three adopted girls within the age range of 0 to 12, the archive contains the most materials about Wang Shu-yu.[40] I focus on her story because we get to know her personality. Shu-yu was the eldest child in her adoptive family. At the beginning of the fieldwork, she was five years old, living with her (adoptive) grandparents, parents, and three younger siblings, one sister and two brothers, including a baby brother. According to Child Observation, she was observed in 306 behavioral interactions with twenty-seven children and several adults. Figure 4.6 represents Shu-yu's behavioral interactions with other people in a network graph: A node represents a person, an edge represents behavioral interactions between two nodes, and the arrow represents the direction of behavior (from initiator to recipient). This ego network graph shows that Shu-yu (#193) interacted most frequently with her sister Wang Shu-lan (#195, 3.5 years younger), brother Wang Jun-hsien (#194, 1.5 years younger), and several other children similar to her in age (e.g., her cousins #206 and #205 and friend #253).

---

[40] These materials include fifty-two episodes of spontaneous, timed observations, eighteen episodes of event-based observations, observations of mother–child interactions, interviews with her and her mother respectively, and two projective tests with her, TAT & Doll Play.

Gendered Morality

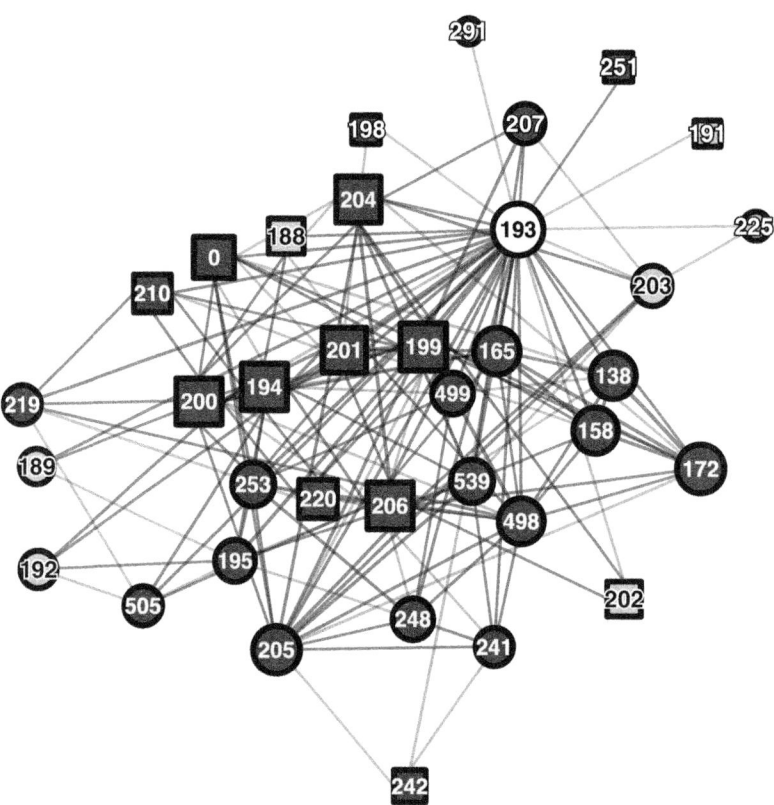

Figure 4.6 An adopted girl's (#193) behavioral-interaction network. The number on each node represents the person's ID. The white node represent the focal child ("ego" node Shu-yu), dark gray nodes represent other children, and light gray nodes represent adults; square nodes represent females and round nodes represent males. The thickness and darkness of the edge is proportional to the weight of this edge, that is, the frequency of interactions between the two nodes. The darker and thicker the edge is, the more interactions between the two people

Shu-yu was adopted when she was only two months old because the family's first child, also a baby girl, died. This custom was called "substitute flower," and part of the purpose was to alleviate the mother's pain and grief of losing a child. The girl was breastfed by the adoptive mother (hereafter "mother"), and after she was weaned, the grandmother took

A Fierce Adoptive Daughter

care of her. This girl, her mom, and paternal grandma formed an interesting triangular relationship that complicates the typical "adopted girl" imagery built from previous studies of Chinese families, including the Wolfs' own works. Unlike the docile *sim-pu-a* (e.g., M. Wolf 1972: 76), Shu-yu seemed quite willful, even stubborn. In her mother's words, she was "touchy," "very fierce." The girl's "unruly" personality might have to do with birth order, her being the oldest child in the family. But a more likely reason, as her mother explained, was that the girl's grandmother, the matriarch of the family, doted on her and protected her:[41]

She is a big girl, but she still asks her grandmother to carry her. … If I hit her, her grandmother will scold me. Her grandmother likes her very much. If her grandmother has special things to eat she always gives them to her. What's left, the grandmother gives to the younger children. Because her grandmother took care of her from when she was very little, she loves her from her heart. Her grandmother is usually very tight-fisted, but if she wants some money she [grandma] gives it to her. Every day she spends about NT$1. Everyday she asks everybody in the family for money.

The mother did not like the girl, perhaps even resented her to some extent: "I don't care whether she is a good girl or not, because she is another's child." In mother's eyes, Shu-yu was not a good, obedient girl: "She is very lazy [meaning not doing chores]. I call her and she doesn't move so I don't like to call her to do something." Mother complained about the ethical burden of raising an adoptive daughter: "She is not my own child. If I tell her to do chores other people would say I don't treat her well." Such reputational concerns bothered her: "If the child was my own I could hit her and others wouldn't say anything." At the same time, mother was always the one exercising punishment toward her because "her grandmother is unwilling."[42] Mother did not want to give in to her. She often scolded the girl and commanded her to take care of younger

---

[41] MI #192, 5/30/1959.
[42] MI #192, 5/30/1959.

siblings. But the girl did not readily comply. She used various strategies to suspend sibling care and enjoy herself when out of her mother's sight. In a jump rope game with other girls, when it was her turn to play, she put her baby brother on the ground. Seeing that scene, mother started scolding her, threatening to hit her and not let her eat dinner. Shu-yu wasn't scared at all.[43] Another time, despite her mother's shouting, she just walked away smiling and went on playing.[44]

More than mischievous, Shu-yu could be really defiant. Shu-yu didn't like to go to school. In 1958, mother sent her to kindergarten,[45] but grandma defended the girl, saying she was too young to study. A year later, she was sent to school again. She was fine on the first day, but soon she got scared in the classroom. According to MC, her teacher made many of her classmates cry, but MC never saw her crying in her classroom. She was tough and strong willed. On September 15, 1959, Shu-yu refused to go to school again. Her grandmother brought her to school, her arms marked from her mom's beatings. Grandma pled to the vice principal. The two of them took her by the arm, trying to lead her into the classroom, but she ran away. MC observed the following scenes at school before her grandmother left:[46]

Grandmother: "First she wants a book bag so I buy it. Then she wants a white blouse so I buy it. Then a dark skirt. She was so interested in school and then yesterday she didn't want to go so her mother beat her. She still wouldn't go. Today she wouldn't go and her mother tied her up and beat her and she still refused."

The vice principal asked Shu-yu to go with her and tell her why she didn't want to come to school, but she wouldn't budge.

---

[43] MO #72, 9/30/1960.
[44] MO #73, 9/18/1960.
[45] Mother did so partly due to her reputational concern. She did not want to be judged by fellow villagers as not treating the adoptive daughter well. But also she believed that the girl could do well in school, as her biological sisters all did well.
[46] SI #45, 9/15/1959.

A Fierce Adoptive Daughter

When the grandmother started to leave, she told Shu-yu: "You stay here because if you go home you'll get beat again. What a stupid granddaughter. Next year you'll see everyone having a good time in school and want to go and your adopted mother will beat you and won't let you go because when you grow up she'll want you to stay home and help her and she won't let you go again. You'll have to pick rocks and it'll break your back."

In this episode grandmother was clearly the affectionate protector, while the mother was a harsh punisher. The triad of Shu-yu, mother, and grandmother complicates the already fraught relationship between the two adult women. This tension between mother-in-law and daughter-in-law was part of the manifestation of what Margery Wolf called "the uterine family" (1972), that women's power in this village came from the social unit between a mother and her son, and from the priority of mother–son tie over the son's conjugal relation. Shu-yu's Doll Play transcript illuminates a young girl's perceptive insights about her family dynamics: "Dad scolded mom [for hitting her child]. Grandmother [scolded her daughter-in-law]: 'Ah! A woman like you, always like this [hitting the kids], such a fierce woman! It'd be better not to marry her. Dad said next time he'll send mom to the police station'."[47] The girl knew well of the tensions in her family. She manipulated such tensions to her own advantage. She would use grandmother's love to shield herself from mother's punishment, and her mother disliked this.[48]

As a girl who was forced upon a complicated journey of adoption, however, she had developed paradoxical sentiments toward the mother. Her fantasy in Doll Play seemed to resemble her own family situation and disclose her hatred toward her mother: "Mom left home after a fight with dad. ... All the children cried, except the elder sister. Because elder sister often got hit, so she didn't cry for her. She was glad to see mom go away."[49] Note that she happened to be the "elder sister" in her

---

[47] Doll Play #193, 9/13/1960.
[48] MI #192, 5/30/1959.
[49] DP #193, 9/13/1960.

own family. On the other hand, she seemed to long for intimate attachment with mother. In one observation, Shu-yu was teasing a baby, and mother scolded her. But this mischievous girl "smiled and stopped and went over and threw herself on her mother's back." Her mom "shook her shoulders annoyed." She then "smiled, went over and sat down by herself."[50] This moment of desire and rejection speaks to the adopted daughter's intricate emotional experience.

Discourses, Statistics, and Personalities

The idea that gender is an integral part of children's moral personhood runs deep in ethnic Han families. Despite all the familiar discourses and imageries about sons and daughters in the so-called "traditional Han Chinese family," few studies have dived into the actual world of childhood and examined, in a systematic approach, how gender intersects with moral development. This archive affords a rare opportunity for comprehensive statistical analysis on gendered behavioral patterns. For example, boys initiate more physical aggression, verbal aggression, and dominance, but girls assert themselves in more subtle or indirect ways, such as through tattling, scolding, and social exclusion. The rich ethnographic materials also allowed me to connect children's behavior, knowledge, and emotions to the larger historical context.

Moreover, I was curious about children's perspectives, the range of experiences that shaped young girls' and boys' understanding of their duties and privileges, rights and wrongs, and the emotional texture of those experiences. Sinological anthropology, or anthropology in general, tend to ignore individual children, or reduce them to family ideologies and childrearing values, such as the trope of filial sons and submissive daughters. In this chapter I recovered the voices of mischievous, naughty, and even fierce boys and girls. Boys observed aggression in their

---

[50] MO #75, 8/25/1960.

everyday life. They learned that misbehaving boys would become hooligans and gangsters (*lo-mua*). Girls learned the rules of patriarchy, often enforced by adult women, but at the same time they developed various strategies to subvert these rules, especially when the enforcers were not around. From snapshots of their everyday life, I tried to understand their personalities. Continuing the journey of rediscovering individual experiences, Chapter 5 will present a case study, centering on two children, a brother-and-sister dyad. This case study highlights sibling relation, a special and significant type of peer relation in this community, in addition to exploring the complexity of gender and individual personalities in family dynamics. Thanks to its "previous life," this unique case also echoes an overall theme of this book, what it means to construct/reconstruct an ethnography.

FIVE

Care and Rivalry

An Untold Tale of a Sibling Dyad

Siblings Matter

On a spring morning, MC observed a brother–sister dyad interacting with another child:[1]

Pai Yan-yan [a seven-year-old girl] was standing in front of a rock with food on it. Wang Yi-kun [a seven-year-old boy] was in a hurry to go away and stuck a paper package into Yan-yan's hand and said: "Here is some face powder [for pretend play]. I give this to you."

Yan-yan: "Alright." She took it.

Yi-kun: "You have to let my [younger sister] Mei-yu play with you." Yi-kun turned and ran off.

His sister Wang Mei-yu [five-year-old]: "You let me play with you, alright?"

Yan-yan nodded her head. She put the powder package under the rubber band that was holding her purse closed.

Mei-yu had a little cosmetic box in her hand. Yan-yan took it from her and said: "We'll put this in my purse, alright? We'll put it with all my other things."

Mei-yu nodded her head in agreement.

This episode, combining elements of kinship, friendship, and gender, provides a glimpse into young siblings' moral life in peer context: The

---

[1] CO #1176, 04/05/1960.

Siblings Matter

young boy Yi-kun "bribed" his peer Yan-yan with the explicit goal of getting Yan-yan to accept his little sister Mei-yu as her playmate. Yan-yan accepted Yi-kun's gift – a popular play object among young girls in the community, as well as his request. Perhaps benefitting from her seniority in age or her position as the desired playmate, Yan-yan also took the initiative to lead the subsequent interactions, commanding the control of resources upon Mei-yu's agreement. Above all, we see a little boy helping his younger sister to make friends with peers, in a social world outside the home, through exchange of gifts and favors.

Sibling relations provide a unique lens through which to examine core questions of learning morality. How do young children learn their first lessons with their siblings, about relating to others and asserting oneself, about cooperation and conflict, and about negotiating parental control and love, within and beyond familial contexts? While many in other species never know or meet their siblings, humans have almost always known and lived with their siblings throughout our evolutionary history. Across cultures, instead of having adults supervise and teach them, children spend a lot of time playing with and learning from other children, and siblings are important agents in such peer learning processes (Maynard and Tovote 2010). Cross-cultural research on child development has long demonstrated that siblings always matter (Weisner 1989).

A special relationship that cuts across the peer world and the family world, sibling relation can shed invaluable light on family dynamics. Despite the fact that Chinese children also spend a lot of time with their siblings, the anthropology of the Chinese family since its inception has obscured the importance of sibling relation. Classic works, shaped by British social anthropology's lineage studies traditions,[2] rarely focused on sibling relations in childhood, only analyzing brother-brother relations as adults.[3] Later research, inspired by

---

[2] In particular, Maurice Freedman's paradigm (1966) on Chinese lineage.
[3] A few classic studies include the following: Maurice Freeman (1966) established the conceptual foundation for explaining the division and unity of Chinese families.

Care and Rivalry

the new anthropology of kinship that emphasizes the lived experience of "relatedness" (Carsten 2000) instead of formal structures, still paid little attention to sibling experience.[4] Neglecting sibling relation reflects a broader problem in the anthropology of kinship, that is, the bias toward the centrality of parent–child and conjugal relations (Alber, Coe, and Thelen 2013).[5]

Studying sibling relations also honors and expands from Arthur Wolf's legacy in biological and evolutionary anthropology. From a bio-evolutionary perspective, sibling experience in childhood is a key component in human kin detection – detecting genetic relatedness (Lieberman, Tooby, and Cosmides 2007). Even today, Arthur Wolf's research on Taiwanese *sim-pu-a* ("little daughter-in-law") (A. Wolf 1970) and communally-reared children in the Israeli Kibbutzim (Shepher 1971) remain two classic cases of "natural experiments" that are often taken to have wider implications for human kinship in general. Drawing from demographic records in the Haishan area, Arthur Wolf found lower fertility rates and higher divorce rates of adult couples who grew up as stepsiblings compared to those who did not. As I mentioned in Chapter 4, he has written extensively to support the Westermarck hypothesis that intimate association in childhood leads to incest avoidance through

---

Margery Wolf (1972) described women's role, how tensions between brothers in a household were amplified by sisters-in-law and led into family division; Myron Cohen (1976) focused on large, joint families are maintained and divided in a Southern Taiwan village; Rubie Watson (1985) traced the formation of inequality among brothers in a single lineage spanning centuries in a Hong Kong village.

[4] For a critique of the inadequate attention on sibling and other sorts of kin and fictive kin relations, see (Stafford 2000). There are a few exceptions in sinological anthropology, such as "same-year siblingship" – fictive kin, friendship (G. D. Santos 2008) and elder sister's sacrifice and support for younger brother in rural China (Obendiek 2013), but these focus on young adults, instead of children.

[5] David Schneider, "the father of the new kinship studies," found that American adults valued sibling relations formed in childhood experience (Cumming and Schneider 1961). But Cumming and Schneider's explanation, that such horizontal solidarity is embedded in a social system that values a high-level of autonomy and freedom, is not generalizable to societies that value children's conformity and obedience.

sexual disgust.⁶ Along these lines, later research based on laboratory experiments further established sibling co-residence experience as a key parameter for kin detection and moral sentiments related to incest (Lieberman and Lobel 2012; Lieberman, Tooby, and Cosmides 2003).

But Wolf's previous research did not explicitly address the linkage between sibling relation and kin-based morality. Sibling-directed morality as altruism, formulated in kin-selection or inclusive fitness theory (Hamilton 1964), is an important prediction of human behavioral ecology.⁷ Help, care and collaboration among siblings are a major focus of this chapter. I will also delve into the dark side of sibling morality. Even though natural selection should lead to kin-based altruism at a very general level and as what's called "an ultimate explanation" (Scott-Phillips, Dickins, and West 2011), in everyday reality kinship is not always "warm and fuzzy." While classic theories on kinship in sociocultural anthropology tend to focus on dimensions of solidarity, many recent reflections have emphasized the negative sentiments, or ambivalence of kinship (see e.g., Bamford 2019; Cartsen 2013).⁸ Sibling relations, especially cross-sex siblings, are constructed simultaneously as equal (shared parenthood) and as different (age, gender, birth order) (Thelen, Coe, and Alber 2013). Exploring sibling relations in childhood can help us understand the "double-edged quality of human kinship"

---

⁶ For a review of Wolf's works and the Westermarck hypothesis in light of human biology, see (Lieberman and Symons 1998).
⁷ Hamilton's rule in theoretical biology states that a trait is favored by natural selection if the benefit to others, B, multiplied by relatedness, R, exceeds the cost to self, C. Kin-based altruism is distinct from reciprocal altruism in nonkin interactions (Trivers 1971). Plainly speaking, while cooperation between non-related people is often maintained through reciprocity, reciprocity is not necessary for people to sacrifice themselves to help their close-relatives, for example, their children.
⁸ Some classic works in anthropology also addressed the negative or ambivalent sentiments of kin relations, but more in the form of ethnographic materials rather than a main focus in theoretical paradigms (Peletz 2002). Within sinological anthropology, Margery Wolf's ethnography "House of Lim" (1968) portrayed vivid scenes of family disputes and conflicts among adults in Xia Xizhou.

Care and Rivalry

(Carsten 2013): love and control, connection and exclusion in everyday practice of relatedness.

I rediscovered the once untold tale of a brother–sister dyad, two main characters in the opening vignette. Their family was featured in Margery Wolf's *A Thrice-Told Tale* (1992), but what happened to the children remained a mystery. This intrigued me. I recovered these children's voices in their family drama. I traced their social network and behavioral patterns. I explored how they looked out for each other and united against their peers but competed and maneuvered at home. Finally, reconstructing the story of these two children also led me to ponder the nature of fieldnotes and ethnography.

A "Crazy" Mother and Her Children

The family of Wang Yi-kun and Wang Mei-yu was featured in Margery Wolf's book *A Thrice-Told Tale: Feminism, Postmodernism, and Ethnographic Responsibility* (1992), including its shorter, article version (M. Wolf 1990b). This family "had lived in the village for nearly ten years, but by village tradition they were still newcomers."[9] In a community bonded through kinship, although sharing the same surname, they didn't belong to the village's prominent Wang lineage (the Wolfs' landlord, the Lims of *The House of Lim*).[10] At the beginning of the Wolfs' fieldwork, this family (see Table 5.1) included father Wang Tian-lai (#47), mother Wang Chen-hsin (#48), and three children: Wang Yi-kun (#49), Wang Mei-yu (#50), and an infant boy Wang Ju-kun (#51).

The protagonist of *A Thrice-Told Tale*, Wang Chen-hsin, a woman who "went crazy," was originally from Keelung, and her mother still

---

[9] M. Wolf (1992): 95.
[10] Margery Wolf used the pseudonym "Tan" in "Thrice-Told Tale" as her protagonist's surname, and the pseudonym "Lim" for the protagonists in *House of Lim*. But according to the demographic data in the Wolf Archive, this newly settled family's actual surname is Wang.

A "Crazy" Mother and Her Children

Table 5.1 *Wang Yi-kun and Wang Mei-yu's family, Household #7*

Name	Person ID	Age by years (in November 1958)	Gender
Wang Tian-lai	#47	32	M
Wang Chen-hsin	#48	30	F
Wang Yi-kun	#49	6	M
Wang Mei-yu	#50	5	F
Wang Ju-kun	#51	1	M

lived there. Her younger sister Wang Hsiu-chu (#52) somehow lived nearby. Her sister and her mother were both around to look after her, during her mental breakdown, an incident featured in "*A Thrice-Told Tale*:"

In the spring of 1960, in a then remote village on the edge of the Taipei basin in northern Taiwan, a young mother of three lurched out of her home, crossed a village path, and stumbled wildly across a muddy rice paddy. The cries of her children and her own agonized shouts quickly drew an excited crowd out of what had seemed an empty village. Thus began nearly a month of uproar and agitation as this small community resolved the issue of whether one of their residents was being possessed by a god or suffering from a mental illness.[11]

This incident was related to a fight among children. Wang Chen-hsin "had quarreled in recent months with a woman from a Lim household when her young son had been slugged by a Lim boy."[12] The "Lim" household in this quote was actually another Wang household (#15b). From multiple women's testimony during village gossip, MC learned that when Chen-hsin went to the other mom Wang Lin-hua (Household #15b) to report that fight, Lin-hua scolded her harshly: "If children fight and kill each other it serves them right. If your children get killed, then

---

[11] M. Wolf (1992): 93.
[12] M. Wolf (1992): 95.

Care and Rivalry

you come and take your children home and bury them. You don't need to come and talk to me about it."[13] During the days of Chen-hsin's mental breakdown, when she acted like a *Tang-ki* (spirit medium), confusing many people, Lin-hua's household did not go to see Chen-hsin as other neighbors did, and Chen-hsin tormented that household.[14] Another woman, according to Chen-hsin's mother, had cursed Chen-hsin due to children's fights: "You are going to go crazy and take off your clothes." Village women also told MC that when Chen-hsin fell into the field, she lay there lamenting: "Just because of children's things other people bully me, other people bully me just because of children's things. I won't forget this! I won't forget this!"[15]

When I reapproached *A Thrice-Told Tale*, I looked everywhere to find clues about the role and experience of Chen-hsin's children. I gleaned sporadic information about her children in the raw fieldnotes section, the second tale of that book.[16] It turns out that Chen-hsin's older boy Wang Yi-kun played a unique part in the development of that story, although Margery Wolf did not write about this child in her final, ethnographic tale. First of all, the boy knew his mom's psychology quite well and seemed more perceptive than his father Tian-lai. Had his father been as insightful as he was, they might have successfully prevented Chen-hsin from "going crazy" this time.[17] On top of a grudge against other mothers accumulated recently, the immediate trigger of Chen-hsin's erratic behavior, on March 4, 1960, was her losing NT$ 90 and believing that a neighbor had stolen it. When she couldn't find the money and

[13] M. Wolf (1992): 62. These same women reported that later when Chen-hsin's child hit Lin-hua's child, Chen-hsin just said the same thing back to Lin-hua.
[14] M. Wolf (1992): 100.
[15] M. Wolf (1992): 62.
[16] *A Thrice-Told Tale* includes three sections, the first is fiction, the second is raw fieldnotes, and the third is ethnographic writing. The raw fieldnotes presented in the second section belong to note-type "G" ("general"), instead of the child-centered notes (Child Observation, Child Interview, etc.).
[17] A villager told MC that something like this had happened to Chen-hsin before (M. Wolf 1992: 62).

A "Crazy" Mother and Her Children

asked Yi-Kun about it, he told mom that his father took it to gamble. But his father denied it. She then plunged into the rice field. Neighbors criticized the husband who, they said, was aware of his wife's illness, because he should not have let her worry. He should have said that he had taken the money even if he hadn't, because she then would not worry about the missing money.[18]

Yi-kun and his mother were very close. He was her confidant. After she fell ill, she once called her son into the house and lay on the bed with him. Yi-kun told his mother that a medicine his father gave her was made of worms, prescribed by local gods. She called her son in, both to confirm that matter and to protect him from being spanked by his angry father. Upon confirming with Yi-kun, she ran out of the house and her children looked scared.[19]

As hard as it could be, her children, both Yi-kun and Mei-yu, were seen helping her when everyone else present was frightened by her possession-like behavior. On March 10, 1960, Chen-hsin drew a crowd in her courtyard, dancing like a *Tang-ki*, making *bai-bai* motions. She summoned MC, hugged her close and praised her for being kind to all the children, but the chaotic scene frightened MC and children in the crowd. Her own children, however, did not see scared. They rushed to pick her up each time she fell down.[20]

Finally, her mental breakdown strained her marital relation, and her children were inevitably involved in. When Chen-hsin found out that her husband was going to send her to the hospital again, as he had when she stumbled into the rice paddy, she kept saying that her husband was too dumb and that she wanted a divorce: "I am a woman and you are a man, so I'll take the one girl (Mei-yu) and you take the boys (Yi-kun and

---

[18] Neighbors thought the husband very dumb and that he could have made the wife feel better. My description of what happened on March 4, 1960 was based on raw fieldnotes that recorded what MC heard from other villagers (M. Wolf 1992: 62).
[19] M. Wolf (1992): 68.
[20] M. Wolf (1992): 76.

Care and Rivalry

his baby brother). I won't have to take your boys [the heirs of the husband's family]. I'm going to take the girl home [to Keelung] with me. I am going to take my girl home with me." A neighbor said she did bring her daughter with her when she tried to run away from the house.[21]

Children's voices were mostly omitted when Margery Wolf transformed the raw fieldnotes into her ethnographic piece, "The Woman Who Didn't Become a Shaman" (M. Wolf 1990b, 1992: 93–126). But children's voices are precious in *this* ethnography: What were Chen-hsin's children like? How did these little ones cope with their life, as part of a marginalized family going through a scandalous crisis? One episode in Child Observation (CO)[22] clearly shows that children were active participants in village gossip. The next day after Chen-hsin made a scene with MC, children from other families, while playing a hopscotch game, teased their "Older Sister" observer.

A boy named Wang Shi-hui asked MC: "Did you really cry yesterday when she [Chen-hsin] caught you? Wang Hsiu-yun [a girl] told everybody that you cried loud. Did you?"

MC (indignantly): "I did not."

Wang Hsiu-yun (angrily): "Now, when did I say that? Now, when did I say that?"

[Another girl] Wang Shu-yu laughed very loud.

[The boy] Wang Shi-hui: "I heard you. Don't you think I didn't hear you." Hsiu-yun seemed quite anxious and probably did say this.

Two days later, on the way to school, MC overheard an eight-year-old girl, Chen Yu-li, telling other children this story:[23]

Last night when she (Chen-hsin) came in I was just getting ready to go to bed and my sister was studying. She banged on the door, and my aunt [a teenager] had to keep asking her to go home. My oldest sister was very

---

[21] M. Wolf (1992): 82.
[22] CO #1009, 04/05/1960.
[23] M. Wolf (1992): 76. Yu-li's grandmother was the one who Chen-hsin accused of stealing her money.

scared and almost fainted when Chen-hsin wouldn't go home. ... She said that my grandmother had stolen her money, and that my grandmother had borrowed NT $900 from her. How could this be? My grandmother says that she gave her back all her money. And how could she steal her money?"

Anthropologists rely on gossip to gather data, for example, MC checking with villagers to understand what happened to Chen-hsin. Children also gossiped among themselves, an important way to establish their own reputation and spread information about other people's reputation. One can only imagine the kind of teasing, mocking or social exclusion Chen-hsin's own children would have experienced. One can further speculate that Chen-hsin's children might have to rely on themselves and support each other at this difficult time. Because Chen-hsin was very shy, Wolf's team did not conduct concentrated observations or interviews with her as they did with some other mothers. Fortunately, her two older children Yi-kun and Mei-yu were quite visible in the archive.[24] CO includes sixty-four timed episodes that involve at least one of the two children, of which seventeen episodes involve both children. Besides, eight episodes of other (un-timed) observations involve one child or both; in terms of projective tests, both children participated in TAT, and the sister also participated in Doll Play. Drawing from the core data, CO, the next section explores these two children's relative positioning in the context of their social networks.

Siblings in Peer Network

Social network analysis of CO reveals patterns of how Yi-kun and his sister Mei-yu interacted with each other and with other children and adults. We have already seen in Chapter 3 that household number

---

[24] The Wolfs' original research defined 3–11 as their target age range and they did not collect much data on infants, so Wang Chen-hsin's youngest child is not my focus here.

Care and Rivalry

is the most important demographic variable for predicting network homophily, more so than gender and age. This pattern holds true in both co-occurrence network, meaning that children from the same household tend to appear together during CO episodes and behavioral-interaction network, meaning that they tend to actually interact together too. Children from the same household are mostly siblings, and some cases include cousins. It is thus clear that sibling relations are significant in children's overall social network structure.

With regards to the dyad of Yi-kun (#49) and Mei-yu (#50), they two belonged to the same clique out of the four cliques mentioned in Chapter 3, suggesting that Yi-kun and Mei-yu often appeared together in play groups. Figure 5.1 depicts a subset of Child Observation co-occurrence network, the union network of Yi-kun and Mei-yu, a regional network with these two children as the focal nodes. Each node in this union network represents a person. The size of a node is proportional to the person's betweenness-centrality, which measures how often a node occurs on all shortest paths between two nodes and represents the person's importance as a "bridge" between other people in the network. Each edge (line) between two nodes represents the co-occurrence of these two people; the thickness of edges is proportional to the frequency of co-occurrence observed.

The union network of Yi-kun and Mei-yu, which includes all the nodes and edges connected to Yi-kun or Mei-yu, displays the following features. First of all, similar to the overall co-occurrence network configuration, children occupied a central position and adults were at the periphery. Moreover, a closer look at this brother–sister dyad's network attributes (Table 5.2), in comparison to the respective maximum numbers observed in the child network, reveals these two children's different social statuses in their peer world: Brother co-occurred with seventy-nine other children in the network (measured by "degree," the number of other nodes he is connected to), many repeatedly (total co-occurrence measured by "weighted degree"), and

Siblings in Peer Network

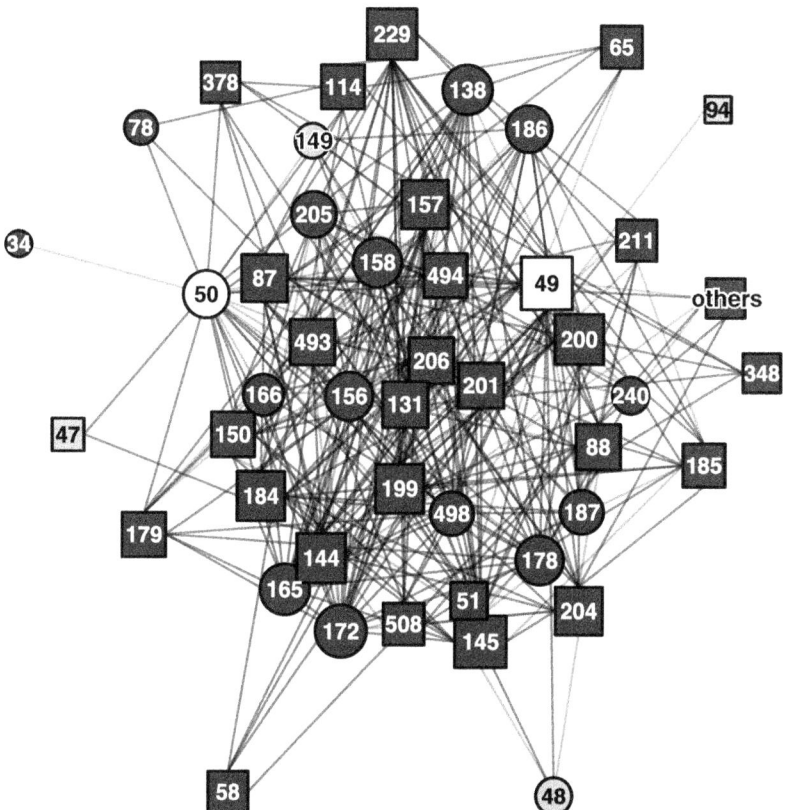

Figure 5.1 Child observation subset (#49 and #50) union network. The number on each node represents the person's ID. White nodes represent the two focal children (#49 and #50), dark gray nodes represent other children and light gray nodes represent adults; Square nodes represent females and round nodes represent males

close to the maximum values observed. This means that Brother was a popular figure in the peer network. But in terms of between-ness centrality, brother was far from being the central hub of connections. Sister ranked much lower in all three attributes compared to her brother, suggesting that she was probably a less important figure in the village play groups.

187

Table 5.2 *Wang Yi-kun (#49) and Wang Mei-yu (#50) in children's co-occurrence network*

Child ID	Co-occurrence degree	Co-occurrence weighted degree	Between-ness centrality
49	79	421	634
MAX*	92	424	1,312
50	56	241	160

Note: * "Max" represents the child/node who had the highest value in each of the three network attributes. The three maxima do not necessarily refer to the same child, but simply serve as references values to compare with those of Wang Yi-kun and Wang Mei-yu.

Departing from simple co-occurrence patterns, social network analysis based on behavioral interactions provides a finer-grained look brother–sister similarities and differences in social life. Figure 5.2 (a & b) juxtaposes brother's and sister's "ego networks," in which a node represents a person, an edge represents behavioral interactions between two nodes, and the arrow of an edge represents the direction of behavior between the two connected nodes (from the initiator to the recipient). In Figure 5.2, each ego network depicts the focal node ("ego")'s "neighborhood," the collection of ego and all nodes ("alters") with whom ego has direct interactions. Besides representing ego-alter ties, the "neighborhood" also includes all of the ties among the "alters" (Hanneman and Riddle 2005).

Comparing these two ego networks reveals the following patterns: (1) These two children have overlapping peer networks and they two often interacted together. But Brother seemed to be a more important character in Sister's circle than Sister was to Brother: In terms of interaction frequency,[25] while Sister was not among the top five children that Brother interacted with, Brother was the third most important

---

[25] See the thickness of edges between nodes in the network.

Siblings in Peer Network

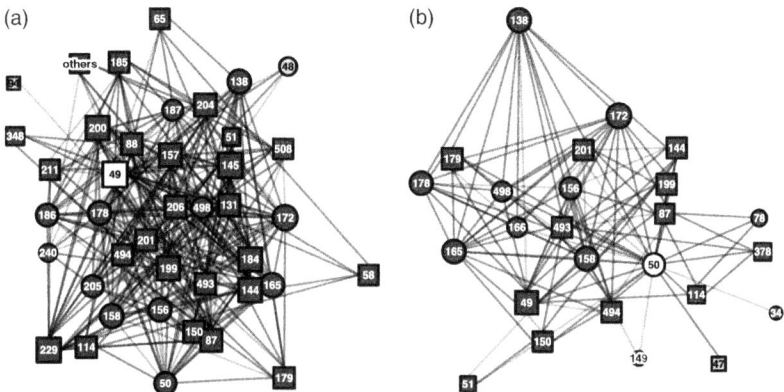

Figure 5.2 (a) #49's ego network of behavioral interactions, (b) #50's ego network of behavioral interactions. The number on each node represents the person's ID. White nodes represent the two focal children (#49 in a and #50 in b), dark gray nodes represent other children and light gray nodes represent adults; Square nodes represent females and round nodes represent males. In these behavioral-networks, the size of a node is proportional to the person's weighted degree centrality, measured by the sum of frequency of behavioral interactions this person has with all other people. The thickness and darkness of an edge is proportional to its weight, meaning the frequency of behavioral interactions between the two nodes (people) connected by the edge

child Sister interacted with. (2) Brother interacted with a wider circle of children than Sister did, measured by the number of alters in each ego network. (3) Brother was the center of his ego network, ranked #1 in weighted degrees, while Sister was not, ranked only #7, next to Brother, in her own ego network. Taken together, Brother was an active figure in the village peer network, despite his mother and family's marginal status, but Sister was a more peripheral figure in the observations and was often observed overlapping with her brother in play. Perhaps Sister was used to trailing her brother, as in MC's observation in the opening vignette of this chapter? To understand what contributed to these patterns – age, gender and/or personality, let's look at the content of observations through NLP (natural language processing) and granular-level behavioral analysis.

Play, Cooperation, and Conflict

I used NLP techniques to analyze linguistic patterns of those CO episodes,[26] where Brother and/or Sister appeared, a subset of the cleaned and preprocessed CO corpus. Figures 5.3 and 5.4 depict high-frequency words in this subset of observations: Figure 5.3 presents the top 100 high-frequency words (in wordcloud format) and Figure 5.4 presents the top 50 high-frequency words (as a bar graph).

Based on these, Figure 5.5 depicts the co-occurrence network of top twenty-two words: Each node represents one high-frequency word, and each edge represents co-occurrence of the two nodes/words. Node size is proportional to the word's frequency and edge thickness is proportional to degree of co-occurrence between the two words. These analyses identify several notable patterns: The words "say" and "play" ranked #1 and #5, indicating the abundance of verbal interactions and the overall

Figure 5.3 Top 100 high-frequency words in the Child Observation subset (#49 and #50)
Note: Analyses in this figure and Figure 5.4 were performed and visualized in the Python programming language.

[26] The cleaned corpus transformed all words to lowercase, removed punctuation, numbers and special symbols, excluded common stopwords and reduced a word to its lemma form.

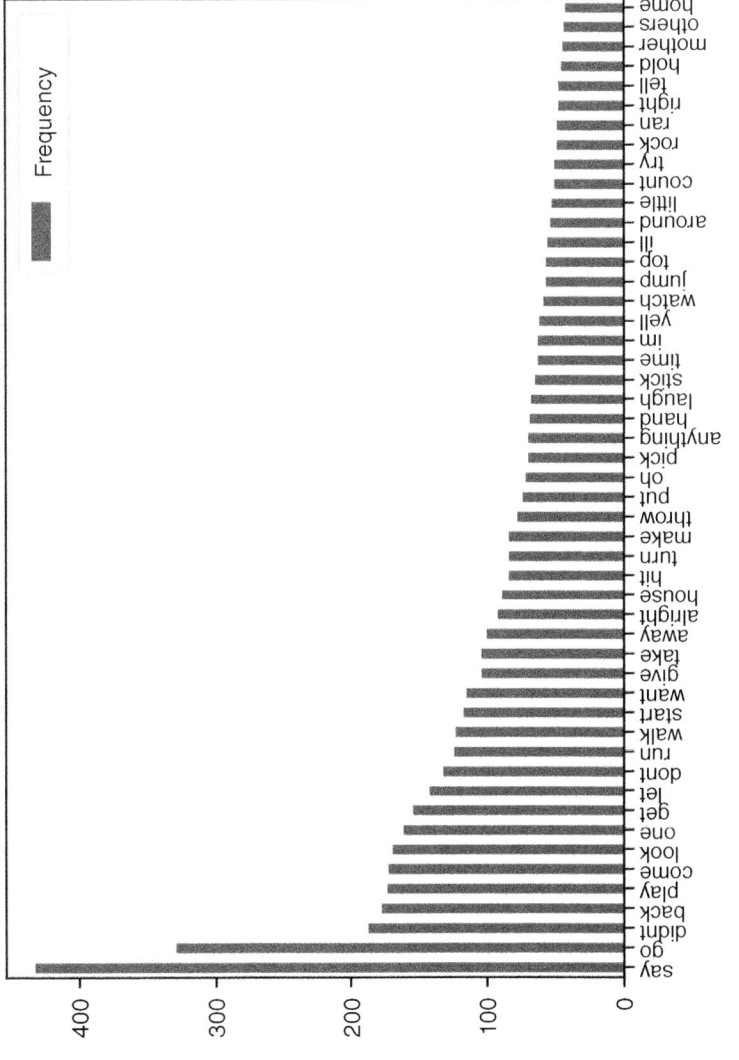

Figure 5.4 Top 50 high-frequency words in Child Observation subset (#49 and #50)

Care and Rivalry

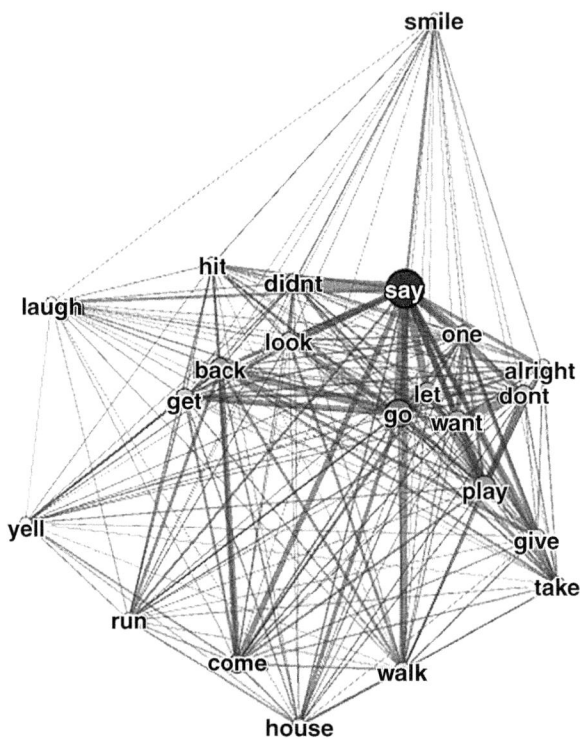

Figure 5.5 Word co-occurrence network in the Child Observation subset (#49 and #50)
Note: The word co-occurrence matrix in this figure was computed in the Python programming language, via word embeddings analysis, and then visualized in Gephi (layout: Force Atlas 2 algorithm).

prevalence of play in their interactional contexts; The word "hit" ranked #21, possibly related to children's fighting and/or pretend play; The words "laugh" and "yell" ranked #20 and #34 respectively, giving us a clue of the emotional texture of children's play; Finally, co-occurring word-pairs with the highest-frequency rankings, such as hit-smile, hit-laugh, and hit-run, offer insights into how different behaviors intertwined in children's naturalistic play.

I also analyzed this subset of CO using a standardized behavioral grading protocol and grouped peer interaction behavioral themes into

Table 5.3 *Behavioral grading results (Child #49 and #50)*

	Brother as initiator	Brother as recipient	Sister as initiator	Sister as recipient
# of behavioral partners	34	30	20	17
# of behaviors	109	108	52	43
# of positive behaviors	72	56	32	24
# of negative behaviors	37	52	20	19
Positivity score*	35	4	12	5
% of positive behavior	66%	52%	62%	51%

Note: After grading all behaviors manually, I exported the behavioral grading data to and completed analysis in R programming language. *Positivity score = number of positive behaviors – number of negative behaviors.

two main categories, cooperation (positive) and conflict (negative). Table 5.3 summarizes the behavioral analysis results. First of all, in terms of absolute numbers, Brother not only appeared in a lot more observations than Sister did, as co-occurrence social network analysis revealed. He was also involved in many more behavioral interactions than Sister was, as the initiator or recipient, and he interacted with more children than Sister did. Moreover, regarding percentage of positive behavior among all behaviors, Brother's and Sister's numbers are similar. Both initiated more cooperative behaviors than receiving cooperative behaviors. Was Brother a more popular person than Sister? Was Brother helping Sister in peer interaction, as the opening vignette portrayed? If both of them were ridiculed or bullied by peers, for what reasons then? To understand what these quantitative patterns mean and what motivated these behaviors, we need to explore the behaviors in ethnographic detail.

Personalities in Coalition

Close reading of naturalistic observation records can flesh out these two young characters and demonstrate the moral lessons these youngsters

Care and Rivalry

Figure 5.6 A boy carrying his baby brother
Source: Photo by Arthur Wolf.

learned. Brother and Sister had distinct personalities. Brother played with many more children and was more active in their peer network. Sister was not popular and less savvy in navigating peer network. On many occasions the sibling dyad often acted in solidarity, like a small coalition facing the world outside their home. Together they learned to coordinate with peers, negotiating fairness and ownership, adapting to respect game rules and submitting to peer leaders.

As behavioral grading results suggest, Brother Wang Yi-kun, although accused by his mother and other adults of being a troublemaker (fighting with other children),[27] was more of a cooperator than an aggressor. Although sibling care was mainly girls' responsibility, Yi-kun also helped take care of his little brother (#51). In one scenario his sister Mei-yu called the observer MS: "See? Big brother can take care of little brother."[28]

---

[27] See episodes of Yi-kun's conflicts with other children in the next sections.
[28] SO #59, 08/02/1959.

Of course, this scenario alludes to her assumption, the local norm that girls, instead of boys, were supposed to take care of younger siblings.

Beyond sibling care, by the age of seven, Yi-kun had already mastered clever skills in negotiating rules of games and access to group play with other kids. He used the principle of reciprocity to his own advantage, reminding playmates of his previous favors to them. For example, when he saw an older girl holding sticks with feathers, he asked: "Give me one of yours, will you? You have two in your pocket." Rejected by that girl, he insisted: "I, I, I did something for you."[29] He joined girls playing house and helped them with what they needed.[30] Across several occasions Yi-kun was found controlling his anger and yielding to other children: One girl Chang Ah-yin (#172, a year and half older than he), a leader in their small group, bullied him, but he did not fight back. That's why a bystander boy teased him: "A boy is afraid of a girl!" At another time, chased, cursed and hit by two naughty boys much younger than he, Yi-kun appeared scared. Those boys' older brother laughed: "Ha ha, the older one is afraid of the younger one."[31]

The following observation, about Yi-kun's unintended conflict with a slightly younger boy Wang Chen-jin (#508), is a vivid illustration of his personality: Chen-jin was quite a dominant character, bulky, strong and popular among boys. Initially they two were playing tag, and Yi-kun accidentally hit Chen-jin on the face. Chen-jin cried. Another older boy came by, scolded Yi-kun and pushed him down. Yi-kun did not respond or avenge. After crying for a couple minutes, Chen-jin walked over to Yi-kun and hit him four times. Yi-kun looked angry, but he still didn't hit back or say anything. Chen-jin repeated that, hitting him three times. Yi-kun just held his emotions and walked away.[32]

---

[29] CO #836, 02/21/1960.
[30] MO #70, 09/20/1960.
[31] CO #1655, 07/28/1960.
[32] CO #306, 11/08/1959.

Care and Rivalry

Mei-yu, on the other hand, had a different personality, which helps to explain why her status in their peer network was more peripheral compared to that of her brother. She did not have many friends, even before the onset of her mother's scandalous insanity. Unlike her brother, she was not easy to get along with. She interrupted other children's play or bullied them, including her big brother. Her brother's friends saw her as a troublemaker, reluctant to include her during their play. She did want to play with other children, though. Once two boys were playing a marble game, using little rocks marbles. She asked to join but was bluntly rejected by one of them. She turned to the other boy, her classmate, attempting to manipulate him: "He (your playmate) doesn't want our Jung (*zhong*) class to play!"[33] The boy who rejected her stayed firm: "Yes, I do. I just don't want *you* to play." During a jumping rope game, one boy explicitly asked the group leader not to let Mei-yu play: "She hit my little brother." Mei-yu walked off, looking unhappy.[34] She was not popular among girls either. She really wanted to play with Pai Yan-yan (#138), the girl who appeared in this chapter's opening scenario. Yan-yan manipulated her: "Give it to me and I'll be your friend. Otherwise I won't play with you." And Mei-yu gave in.[35] Girl leader Ah-yin (#172) did not allow her to join their tree game, which is, to make "boats" out of bamboo leaves.[36]

One day, Mei-yu was excluded by her peers again. Three children were playing house. She walked up to watch, but a girl shouted at her (angrily with a threatening look): "Get out of here! I don't want you to look." She looked sad and walked away. But her brother Yi-kun happened to be there. He tattled, yelling to his mother, trying to protect his sister.[37] Yi-kun appeared as a brother with a caring heart: In dyadic interactions, he yielded to Mei-yu many times even when she grew aggressive. In

---

[33] CO #277, 10/29/1959.
[34] CO #492, 12/30/1959.
[35] CO #35, 08/05/1959.
[36] CO #1159, 03/30/1960.
[37] CO #313, 11/19/1959.

Personalities in Coalition

multi-person interactions, he used his social skills to help her. The opening vignette is a great example: He "bribed" a girl with face-powder so that she would agree to play with his little sister.

Sometimes help was mutual and cooperation was fruitful: Playing house with other children, they partnered in crime, taking away a small boy's stones and teasing him.[38] But seeing another child cheating a younger one when playing tops, Sister echoed her brother to mock and condemn the cheater.[39] In hide-and-seek games, they two coordinated together to cheat, sister on the watch for brother who was the "ghost" trying to catch hiding children.[40]

But since neither of them was a leader in their peer group, negotiating with peers could be difficult. In the following observation, their negotiations failed.[41]

Children were playing "cars" on a 2-seat tricycle. Yi-kun was in the front seat and another little boy was pushing. Sister came and sat down.

Yi-kun told the child who was next in line to get on the trike: "Come and get in your seat. Next time it's my sister's turn."

An older girl Pai Yan-yan disagreed: "No, it's not, it's mine. We have to line up."

Yi-kun countered: "No. We pretend she (Mei-yu) is my daughter so I have to give her a ride first and she doesn't have to pay for a ticket"

Yan-yan rejected: "No, you can't do that. We have to line up."

Yi-kun: "It's my tricycle!"

Note that Yan-yan, the girl quite skilled at manipulating Mei-yu, was not persuaded by Yi-kun's reasoning. Disagreement continued, until their playgroup leader Ah-yin (#172), a quite dominant girl, intervened and reinstated the importance of turn-taking rules. Brother attempted various methods to help his sister skip the line, improvising fictive

---

[38] CO #32, 08/04/1959.
[39] CO #497, 01/01/1960.
[40] CO #1640, 07/20/60.
[41] CO #72, 08/13/1959.

Care and Rivalry

parent–child kinship (apparently the real sibling tie was not enough) and asserting his ownership. But in the end, they had to submit to more "powerful" children, even though they were playing on his tricycle. In this quite serious pretend play scenario, we not only see children's rich imaginative world – riding tricycles as cars and using leaves as tickets, but also how they learned to coordinate with peers and comply with rules.

Sibling Rivalry: Storytelling in Projective Tests

What about life inside their family? As I mentioned earlier, the Wolfs' team didn't manage to interview their mother or observe their family interactions at home, because their mother was very shy. But fortunately, these children participated in projective tests. Transcripts from Doll Play and TAT, based on verbal communication records, offer a precious window into children's thoughts and emotions. In both tests, children were asked what they thought people in the scenarios were doing. Doll Play explicitly focused on family life, but some TAT drawings were also interpreted as interactions between family members. Narratives in these two projective tests shine light on children's own perspectives about their family relations, especially sibling rivalry at home, which poses a contrast to sibling solidarity during peer interactions in the outside world.

In Mei-yu's Doll Play test, a salient theme is brother dominating and bullying sister. At the first sight of dolls, she looked carefully, checked the dolls' clothes, and started to tell this story spontaneously[42]:

A: Big sister was arguing.
Q: With whom?
A: Big brother.
Q: Why?
A: Brother ate her candy.

---

[42] DP #50, Session I, 10/07/1960.

Sibling Rivalry: Storytelling in Projective Tests

Q: Then they started to argue, right? How?
A: They fought on and on. Brother hit sister; he's bad.
Q: How did they fight? Can you show me?
A: Like this, like this! (Holding B-boy doll and G-girl doll, crashing them)
Q: How's the sister?
A: She cried.
Q: Did the sister hit the brother?
A: No. Sister didn't. It was brother all the time.

Mei-yu was tested in two sessions. In both sessions, she spontaneously pivoted the conversation to the same topic: Brother is mean to sister, and he deserves to be punished. Unlike "brother eating sister's candy" or "brother hitting sister" in the earlier discussed excerpt, in some other segments she didn't even articulate a specific explanation. For example, she just repeated: "He (brother) is so bad." This deviates from the imagery of a protective brother and the pattern of brother–sister solidarity that emerged in peer play outside the home setting.

One might wonder, though, if this had anything to do with Mei-yu's real experience, or it was just purely imaginary. Yes, these utterances were a product of children's storytelling exercise, most likely reflecting Mei-yu's self-serving bias, that Brother was always the villain at home. But there are several reasons to doubt that stories she told were mere fantasies: In Mei-yu's two sessions, the names she gave the dolls mapped exactly onto her family's real situation. For example, she called the boy doll "big brother," the girl doll "big sister" and the baby doll "little brother."[43] Moreover, the scenario of brother–sister fighting, especially over candy, appeared not only in Doll Play. It also surfaced in Mei-yu's

---

[43] These kinship terms were translated from the Chinese transcript. Without access to the original audiotapes, it remains unclear whether she used Taiwanese or Mandarin terms in the actual conversation, although both languages have distinct terms for older and younger brothers/sisters. According to Mr. Huang Chieh-Shan, some children were better than others in Mandarin, and some might have spoken a mixture of both languages in projective tests.

Care and Rivalry

TAT session conducted several months earlier, and in surprisingly similar ways. Compare the following two excerpts: The first one was from her Doll Play transcript and the second from her TAT transcript.

Doll Play excerpt:

A: Big brother wanted money for food.
Q: Who gave him money?
A: He asked her. (Pointing at M, "mother" doll)
Q: What did the brother say to mom?
A: He said, "mom, give me one cent."
Q: What did mom say?
A: Mom said, "why did you fight."
Q: And the brother?
A: And sister came told mom brother took her candy away.
Q: What did mom say then?
A: Mom said she would not give him one cent.
Q: What did the brother do next?
A: He cried.
Q: And how's mom?
A: Mom said, "why did you take your sister's candy?" Big brother stopped crying.

The following TAT excerpt[44] is especially intriguing. The research assistant Mr. Huang showed Mei-yu the fifth drawing in the set,[45] which featured a girl, a broken bowl on the floor, and an adult woman. Mei-yu interpreted the drawing as about the girl breaking a bowl and her mom reacting to it, including beating her. When the research assistant asked what the girl in the picture would feel when her mom hit her for breaking the bowl, Mei-yu went silent. Then, the research assistant repeated his question: "What will the girl feel?" Surprisingly, Mei-yu pivoted her answer to an apparently irrelevant topic, big brother taking her candy:

---

[44] TAT #80, P50, summer 1960.
[45] This drawing is missing in the Wolf Archive.

Sibling Rivalry: Storytelling in Projective Tests

Figure 5.7 TAT Drawing #5
Source: The Wolf Archive.
Photo by Jing Xu.

A: She wants to fight someone.
Q: Does she want to fight someone?
A: Yes.
Q: Who did she fight with?
A: Her brother.
Q: Why her brother?
A: Because her brother took her candy.
Q: Did the brother really take her candy?
A: Yes.
Q: Why?
A: There was a lot of candy, so he took all of them.

Another detail in the story Mei-yu told, about the girl character breaking a bowl, alludes to her own family's experience. Right before the earlier segment in her TAT transcript, Mei-yu mentioned that the girl's mother found out she broke a bowl. Asked what would happen then, Mei-yu answered: "When mom found out, she didn't feel well." When asked why

Care and Rivalry

mom didn't feel well, she pivoted, again, to the topic of fighting, the girl fighting with her big brother. Children fighting and mom feeling unwell was not something portrayed in that particular TAT drawing at all, but it encapsulated what happened to Mei-yu's mother in real life, as shown in *A Thrice-Told Tale*: Her estranged relation with certain neighbors, due to her boy Yi-kun's fight with neighbors' children, was a major contributing factor to her mental illness. Coincidentally, Mei-yu's TAT session was conducted in summer 1960, just a few months after her mother's "erratic behavior." Pressed by the research assistant twice to explain why, in the drawing, the mom would feel unwell upon her children's fighting, Mei-yu kept silent. This little girl's nuanced reactions, her utterances and hesitancy, hint at the lingering impacts of the chaos in the adult world on these young children's emotional and moral experience.

Mei-yu's reactions in projective tests share a similar quality to what I found in many other children's projective tests transcripts, that is, the quality of "reality-based fantasy." Sibling conflict is one of the most common themes across all Doll Play transcripts (nearly fifty children), which probably reflects its prevalence in this community. Moreover, the stories children told are closely related to, or mapped from, the reality of sibling rivalry at home. CO abounds with stories of siblings fighting for fairness in resource distribution and tattling to parents about sibling-inflicted injustices. Readers might feel sympathetic for the young mother in the following scenario, who had to settle disputes between her children over some peanuts or ten cents:[46]

Shih Mei-lin (a 7-year-old girl) was walking toward home eating peanuts. She met her younger brother Shen-min (5-year-old) on the way. Shen-min came up to Mei-lin and said: "Give me some," sticking his hands out demandingly.

Mei-lin darted away and said: "No." She went her way.

Shen-min followed her and said: "I'm going to tell mother then. I'm going to tell mother."

---

[46] CO #1036, 03/15/1960.

Mei-lin didn't seem to care or look worried and continued to eat. Her younger sister Mei-yun came by. Mei-lin stopped and gave her some peanuts.

Shen-min walked on into the kitchen door and said to mother: "Your Mei-lin & Mei-yun both have 10 cents. I want some too."

Mother picked up a bamboo fan and held it threateningly and said: "Haven't you had enough today? Come on. Come on!"

Shen-min looked sulky and ran. Mei-lin started to smile and quickly closed her mouth. Mother could see her.

Shen-min: "They all have something to eat. Your Mei-lin has another 10 cents and I don't!" Mother ignored him.

Mirroring observational records, sibling rivalry emerged as a main theme during children's spontaneous narratives in projective testing. Some children in their answers even explicitly inferred about parental favoritism. This sheds light on a key mediator of sibling disputes, that is, parental interference. One drawing in TAT featured one big boy (B1) standing behind a tree and watching a smaller boy (B3) playing with other kids in a ball game (see Figure 5.8). When asked to describe what happened in that scene, ten-year-old Cheng Ling-hui answered that the big boy (B1) was about to sneak out and hit the younger one (B3), and that they two were brothers.

Asked why they would get into a fight, Ling-hui told this story:[47]

A: Because of a plum.
Q: They fought for a plum?
A: Their mother gave more money to B3, and less to B1. That's why [B1] wants to hit him [B3]. … He [B1] was not afraid of their mother punishing him, therefore he would hit his little brother [B3].
Q: What do you think his mother will do when she finds out this?
A: [She] will be angry.
Q: Just angry?
A: [She] will tie him up [with ropes] and hit him.

Proceeding to another drawing in TAT (see Figure 5.9), Ling-hui again used the same lens to interpret a different scene: Three boys (B1,

[47] TAT #18, P387, summer 1960.

Care and Rivalry

Figure 5.8 TAT Drawing #2
Source: The Wolf Archive.
Photo by Jing Xu.

Figure 5.9 TAT Drawing #8
Source: The Wolf Archive.
Photo by Jing Xu.

B2, and B3) were fighting for some fruits and their mother (F1) came out to see what happened. Mother went back home and told their dad, and dad would tie the oldest child up and beat him. Given that Ling-hui was indeed the oldest child in his family, it is reasonable to infer that this imaginative narrative was partly inspired by his real-life experience. Such storytelling experience probably provided many children like Mei-yu and Yi-kun an opportunity to express their negative sentiments toward their siblings and parents.

"A Fiercely Protective Mother"

The tragic story of Wang Chen-hsin – the mother of Yi-kun and Mei-yu, illustrates the extent to which children can disrupt adults' relationships with neighbors. In their projective tests these two children painted a picture of their mother as a ruthless punisher at home. Mother's punishment appeared in both Mei-yu and Yi-kun's TAT transcripts: For example, when shown the drawing of a girl character, a broken bowl and an adult woman character, Yi-kun mentioned the same scenario as Mei-yu did, that mother would beat up the girl; Presented with other drawings featuring multiple children, both Brother and Sister inferred that children were fighting and would be punished by the mother figure.[48] When Yi-kun or Mei-yu were playing with other children outside, however, their mother appeared more often as their defender. The following is an excerpt of one episode observed right in front of their house.[49] In this scenario a little boy attempted to tattle to Yi-kun's mother about Yi-kun's misbehavior, stealing flowers. We see Yi-kun's naughty disobedience: He ignored mom's threat and punishment. But we also see why Margery Wolf described Chen-hsin as "a fiercely protective" mother[50] – she cursed the tattler and gave the flower back to Yi-kun:

[48] TAT #56, summer 1960.
[49] CO #137, 08/25/59.
[50] M. Wolf (1992): 95.

Care and Rivalry

Wang Yi-kun came back with a branch with a flower on it. Wang Ching-fu [a 6-year-old boy]: "I know whose flower that is. I'm going to tell him. I'm going to go tell that you're stealing his flowers."

Yi-kun: "I didn't steal it. I found it."

Yi-kun's mom came out and asked him: "Where did you get that flower." When Yi-kun saw his mother coming, he threw the flower on the ground. Ching-fu's brother Ching-chi [an 8-year-old boy] and another boy Wang Yu-lu ran to get it.

Ching-fu was still yelling: "You stole somebody's flower. I'm going to tell somebody. Something's going to happen to you."

Yi-kun's mom yelled at Ching-fu: "Tell your going to die! What would you get if you told? You'd get a sex organ [cursing]."

Ching-fu stopped yelling and looked a little confused. Mom went to Yi-kun and said: "Where did you get it? How could it get in there. The gate is closed. If you do it again I'm going to beat you."

Mom took the flower from Wang Yu-lu and said to Yi-kun: "Go home."

Mom and Yi-kun walked into the house. Yi-kun hadn't said a word. He looked a little bewildered. As they went into the house mom said: "Next time I'm going to tie you in the house."

Mom walked into the kitchen and Yi-kun came out again. Ching-fu stood and watched all this. Ching-fu saw a dragon fly and ran to catch. Yi-kun ran also to get it.

Ching-fu: "No. It's mine."

Yi-kun: "No. It's mine." They pushed at each other.

Yi-kun's mom had come to the door again. She yelled: "Whose? It belongs to the one who catches it."

She told Yi-kun: "Don't catch it. What do you want that for? If you don't have rice you can't live. If you don't have a dragonfly you'll live. Come back."

Yi-kun: "No!"

This episode was observed in summer 1959, nine-months before Chen-hsin' mental breakdown recorded in *A Thrice-Told Tale*. The kinds of quarrels Chen-hsin got herself into, with other mothers, probably all evolved from children's conflicts over trivial things, like this argument about a flower and a dragonfly. *A Thrice-Told Tale* only

"A Fiercely Protective Mother"

presented fieldnotes up to March 15, 1960.[51] That ethnography did not tell us what happened to Chen-hsin after her outbursts of "insanity," but I was curious about it. The last episode of CO where Chen-hsin appeared in was March 30, 1960, twenty-four days after she plunged into the rice paddy. In this episode,[52] Wang Yi-kun was playing with Wang Ching-fu and some other children again, climbing the guava tree. Chen-hsin was commanding Yi-kun to get down, come home and do his homework. Shaking a stick, she threatened to beat him up. But when her son got caught in the tree, she laughed and came up to hold him until he could get down. A couple of weeks ago she was still jumping around and doing *bai-bai* motions like a spirit-medium, or like a crazy woman who needed to be tied up in a mental hospital.[53] Now she seemed to have restored her sanity. Wolf's "general observations" (type "G" notes), focused on adult life, also include further traces of her, although Margery Wolf did not report these in her ethnography. For example, on June 13, 1960, Chen-hsin was gossiping with a group of women about other adults and children, even teasing her own daughter Mei-yu lightheartedly.[54]

On September 20, Yi-kun climbed up a neighbor's fence to get some leaves for the girls who were playing house nearby. The neighbor, a thirty-two-year-old woman, scolded Yi-kun and reported to his mother, but Chen-hsin did not do anything about it:[55]

The neighbor came out of the house and started shouting: "You children, that fence is old and about broken down and you're always climbing it, I tell you not to do it but you won't listen this time I'm really going to hit someone!" She hurried toward the fence with a stick.

---

[51] Margery Wolf did not leave Xia Xizhou until the end of summer 1960.
[52] CO #1157, 03/30/1960.
[53] Chen-hsin's husband had sent her to a hospital and she was terrified by that experience (M. Wolf 1992: 62, 81–82).
[54] G-930.
[55] MO #70, 09/20/1960.

Care and Rivalry

The girls all said, "It wasn't me, it's not me, it's Yi-kun, it's Yi-kun." The neighbor chased Yi-kun, but he ran away and she couldn't catch him.

She then turned angrily to the girls: "Oh, you didn't do it, you didn't do it, you just didn't get caught, I tell you not to climb up there but you won't listen, next time I catch you on there I'm really going to beat you up." She was walking away as she said this. The girls just stood and looked at her and didn't seem to be frightened.

The neighbor then went over and told Chen-hsin about what had happened: "Your Yi-kun really has to be beaten, climbing all the way up on that fence getting flowers for all of those dead children!"

Chen-hsin didn't seem to be very concerned and just asked: "Where, where is he?"

The neighbor was really mad and answered: "He already ran a long way away, I kept telling him not to climb up on that fence, it's about broken, but he never listens."

Chen-hsin just kept asking: "Where? Where is he?"

Finally the neighbor answered, very angrily: "There, there, over there!" [as though anyone couldn't see him] and then she turned and ran into her own house.

Her [the neighbor's] seven-year-old daughter followed her, saying: "That Yi-kun was always climbing on the fence, and whenever you tell his mom, she doesn't do anything about it."

Chen-hsin, "the woman who did not become a shaman" (M. Wolf 1990a), was still around in the village by the end of the Wolfs' fieldwork. She did not divorce her husband. She did not leave her boys behind and run away to her natal home with her daughter. She continued to gossip with her neighbors and sometimes quarreled with her neighbors over children's issues. She was still known as a protective mother, even by the village children.

An Untold Tale

My motivation to pursue the story of this brother–sister dyad partly originates from personal experience, growing up as a Han Chinese daughter. Being an only child, among the first generation of singletons born under China's One-Child Policy, I always wondered what it would be like to have a sibling. I asked my mother why she did not give me an older brother. I was also terribly naïve about sibling relations. To me, having an older brother meant having someone to protect you and rely on. But my mother always jokingly warned me: "You are lucky not to have an older brother! Otherwise, your father would have favored him." My young mind could not fathom the profound sentiment of sibling rivalry: Not only did I not have the first-person experience, other children in my peer world were mostly singletons too, so I did not even have opportunities to observe sibling dynamics or hear relevant testimonies. Now my son, an only child living in America where most of his friends do have siblings, told me: "My friends all say that I am lucky not to have any siblings." From the viewpoint of this case study, both my mother and my son were half right: Many if not all families in Xia Xizhou favored a son over a daughter. In Mei-yu's storytelling, her brother was quite annoying at home. Yet when playing with other children, Yi-kun seemed like a caring elder brother and they two often supported each other. Going beyond general patterns of gender, this might reflect individual children's personalities and circumstances, but it also points to the ambiguous nature of sibling relation, tension at home and solidarity in the outside world.

This personal curiosity aligns with my scholarly interests: Prior research on "the Chinese family" or Chinese moralities rarely focused on sibling dynamics in childhood. The duality of care and rivalry in the early shape of sibling relation contributes to children's developing moral knowledge and emotions. Siblings learn to care for each other and build coalitions. Through constant negotiations of how resources and responsibilities should be distributed, they also gain intimate understanding of fairness and justice, authority and hierarchy. The contradictory dimensions of love and power are particularly pronounced in cross-sex sibling relation in patriarchal societies due to differential statuses of boys and girls (see e.g., Joseph 1994). Therefore, the ambivalence of sibling relation in this case study can help us understand the complex, double-edged quality of human kinship more generally.

Besides weaving together various aspects of learning morality, including parent–child dynamics, peer interactions, gender, and siblings, this case study also accentuates critical reflections on ethnographic epistemology. The case recovered what was obscured from a classic ethnography, *A Thrice-Told Tale*, which was already infused with meta-reflections on ethnographic authority. In that book Margery Wolf reflected on the role of the anthropologist as writer and the position of ethnography as a genre of writing. Every ethnography has its omissions and silences (Silverman 2020). *A Thrice-Told Tale* is no exception. Not to mention that the anthropologist relied on her intermediary MC, the confidant of village women, to gather evidence concerning a scandal. To Margery Wolf, all the important characters were adults. She distinguished her ethnographic tale from both fiction and raw fieldnotes, reconstructing a plot based on selected materials from what was called "general observations" in their fieldwork, the only type of fieldnotes focused on adults. But even in these raw fieldnotes listed in *A Thrice-Told Tale*, I discovered traces of children: The protagonist's children played a role in the unfolding of their family drama. Other children witnessed that drama and participated in gossip. These traces were perhaps less relevant to Margery Wolf's question, whether the woman in question became a shaman or went crazy. But they are central to my question.

To put children under the spotlight, I systematically searched for and analyzed the voices and behaviors of Yi-kun and Mei-yu in the Wolf Archive. My narrative centered on children's agency in learning morality: The brother and sister helped each other in peer interactions, longing for social inclusion; they told stories of sibling conflicts, stories laden with moral judgments; they cared for their mother when she was going through a difficult time; they also maneuvered against her punishment. My narrative reflects my intentional choices and implicit biases, just as *A Thrice-Told Tale* reflects the choices and biases of my predecessor. This untold tale therefore bears witness to the limitations, possibilities, and charm of ethnography.

Epilogue: Taking Children Seriously

On an early September morning, a group of young girls went to the ditch to wash clothes. Chen Shi-lin, a four-year-old girl, was washing diapers of her aunt's baby. She started a most hilarious game:[1]

Shi-lin started to wash a very dirty diaper and put lots of soap on it. She gathered the soap suds in her hands and said: "Who wants to eat this? Who wants to eat feces?"

She turned to Wang Su-chen, another four-year-old girl: "Do you want to eat it?"

Su-chen burst out some dirty words, and said: "You eat it!" She shouted to the other girls: "Chen Shi-lin always likes to play with feces. Dirty Girl! She's feces' child!"

Su-chen's mom scolded her: "Su-chen! Why do you always say those...." Su-chen interrupted before her mom finished the sentence: "Those dirty words? Is that what you mean?"

Mom laughed and said: "Oh you!"

But Shi-lin continued her funny game, holding up the diaper with feces all over her hand and laughed out: "Who wants to eat feces?" She held it under Su-chen's nose and Su-chen cursed her again, and after a few rounds Su-chen got angry at her. Then Shi-lin turned to MC: "Sister Chen likes it!" She kept teasing MC.

[1] CO #194, 09/03/1959.

Epilogue: Taking Children Seriously

Somehow this scene stuck in my mind ever since I first read it. As a spoiled young girl, a singleton child growing up in postreform China, I never had to handle diapers for any relative's babies. To my own child born in the 2010s U.S., the idea of washing a filthy diaper is probably nothing but disgusting,[2] not to mention that he never had to take care of any diapers. Yet there they were, some four-year-old girls turning their moral responsibility of a dirty chore into a mischievous game. Different historical contexts bring different material, symbolic, and structural constraints to children's lives. But we can learn some timeless truths from children: their creativity and spontaneity, their ability to find joy, have fun, and even humor themselves under all kinds of circumstances. All these are connected to, and probably propelled by, their insatiable curiosity about the world, their capacity for learning.

I told this story to my mother, who was also born in the 1950s, like the protagonists of this book. My mother excitedly shared with me her memories:

When I was ten, the year Cultural Revolution began, my niece was born and I had to wash her diapers. I did not clean them very well, just muddling through. But I remember walking across the woods by my house, beautiful woods, still somewhat green in the winter. I carried the cloth diaper with two fingers, put it in the stream, and saw it swinging with the water. In that moment I forgot everything.

Shi-lin's lifeworld is not the same as my mother's world, or my world, or my child's world. But no matter what world, in every child's life journey toward adulthood, in that irreversible unfolding of growing up, there must have been many such moments of "forgetting everything," of being genuinely engaged in the present, being thoroughly absorbed in the moment, and being playful and imaginative. A child's life is full of surprises to the adult eye. What looks like the most mundane everyday

---

[2] These were old-style cloth diapers in mid-twentieth century rural Taiwan, not the fancy ones in today's middle-class American families.

Epilogue: Taking Children Seriously

life, as the Wolf Archive documents, presents numerous surprises to me. The desire to spotlight these intriguing experiences of childhood and make sense of them prompted me to write this book.

Rethinking Chinese Childhood, Family, and Morality

The washing diaper scene, like the "opening an orange" scene in Introduction and many other scenes I portrayed throughout the book, of children teasing, maneuvering, and fighting, together provide a rare picture of "unruly" children in mid-twentieth century Taiwan. Unlike mainstream sinological anthropology, which prioritizes parenting and parent–child ties, I take children's active learning as a central concern and rediscover voices of children who defy parental expectations – therefore "unruly," who negotiate with peers and siblings and develop their own moral understandings – that's why I use quotation marks around "unruly." By offering this revisionist account of the so-called "traditional Chinese family," from the learners' instead of parents' perspective, the story of "unruly" children sheds new light on Chinese and East Asian childhood, family, and morality from the past to the present.

"Unruly" children have always been there, but somehow sinological research rarely focused on this topic, because it goes against the orthodox discourse: Philosophical views extending from the innocent child representing the bright human nature, historiography of the filial sons and daughters in the past, and ethnography of obedient children stressed out by academic competition today. Together with a few other studies that looked at less well-behaved children,[3] this book reminds us of "the darker, less regimented, certainly funnier, possibly crazier – and in some respects very un-Confucian" (Stafford 2011) aspects of

---

[3] For a brief review, see (Xu 2020b). A recent edited volume looked at "bad children" in early and medieval China (Rothschild and Wallace 2017). Missionaries also noticed the ubiquitous presence of *taoqi* children in late-imperial China (Headland 1901: 35–36).

Epilogue: Taking Children Seriously

those small, close-knit communities organized by patriarchal kinship system. Moreover, the general public in the West today still rely on the lens of essentialized "Confucian" morality, encapsulated in the values of obedience and conformity, to understand East Asian childhoods in general, leading to racial biases and stereotypes. This alternative account of childhood, based on systematic evidence, can offer critical reflections on popular Western discourses crystalized into the Model Minority myth.

Given the duality of the Wolf Archive – its significance in anthropology and its unique historical nature, these ethnographic fieldnotes provide an extraordinary archival source about children's actual life, rather than mere discourses, impressionistic generalizations, or anecdotal recollections about childhood in most other sources. Young children are "the most blatant, intellectually innocent, and professionally overlooked among the unrepresented" people in historiography" (Hsiung 2005: 261). What's more, ethnographies that focused on young children's experience did not exist in prior studies of "the Chinese family." As Arthur Wolf proudly remembered, his work in Xia Xizhou was "the first attempt ever to record in a systematic manner the behavior of Chinese children" (n.d.: 37). His archive offers a unique opportunity to tell stories of children in rural communities at the historical margins, stories that would otherwise unlikely figure into scholarly accounts.

This book presents systematic examination of children's moral life in an authoritarian, patriarchal society, before industrialization, urbanization, rapid economic growth, political democratization, and transformations of family values took place in postwar Taiwan. Also, departing from Wolf's vision of looking through Taiwan to see a timeless "traditional Chinese" society, I demonstrate how the historical context of Martial Law Era shaped even the youngest children's moral consciousness. When he revisited what used to be Xia Xizhou village thirty-five years later, Arthur Wolf realized the irreplicable nature of his original research (n.d.: 36):

Epilogue: Taking Children Seriously

The path I walked from the train station to the village is now a paved thoroughfare lined with high-rise apartment buildings. The school my subjects attended has been demolished and replaced with a modern multi-storied facility. Three of the village houses still stand but only because a strip of land along the river has been designated a green area. They are unoccupied. A few of the villagers live in apartment buildings near their old homes, but the majority have moved away. What I knew as a village is now an ill defined urban neighborhood.

Maria Duryea, then an anthropology doctoral student from the University of Washington, accompanied Wolf on this trip, hoping to replicate the research methods for longitudinal comparison (Duryea 1999). However, Duryea was not able to do systematic observations and interviews with children as Wolf's team had done earlier, the main reason was that children's social lives, "increasingly removed [as they were] from the interstices of the residential neighborhood," were not as readily accessible (1999: 105). Today, the original community is thoroughly urbanized, economic conditions have greatly improved, and many of the children in the original research have become grandparents. When I met some of them in September 2023, they recalled Wolf's research as a fun childhood memory, but their childhood is very different from that of their grandchildren today.

This ethnographic case also contributes to understanding childhood in East Asia more broadly. "The child" is a key "sign of value" (Anagnost 2008) in the long project of modernization and national development in China (Jones 2011), Taiwan (Lan 2018; Stafford 1992), Japan (Arai 2016; Tanaka 1997), and South Korea (Jung and Ahn 2021). Children today have much better material resources at their disposal and fewer siblings to compete for resources. But they also face much higher educational pressures. As East Asian societies are grappling with a complicated history of familism and compressed modernity, fertility rates have reached ultra-low levels (Cheng 2020; Ochiai 2011). Childrearing has become an important issue in public discussion, generating enormous anxiety for policymakers and individual families. The story of Xia Xizhou childhood (1958–60) provides a precious reference to compare and contrast with both historical representations about and contemporary transformations to family values and children's lives in East Asia.

As families and societies are coping with changing material and structural conditions today, the change and continuity of Chinese moralities have become a prominent topic.[4] Presenting a more accurate picture of how children learn everyday morality provokes us to rethink our shared assumptions about the past, the starting point of our vision of contemporary moral transformations. Also, the study of Chinese moralities tends to emphasize the authoritarian state and how the state incorporates Confucian discourses to control the society, whether it is the CCP in the PRC or the KMT in Martial Law Era Taiwan.[5] This book brings to light a rare, vernacular account of everyday morality and explores the complex reality beneath moral ideologies, even for children, the least powerful actors in a society. It adds a much-needed perspective of moral life that transcends the authoritarian state framework, especially given the heightened focus on geopolitical tensions today, both in scholarly and public discourses.

Where Does Knowledge Come from?

This book is not just about one particular society. It also explores some universal aspects of humanity through directing our attention to the experience of children. If lack of direct access to the world of the young

---

[4] Nichols (2022); Yan (2009, 2014, 2017); Kleinman (2011); Kleinman et al. (2011); Ning and Palmer (2020); Kuan (2015); and Xu (2017).
[5] For an anthropological review on the state and morality in the PRC, see Yan (2020). State-led moral and political socialization in Taiwan used to be a prominent research topic before Taiwan's demographic transition, see for example (Meyer 1988).

Epilogue: Taking Children Seriously

contributed to the relatively marginalized status of children in historiography, the problem with sociocultural anthropology is perhaps of a different nature: The reluctance to recognize children's critical role and unique capacity in the acquisition, transmission, and creative transformation of cultural knowledge (Hirschfeld 2002). We look past children. We take them for granted. Cognitive anthropologists have reasserted the significance of studying children as part of "taking people [who we study] seriously": This means understanding the multiple sources of children's knowledge and the different ways of knowing that they mobilize in particular contexts, for particular purposes, at different ages, and fueled by different kinds of experience and cognitive resources (Astuti 2017).

Following these cognitive anthropologists' footsteps, I anchor this book in the fascinating world of children's socio-moral cognition. I make sense of "unruly" children through the lens of learning morality. I take inspiration from children's learning to interrogate the nature of anthropological knowledge. Although morality has become an explicit theoretical focus in anthropology, my book highlights a child development perspective that is still underappreciated. I show how children's emerging social cognition – "cognition" as a general term that also encompasses emotional and motivational processes – underpins their moral intuitions, evaluations, and reflections in everyday speech and action. Reconstructing this ethnography of children is also an opportunity for me to experiment new methodologies and reflect on the question of how we know what we know. I rediscover the ethical textures inherent in fieldwork experience and fieldnotes making through children's eyes. I further show that the ways children learn to discern layered intentions, moral sentiments, and cultural meanings constitute the foundation for ethnographic epistemology. In a word, I urge anthropologists to take children seriously and interrogate where humans' complex social knowledge and moral sensibilities come from.

Such an approach distinguishes this book from the one that Arthur Wolf would have written. His draft manuscript was entitled *Chinese*

Epilogue: Taking Children Seriously

Children and Their Mothers, about childrearing and childhood in a generic sense, whereas my book pursues the specific question of learning morality. Even though he did not live to write the content chapters, the "Table of Contents" he left behind shows how he would have organized his manuscript: The four content chapters were intended to focus on four types of materials, children's words (CI), children's behaviors (CO), mothers' words (MI), mothers' behaviors (MO), and half of the book was devoted to topic of parenting. This book, of course, is organized quite differently: All the chapters center on children's active learning experience, with each chapter featuring one important aspect of children's moral life. Each chapter integrates materials from various types, including projective tests data that Wolf did not plan to systematically write about.

To fully understand children's learning in diverse contexts requires conversation and collaboration between anthropology and psychology. While psychology tends to focus on individual cognitive mechanisms and anthropology on sociocultural environments, this book facilitates dialogues between the two disciplines. It integrates ethnographic thick description and systematic behavioral analysis and shows how sociocultural contexts filter through children's minds to shape children's early moral experience.

In particular, I highlight the role of peer learning in moral development, an understudied topic across anthropology and psychology. We tend to focus on intergenerational, adult–child ties in the transmission of cultural norms and moral values. But recent interdisciplinary research has emphasized the significance of peer learning, how children transmit and acquire instrumental skills and social knowledge in peer interactions, for the evolution and development of human cultures (Lew-Levy et al. 2023). Children not only learn *from* peers, they learn *with* peers, especially in face-to-face interactions, syncing at behavioral, cognitive, and neural levels (De Felice et al. 2022). Peer play, including sibling interactions, is a vital site where children negotiate social norms

Epilogue: Taking Children Seriously

and develop subtle moral sensibilities. Children complain to their peers about adults' unfair punishment. They gossip about other children. They form coalitions. They navigate cooperation and conflict and blend the two in spontaneous teasing and pretend play that is full of creativity and humor.

The story of "unruly" children also urges us to look beyond children's prosocial behavior in neatly controlled psychological experiments, a recent trend in moral development studies, or adults' moral socialization beliefs and strategies, what anthropologists have focused on. I spotlight the darker side of children's realistic experience, that is, defiance, dominance, and fighting, through the lens of their own reasoning and feelings, in a community where parents prohibit children's fights for the sake of neighborly harmony. By doing so the book speaks to the inherent tension between moral ideology and practice, and between cultural model and its discontents. It also reveals the influence of authoritarian political atmosphere and local patriarchy on children's understanding of violence, explores the role of children's moral psychology in mediating such influences, and shows how those in a disadvantaged position, for example, young girls, assert their agency.

This book is not a conventional ethnography. It uses new methods to reinterpret old fieldnotes. Without first-person fieldwork experience, I have resorted to computational techniques and standardized measurements to complement ethnographic analysis. These methods, especially NLP "text-as-data" and social network analysis, are not common in sociocultural anthropology yet, but they are becoming increasingly popular and important in almost all other disciplines that study human behavior in the past or present.[6] These new methods helped me to piece together some parts of the puzzle in the fieldnotes, when all I

---

[6] This methodological movement is gaining impetus in social sciences (Grimmer, Roberts, and Stewart 2022), psychology (Jackson et al. 2021), and humanities like Chinese studies (Fuller 2020).

Epilogue: Taking Children Seriously

had were snapshots of children's life in a discrete array of temporal–spatial points, rather than a continuous flow of actual experience in the field. For example, I was quite overwhelmed by the several hundred persons' ID numbers appearing almost stochastically in the thousands of pages of fieldnotes. Computational results, such as each child's overall behavioral patterns and social network connections, helped me to focus on, and thus understand, a specific child's personality features and social circles. Computational approaches also provide an interesting angle to reflect on the nature and value of ethnographic method, for example, the comparison of human interpretation and machine-learning algorithms, including LLMs (large-language-models), in detecting children's nuanced teasing in peer play. But above all, humanistic close reading, dear to us ethnographers, remains indispensable to actually make sense of these fieldnotes: Tracing the stories of multiple authors, discerning the archive's polyvocality, contemplating how a certain text came into being, and pondering its context and subtext. It was through many rounds of reiterations, traveling back and forth between ethnographic details and computational patterns, and between the process of fieldwork and the product of it, that I slowly transformed the abstract person IDs into concrete personalities. This human–machine collaboration in "reading" children's social worlds via texts is a form of experimentation, an invitation for anthropologists to embrace new methods and explore different ways of knowing. To "know" is a never-ending process. This kind of experimentation will not compromise but augment the value of ethnography. This point applies not only to reanalyzing old fieldnotes, but to all ethnography, to any study of human behavior that requires an effort of interpretation.

The Wolfs' works span from bio-evolutionary to sociocultural anthropology and connect to the SCS (Six Cultures Study), a landmark project in American anthropology. Today, new synergy between evolutionary anthropology and cognitive science is reviving the SCS' legacies of examining childhood learning from a cross-cultural perspective. Many

Epilogue: Taking Children Seriously

researchers bring standardized psychological experiments to different fieldsites or promote the "big data" approach, using NLP text-analysis methods to synthesize previous ethnographies in eHRAF database (Amir and McAuliffe 2020; Henrich 2020). But neither approach has seriously addressed the question of how *fieldwork* itself bears on the knowledge it produced. My book therefore injects a core sociocultural anthropology concern, the question of meaning, into this cross-disciplinary conversation. At a time of divisiveness in anthropology (Horowitz, Yaworsky, and Kickham 2019), I hope to build linkages between multiple subfields and bring new insights to anthropological theory, history, epistemology, and methodology.

But the ultimate challenge and charm of this project is children. Young children are not easy to study. They probably cannot give a researcher elaborate answers about their own beliefs, life circumstances, and their society's problems, as many adult interlocutors can do. Perhaps that is one reason why anthropologists don't study them? Even for experimental psychologists, it is much easier and more efficient to get data from adults than from young children: For some inexplicable reason a child might decide not to cooperate in an experiment, or behave in a way that is hard to interpret. Still, some ethnographers might think that young children are too easy to study because they are so simple minded: What, then, is there to learn from young children about the mysterious thing called ethnography that is so contingent upon intersubjective encounters between complex minds? But as we've seen in this book, young children were scared by the anthropologists who looked too different and did not speak their language, even though they were curious about such strange people and gossiped behind their backs. Or, for an ethnographer like the teenage Taiwanese girl MC, who became children's good friend, these young interlocutors might cause trouble: They just wanted her to play with them, not observe/study them. They might even give her "feces" – throwing a dirty diaper toward her. After all, young children are more complicated than what we assume and more unpredictable. That is exactly why they are fascinating. Scientists today turn to children to decipher many fundamental mysteries, from figuring out what is unique about Homo sapiens (Tomasello 2019) to making AI more human (Gopnik 2017). Children have much to teach us, with their unique positionality and enigmatic minds, about morality, learning, culture, and human knowledge in general. At the end of the day, many abstract anthropological concepts and theories would all fade away. But the stories of human children will live on.

Afterword

What can the article *Twitching in Sensorimotor Development from Sleeping Rats to Robots* (Blumberg 2013) teach us about the development of morals in Taiwanese children? Quite a lot, it seems, as I will outline later. We could not learn these lessons, however, until biologists and psychologists had built an infrastructure of ideas and the tools to test them. Dr. Xu Jing stands on this platform, raising it skillfully with evidence collected by Arthur Wolf at the beginning of his career. A bit of perspective on anthropology across the twentieth century will help frame and honor her achievement.

When I was being taught the basics of anthropology (my B.A. dates from 1963), our still relatively new discipline promised a holistic investigation of the human career using four interconnected but distinct domains and methods. At a time when interdisciplinarity was trumpeted as the next big thing, biological anthropology, archaeology, linguistics, and cultural anthropology, the "four fields," examining humanity through both scientific and humanistic lenses, would make anthropology the Queen of Disciplines.

Early anthropologists, doing fieldwork in the midst of the changes unleashed on the precolonial world (and on Western working classes), had often made stupid and harmful assumptions about "race." Markedly after World War II, some concluded that for too long, biology had been

Afterword

used to legitimize racism and sexism. Investigations of human biology, they feared, would foster these socially distorting positions. We learned to set peoples in their historical, environmental, and technological contexts, showing that culture, not biology or evolutionary processes, explained most behavior formerly attributed to "race." This laudable support of human equality has been anthropology's greatest gift to contemporary society.

By the late 1970s, an influential core of researchers began to ring-fence the concept of culture as anthropology's true and sole focus, eschewing the four-field model with its implicit historical materialism. Influenced by learning theory, they argued that human behavior was constructed from experience after birth, particularly with already-enculturated adults; babies were blank slates. In many anthropology departments, efforts were made to preclude potentially risky findings by excluding the other three wholesale from what they called "cultural studies."

The culturological position has serious weaknesses. "Culture" is an extraordinarily labile concept (Kroeber and Kluckhohn 1952), meaning anything from the collective immaterial contents of minds to this encompassing position, as Beatrice Whiting defined it:

> The ecology of the area determines the maintenance systems, which include basic economy and the most elementary variables of social structure.... [T]he type of crops grown, the presence or absence of herding, fishing, and so on, depend on the nature of the terrain, the amount of rainfall, the location of the area *vis-à-vis* centers of invention and diffusion. These basic economic conditions determine in part the arrangement of people in space, the type of houses, and household composition. These in turn set the parameters for child-rearing practices. (B. Whiting 1963: 4)

This materialist hierarchy of formative factors encompassing and generating cultural matters was familiar to me as an undergraduate (Beatrice Whiting supervised my undergraduate thesis). The model floated loosely among other anthropology faculty members as well. To my best knowledge,

Afterword

it was not taught, however, as a "theory" of culture.[1] The culturological position has also led to the unnecessary pinching off of research initiatives – those raised by genetics, for example – that were flourishing in other disciplines. Now in the twenty-first century, a hint of buyer's remorse has surfaced (Luhrman 2023). Scholars like Dr. Xu are showing how knowledge that lies beyond culture reintegrates the human person.

Arthur Wolf, the Lucile and David Packard Chair of Anthropology, was a part of the postwar flourishing, focusing initially on child development. He believed, and his work shows, that American anthropology has been a discipline with a purpose. We are to document the many and remarkable ways in which human beings arrange their collective lives; to explain how and why these variations come about; and to use that knowledge to support socially liberal actions and values. He thought it intellectually feeble to treat human beings as bodiless supernaturals.

In 2013, Wolf was interviewed by Carlos Seligo (Wolf et al. 2017) about Stanford University's Human Biology Program where he had taught for more than thirty years. With the largest number of undergraduate majors at Stanford and some of the university's most eminent scholars as teachers, it alerted budding doctors to their human side and gave Wolf a forum for assessing the integration he sought in his own work.[2]

---

[1] The quote from Beatrice Whiting swerves very close to "vulgar" Marxism. But while the materialist causal hierarchy was a matter of interest among anthropologists, it radiated tension because of the peculiarly virulent American anticommunism that censored my education. As an undergraduate researching for a professor's project, I was told not to use its language in my notes. In two classes, profs. quizzed me, nervously, about whether I "had been reading Marx?" In a course on nineteenth-century political history, a renowned professor waved Marx away with the single comment, "He was wrong." Nothing I was tasked to read in four years at Harvard would have led me to the historical materialist tradition of scholarship. An excellent study of why this might have been so is David Price's *Cold War Anthropology* (2016).

[2] This interview was part of a project to document Stanford's Human Biology Program. I was asked by the Shih Ho-cheng Folk Culture Foundation in Taiwan to edit and comment on it, after which Professor Chen Shujuo of Taiwan's National Museum of Natural History translated it for bilingual publication. I have borrowed from it in this *Afterword*.

Afterword

Arthur Wolf:
I began teaching in the Human Biology Program in 1971.... [with people] from the biological sciences and ... the medical school.... They wrote a proposal to the Ford Foundation for funding ... quite a few millions.... The proposal was not even a whole page long. It was from people with very considerable reputations, and, of course, the Ford Foundation funded the program. What was missing, certainly from my perspective, was ... that a lot of the more significant problems that we face in this country and elsewhere have their origins in society. They are not going to be solved necessarily by "fixes" of a medical or biological sort. They might have to be solved by social means.... [Later] it had much more the tone that it has today, of two kinds of science: biological and medical on the one hand [t]he "A side"] and psychological and social on the other [the "B side"]....

*[An example of how we brought A and B together] was when Craig [Heller] and I [debated the relationship between] aggression and war. .... [Professor Heller, a behavioral biologist] saw war as an expression ... **just of aggression. He didn't see it in social/political** terms. Coming from my perspective ... war isn't like children fighting on a playground. It's not just an expression of a human tendency. **There's obviously something in human nature that allows it to happen and makes people willing to do it, but that isn't what creates war**. (**bold** mine: HG). War comes from larger social/political problems. War probably has more to do with obedience, with strange kinds of loyalties and so forth than it has to do with aggression.*

[For an example of how an evolved tendency against sexual relations with close kin (incest) can overcome cultural pressures to engage in it] I have ... spent the greater part of my career in studying the effect of early association [between children] on sexual attraction.... Imagine a world in which we could experiment on a large population. We would take [girl/boy pairs of] children in one large set and rear them together. In another large set, we would not introduce [the girl/boy pairs] until they became adults. [Then arrange marriage for both kinds of couples] and see what effect that early association vs. no early association had on their sexual interest in one another. We can't do that; we shouldn't be allowed to do it. Nonetheless, that is the obvious and only convincing way to go about [seeing if there is a difference]. That I have succeeded in addressing that problem is only because, in fact, the Chinese did it. In large parts of [traditional] China, people raised their sons' wives. Couples of boys and girls who were reared together were (actually, in this case) forced

to marry. Such couples can be compared with [those in] the other form of marriage in the same communities. In these, parents married their sons to girls that they [the parents] brought into the family at seventeen or eighteen years of age. Now, even given that natural experiment, [it is difficult] to measure the effects of association or non-association. You can look at fertility rates, you can look at divorce rates, you can look at the frequency of adultery. But if you had to go out and collect that data through interviews, it would be extremely difficult. And it would cost something like an aircraft carrier to collect.... I have been able to do it because the Japanese colonial government on Taiwan set up a household register system in which they did it for me. ... [getting appropriate data to test is hard, and that] problem ... enormously inhibits social science research: First, to find the natural situation, which is rare and, in many cases, does not exist; and second, to actually collect the data....

You take a human being: a human being is not psychological, or biological, or anthropological, or sociological. These divisions were made in the history of the development of the Western sciences. I see the major task of the Human Biology program is to bridge, to overcome, what are basically really artificial distinctions. The program does not always succeed in this, as the [disciplinary boundaries] are very difficult to overcome.

With the exception of accepting some imports of theory from (Western) literary criticism in the 1980s, American anthropology built itself a mighty fortress against extra-cultural evidence.[3] Many scholars remained outside those walls, however, rearing new generations willing to see humans as complete evolved creatures and to explore aspects of culture that their perspective makes researchable, as Dr. Xu has done with morality.

Which brings me to those twitchy rat pups. In Blumberg et al. (2013), researchers tested an approach to mammalian development that undermined the old assumption about the passivity of the very young. Even

---

[3] The siloing of cultural anthropology in the United States also owes much to the massive expansion of postsecondary education that followed the Soviet Union's first entry into space. Colleges and universities grew like bamboo shoots with government money watering them copiously (Price 2016). Competition for academic real estate (corner offices) and student body count motivated faculty to tighten disciplinary lines. A major anthropologist has recently voiced some buyer's remorse for fifty years of slighting scientific approaches (Luhrman 2023).

Afterword

before birth, mammals self-initiate important activities, not relying on stimuli from outside themselves. Rat fetuses spend most of their intra-uterine time sleeping, often in the "rapid eye movement" (REM) mode associated with brain activity but body paralysis. Their muscles twitch and spasm constantly. Blumberg concludes that a still rudimentary rat brain sends neural signals to rat muscles, one at a time, thereby teaching itself where their muscles are and how they function. Twitching and self-initiated exploration of the body persist as the body changes through growth and injury, keeping the brain updated and teaching muscle groups to work together. The fetal forms of many animals, including ourselves, do the same. From the third trimester of pregnancy, the human fetus initiates behavior that informs it about itself and its environment. Some learning is self-motivated, even before there is much of a self.

Such insight makes intellectual space that invites exploration by developmental researchers. In our present case, Dr. Xu has analyzed Wolf's data to reveal the agency of Taiwanese village children as they encounter their world. That world is part of an old and widespread Han Chinese civilization where adults believe infants are born a blank slate. Children inherit the teachings of respected sages made legible by symbolism ornamenting buildings, books, and visual arts. Their wisdom is purveyed through proverbs, comic books, theater, and the minatory observations of their elders. Historically, and still in 1950s and 60s Taiwan, instructions on how to behave, what is moral, and what creates the capacity to *zuo ren* – to act as a good, properly developed human being – are assumed to move in only one direction: from enculturated adults to obedient children.

Through Wolf's careful documentation of the words and actions of children themselves, Dr. Xu can watch them forming their sense of what is good or bad. They learn from adult teaching, certainly, but also from their alertness to the imperfections of adults who fail to adhere to their stated principles. Some moral templates are stated, others observed. Some aspects of morality may be innate: a sense of fairness, possibly; compassion, likely. How a person *zuo ren* will be assembled from many

Afterword

and often-inconsistent elements. One might conclude that the morality practiced by ordinary Chinese people (and the rest of us?) is reinvented by each generation.

Hill Gates[*]

Cited Sources

Blumberg, Mark S., Hugo Gravato Marques, and Fumiya Iida. 2013. "Twitching in Sensorimotor Development from Sleeping Rats to Robots." *Current Biology* 23: R532–R537.

Kroeber, A. L., and Clyde Kluckhohn. 1952. Papers. Peabody Museum of Archaeology and Ethnology. *Harvard University* 47 (1): viii, 223.

Luhrman, T. M. 2023. "Unravelling a Web: The Interpretation of Cultures by Clifford Geertz, Fifty Years On." *The Times Literary Supplement*, 6284 (September 8): 21. www.the-tls.co.uk/issues/september-8-2023/

Price, D. 2016. *Cold War Anthropology: The CIA, the Pentagon, and the Growth of Dual-Use Anthropology*. Durham, North Carolina: Duke University Press.

Whiting, Beatrice B., ed. 1963. *Six Cultures Studies of Child Rearing*. Laboratory of Human Development, Harvard University. New York and London: John Wiley and Sons, Inc.

Wolf, Arthur, Carlos, Seligo, Hill Gates, and Chen Shu-juo, [陳叔倬]. 2017. Interview of Professor Arthur P. Wolf (1932–2015) on Stanford's Human Biology Program. *Minsu Quyi* [民俗曲藝] Taipei: September: 11–38.

---

[*] Hill Gates is the owner of the Wolf Archive. Born in Canada in 1942, she received her B.A. from Harvard/Radcliffe (1963), M.A. from the University of Hawai'i (1966), and Ph.D. at the University of Michigan (1973). Her works include *China's Motor: A Thousand Years of Petty Capitalism* (1996), *Footbinding and Women's Labor in Sichuan* (2015), and *Bound Feet, Small Hands: Tracking the Demise of Footbinding in Village China* (2017, coauthored with Laurel Bossen). Now retired, she is preparing *Hypergendering: Footbinding, Veiling, FGM, and the Mother-in-law Belt*, a book about female labor discipline in the old Eurasian civilizations as their economies intensified. Retired as Professor Emerita from Central Michigan University in 1991, she has also taught at Johns Hopkins University, Minzu University of China, Datong University (China), and Stanford University where she shared a position with Arthur Wolf.

Appendix: Topic Modeling List (Corpus: Child Observation)

Topic no.	No. of texts under this topic	Percentage of the corpus	Top ten keywords
0	129	0.08	push, cry, stop, fall, sit, tree, stand, start, back, child
1	186	0.11	play, card, throw, top, ball, game, lose, time, anymore, put
2	104	0.06	laugh, jump, pull, start, rope, make, time, finally, hand, leg
3	130	0.08	give, eat, hand, swing, buy, ill, box, alright, store, candy
4	74	0.04	watch, hold, stand, walk, hand, boy, back, girl, bit, end
5	112	0.07	run, catch, back, start, yell, hurry, stop, high, child, count
6	92	0.05	turn, walk, smile, start, back, point, watch, notice, write, answer
7	107	0.06	hit, mother, hard, angry, back, head, copulate, laugh, angrily, fight
8	121	0.07	stick, make, pick, put, break, mud, piece, big, find, work
9	122	0.07	put, sit, back, pick, carry, paper, leaf, door, tie, open
10	83	0.05	walk, house, home, call, wait, follow, answer, care, leave, talk
11	136	0.08	water, walk, put, hand, ditch, hurry, dirty, basket, pump, foot
12	195	0.12	turn, play, tile, throw, step, die, line, draw, start, square
13	87	0.05	move, start, pick, throw, rock, shoot, back, close, marble, time

Glossary

Anxi	安溪
bai-bai	拜拜
Banqiao	板橋
baomi fangdie	保密防諜
Baye	八爺
benshengren	本省人
cai	菜
chezhang xiaojie	車掌小姐
Chiang-chiu-a (H.)	漳州仔
da xue	大學
Dahan River	大漢溪
Di di da da	滴滴答答
Fujian	福建
Gua-sieng-a (H.)	外省仔
guan	管
guanjiao	管教
gunbang zhixia chu xiaozi	棍棒之下出孝子
guowen	國文
guoyu	國語
jia ba bue (H.)	你吃飽沒？
jiaohua	教化
jiefang taiwan	解放台灣
Jinmen	金門
Kan (H.)	姦
Liu Tzu-jan	劉自然

Lo Ta-yu	羅大佑
lo-mua (H.)	流氓/鱸鰻
Mazu	媽祖
ming ming de	明明德
qi	氣
Qiye	七爺
quan jia	勸架
Sanminzhuyi	三民主義
sannian ziran zaihai	三年自然災害
Sha ji jing hou	殺雞儆猴
Shalun	沙崙
shidi	史地
Shulin	樹林
shuncong	順從
sim-pu-a (H.)	媳婦仔
Tamsui River	淡水河
tang-ki (H.)	童乩
tongnian	童年
tongyangxi	童養媳
Tucheng	土城
tudigong	土地公
waishengren	外省人
Wang Shiqing	王世慶
Xia Xizhou	下溪洲
Xiao-ban	孝班
xiaomie gongfei	消滅共匪
Yeh Hong-jia	葉宏甲
Zhong-ban	忠班
zuguohua	祖國化
zuo ren	做人

References

Alber, E., C. Coe, and T. Thelen. 2013. *The Anthropology of Sibling Relations: Shared Parentage, Experience, and Exchange*. New York: Palgrave Macmillan.

Allerton, Catherine, ed. 2016. *Children: Ethnographic Encounters*. 1st edition. New York: Routledge.

Amir, Dorsa, and Katherine McAuliffe. 2020. "Cross-Cultural, Developmental Psychology: Integrating Approaches and Key Insights." *Evolution and Human Behavior* 41 (5): 430–44. https://doi.org/10.1016/j.evolhumbehav.2020.06.006.

Anagnost, Ann. 2008. "Imagining Global Futures in China: The Child as a Sign of Value." In *Figuring the Future: Globalization and the Temporalities of Children and Youth*, edited by Jennifer Cole and Deborah Durham, 49–73. Santa Fe, NM: School for Advanced Research Press.

Arai, Andrea Gevurtz. 2016. *The Strange Child: Education and the Psychology of Patriotism in Recessionary Japan*. Stanford, CA: Stanford University Press.

Archer, John. 2004. "Sex Differences in Aggression in Real-World Settings: A Meta-Analytic Review." *Review of General Psychology* 8 (4): 291–322. https://doi.org/10.1037/1089-2680.8.4.291.

Astuti, Rita. 2017. "Taking People Seriously." *HAU: Journal of Ethnographic Theory* 7 (1): 105–22. https://doi.org/10.14318/hau7.1.012.

Astuti, Rita, and Maurice Bloch. 2010. "Why a Theory of Human Nature Cannot Be Based on the Distinction between Universality and Variability: Lessons from Anthropology." *Behavior and Brain Sciences* 33 (2–3): 83–84.

Ayars, Alisabeth, and Shaun Nichols. 2017. "Moral Empiricism and the Bias for Act-Based Rules." *Cognition* 167 (October): 11–24. https://doi.org/10.1016/j.cognition.2017.01.007.

Bai, Limin. 2005. *Shaping the Ideal Child: Children and Their Primers in Late Imperial China*. Hong Kong: The Chinese University Press. http://libcat-ind.wustl.edu/?itemid=; iii; b2980294.

References

Bakken, Børge. 2000. *The Exemplary Society: Human Improvement, Social Control, and the Dangers of Modernity.* New York: Oxford University Press.

Bamford, Sandra. 2019. "Introduction: Conceiving Kinship in the Twenty-First Century." In *The Cambridge Handbook of Kinship,* edited by Sandra Bamford, 1–34. Cambridge Handbooks in Anthropology. Cambridge, UK: Cambridge University Press. https://doi.org/10.1017/9781139644938.001.

Barrett, H. Clark. 2020. "Towards a Cognitive Science of the Human: Cross-Cultural Approaches and Their Urgency." *Trends in Cognitive Sciences* 24 (8): 620–38. https://doi.org/10.1016/j.tics.2020.05.007.

Barrett, H. Clark, Tanya Broesch, Rose M. Scott, et al. 2013. "Early False-Belief Understanding in Traditional Non-Western Societies." *Proceedings of the Royal Society B: Biological Sciences* 280 (1755): 20122654. https://doi.org/10.1098/rspb.2012.2654.

Barrett, H. Clark, and Rebecca R. Saxe. 2021. "Are Some Cultures More Mind-Minded in Their Moral Judgements Than Others?" *Philosophical Transactions of the Royal Society B: Biological Sciences* 376 (1838): 20200288. https://doi.org/10.1098/rstb.2020.0288.

Bateson, Gregory. 2000. *Steps to an Ecology of Mind: Collected Essays in Anthropology, Psychiatry, Evolution, and Epistemology.* Chicago, IL: University of Chicago Press. https://press.uchicago.edu/ucp/books/book/chicago/S/bo3620295.html.

Bennardo, Giovanni, and Victor De Munck. 2020. "Cultural Model Theory in Cognitive Anthropology: Recent Developments and Applications." *Journal of Cultural Cognitive Science* 4(1): 1–2.

Björkqvist, Kaj. 2018. "Gender Differences in Aggression." *Current Opinion in Psychology, Aggression and Violence,* 19 (February): 39–42. https://doi.org/10.1016/j.copsyc.2017.03.030.

Blake, P. R., K. McAuliffe, J. Corbit, et al. 2015. "The Ontogeny of Fairness in Seven Societies." *Nature* 528 (7581): 258–61. https://doi.org/10.1038/nature15703.

Blei, David M. 2012. "Probabilistic Topic Models." *Communications of the ACM* 55 (4): 77–84. https://doi.org/10.1145/2133806.2133826.

Blum, Susan D. 2019. "Why Don't Anthropologists Care about Learning (or Education or School)? An Immodest Proposal for an Integrative Anthropology of Learning Whose Time Has Finally Come." *American Anthropologist* 121 (3): 641–54. https://doi.org/10.1111/aman.13268.

Borneman, John. 2016. "Foreword." In *Children: Ethnographic Encounters,* edited by Catherine Allerton, ix–x. Bloomsbury Academic.

Boyer, Pascal. 2018. *Minds Make Societies: How Cognition Explains the World Humans Create.* 1st edition. New Haven and London: Yale University Press.

References

———. 2020. "Why Divination?: Evolved Psychology and Strategic Interaction in the Production of Truth." *Current Anthropology* 61 (1): 100–23. https://doi.org/10.1086/706879.
Brandtstädter, Susanne, and Gonçalo D. Santos, eds. 2011. *Chinese Kinship: Contemporary Anthropological Perspectives*. 1st edition. London: Routledge.
Briggs, Jean L. 1999. *Inuit Morality Play: The Emotional Education of a Three-Year-Old*. New Haven and London: Yale University Press.
Broesch, Tanya, Alyssa N. Crittenden, Bret A. Beheim, et al. 2020. "Navigating Cross-Cultural Research: Methodological and Ethical Considerations." *Proceedings of the Royal Society B: Biological Sciences* 287 (1935): 20201245. https://doi.org/10.1098/rspb.2020.1245.
Card, Noel A., Brian D. Stucky, Gita M. Sawalani, and Todd D. Little. 2008. "Direct and Indirect Aggression during Childhood and Adolescence: A Meta-Analytic Review of Gender Differences, Intercorrelations, and Relations to Maladjustment." *Child Development* 79 (5): 1185–229. https://doi.org/10.1111/j.1467-8624.2008.01184.x.
Carsten, Janet, ed. 2000. *Cultures of Relatedness: New Approaches to the Study of Kinship*. Illustrated edition. Cambridge, UK and New York: Cambridge University Press.
———. 2012. "Fieldwork Since the 1980s: Total Immersion and Its Discontents." In *The SAGE Handbook of Social Anthropology*, 7–20. London: SAGE Publications. https://doi.org/10.4135/9781446201077.
———. 2013. "What Kinship Does—And How." *HAU: Journal of Ethnographic Theory* 3 (2): 245–51. https://doi.org/10.14318/hau3.2.013.
Chang, Bi-yu. 2015. *Place, Identity, and National Imagination in Post-War Taiwan*. London: Routledge.
Chao, R. K. 1994. "Beyond Parental Control and Authoritarian Parenting Style: Understanding Chinese Parenting through the Cultural Notion of Training." *Child Development* 65 (4): 1111–19.
Chapin, Bambi L. 2014. *Childhood in a Sri Lankan Village: Shaping Hierarchy and Desire*. New Brunswick, NJ: Rutgers University Press.
Chapin, Bambi L., and Jing Xu. Forthcoming. "Children in Social Change: Socialization and the Shifting Contexts of Childhood." In *Cambridge Handbook of Psychological Anthropology*, edited by Edward Lowe. Cambridge University Press.
Chen, Chun-Ying. 2007. "Woguo Weiquan Tizhi Jiangou Chuqi Zhi Jingzheng (1949–1958) [The Police Administration in the Early Stage of Structuring of Authoritarian Regime in Taiwan (1949–1958)]." *Renwen Shehui Xuebao* (3): 45–72.

References

Cheng, Yen-hsin Alice. 2020. "Ultra-Low Fertility in East Asia: Confucianism and Its Discontents." *Vienna Yearbook of Population Research* 18: 83–120.

Choi, Yejin. 2022. "The Curious Case of Commonsense Intelligence." *Daedalus* 151 (2): 139–55. https://doi.org/10.1162/daed_a_01906.

Chou, Wan-Yao. 2011. *Pioneer in Taiwanese History: The Life Journey of Mr. Wang Shiqing*. 臺灣史開拓者:王世慶先生的人生之路. New Taipei: New Taipei Bureau of Culture.

Cline, Erin M. 2015. *Families of Virtue: Confucian and Western Views on Childhood Development*. New York: Columbia University Press.

Cohen, Myron L. 1976. *House United, House Divided: The Chinese Family in Taiwan*. New York: Columbia University Press.

Coles, Robert. 1986. *The Political Life of Children*. Boston: Atlantic Monthly Press.

Colle, Livia, Gerlind Grosse, Tanya Behne, and Michael Tomasello. 2023. "Just Teasing! – Infants' and Toddlers' Understanding of Teasing Interactions and Its Effect on Social Bonding." *Cognition* 231 (February): 105314. https://doi.org/10.1016/j.cognition.2022.105314.

Croll, Elisabeth. 2000. *Endangered Daughters: Discrimination and Development in Asia*. London: Routledge.

Cumming, Elaine, and David M. Schneider. 1961. "Sibling Solidarity: A Property of American Kinship." *American Anthropologist* 63 (3): 498–507. https://doi.org/10.1525/aa.1961.63.3.02a00030.

Curry, Oliver Scott, Daniel Austin Mullins, and Harvey Whitehouse. 2019. "Is It Good to Cooperate?: Testing the Theory of Morality-as-Cooperation in 60 Societies." *Current Anthropology* 60 (1): 47–69. https://doi.org/10.1086/701478.

Cushman, Fiery, Victor Kumar, and Peter Railton. 2017. "Moral Learning: Psychological and Philosophical Perspectives." *Cognition, Moral Learning* 167 (October): 1–10. https://doi.org/10.1016/j.cognition.2017.06.008.

D'Andrade, Roy G. 1981. "The Cultural Part of Cognition." *Cognitive Science* 5 (3): 179–95. https://doi.org/10.1207/s15516709cog0503_1.

———. 1987. "A Folk Model of the Mind." In *Cultural Models in Language and Thought*, edited by Douglas Hollan and Naomi Quinn, 112–48. Cambridge, UK: Cambridge University Press.

D'Andrade, Roy G., and Claudia Strauss, eds. 1992. *Human Motives and Cultural Models*. Illustrated edition. Cambridge UK and New York: Cambridge University Press.

De Felice, Sara, Antonia F. de C. Hamilton, Marta Ponari, and Gabriella Vigliocco. 2022. "Learning from Others Is Good, with Others Is Better: The Role of Social Interaction in Human Acquisition of New Knowledge." *Philosophical Transactions of the Royal Society B: Biological Sciences* 378 (1870): 20210357. https://doi.org/10.1098/rstb.2021.0357.

References

Dehaene, Stanislas. 2020. *How We Learn: Why Brains Learn Better Than Any Machine ... for Now*. New York: Viking.

Diamond, Norma. 1969. *Kun Shen – A Taiwan Village*. Later printing. New York: Holt, Rinehart & Winston. www.biblio.com/book/kun-shen-taiwan-village-diamond-norma/d/1408903650.

Du, Keli. 2019. "A Survey on LDA Topic Modeling in Digital Humanities." Text, 2019. https://dev.clariah.nl/files/dh2019/boa/0326.html.

Dunfield, Kristen A. 2014. "A Construct Divided: Prosocial Behavior as Helping, Sharing, and Comforting Subtypes." *Frontiers in Psychology* 5 (September). https://doi.org/10.3389/fpsyg.2014.00958.

Dunfield, Kristen A., and Valerie A. Kuhlmeier. 2013. "Classifying Prosocial Behavior: Children's Responses to Instrumental Need, Emotional Distress, and Material Desire." *Child Development* 84 (5): 1766–76. https://doi.org/10.1111/cdev.12075.

Duryea, Maria. 1999. "Changing Lives and Life Changes on Taipei's Urban Border 1959–1994." PhD diss., Seattle: University of Washington.

Eagly, Alice H. 2009. "The His and Hers of Prosocial Behavior: An Examination of the Social Psychology of Gender." *The American Psychologist* 64 (8): 644–58. https://doi.org/10.1037/0003-066X.64.8.644.

Ebrey, Patricia Buckley, and James L. Watson. 1986. "Introduction." In *Kinship Organization in Late Imperial China, 1000–1400*, edited by Patricia Buckley Ebrey and James L. Watson, 1–15. Berkeley: University of California Press.

Eckert, Johanna, Sasha L. Winkler, and Erica A. Cartmill. 2020. "Just Kidding: The Evolutionary Roots of Playful Teasing." *Biology Letters* 16 (9): 20200370. https://doi.org/10.1098/rsbl.2020.0370.

Edwards, Carolyn Pope. 2000. "Children's Play in Cross-Cultural Perspective: A New Look at the Six Cultures Study." *Cross-Cultural Research* 34 (4): 318–38.

Ellis, Shari, Barbara Rogoff, and Cindy C. Cromer. 1981. "Age Segregation in Children's Social Interactions." *Developmental Psychology* 17: 399–407. https://doi.org/10.1037/0012-1649.17.4.399.

Ember, Carol R., and Melvin Ember. 2005. "Explaining Corporal Punishment of Children: A Cross-Cultural Study." *American Anthropologist* 107 (4): 609–19.

Endendijk, Joyce J., Marleen G. Groeneveld, Lotte D. van der Pol, Sheila R. van Berkel, Elizabeth T. Hallers-Haalboom, Marian J. Bakermans-Kranenburg, and Judi Mesman. 2017. "Gender Differences in Child Aggression: Relations With Gender-Differentiated Parenting and Parents' Gender-Role Stereotypes." *Child Development* 88 (1): 299–316. https://doi.org/10.1111/cdev.12589.

Fabes, Richard, and Nancy Eisenberg. 1998. "Meta-Analyses of Age and Sex Differences in Children's and Adolescents' Prosocial Behavior," January.

Fassin, Didier. 2012. *A Companion to Moral Anthropology*. Hoboken: John Wiley & Sons.

References

Fong, Vanessa L. 2004. *Only Hope: Coming of Age under China's One-Child Policy.* Stanford, CA: Stanford University Press. http://libcat.wustl.edu/?itemid=; iii; b2913568.

Frank, Michael C. 2023. "Bridging the Data Gap between Children and Large Language Models." *Trends in Cognitive Sciences*, August. https://doi.org/10.1016/j.tics.2023.08.007.

Freedman, Maurice. 1966. *Chinese Lineage and Society: Fukien and Kwangtung.* 1st edition. The Athlone Press.

——— 1968. "Foreword." In *The House of Lim: A Study of a Chinese Farm Family*, edited by Margery Wolf, vii–xii. Upper Saddle River, NJ: Prentice Hall.

Fuller, Michael A. 2020. "Digital Humanities and the Discontents of Meaning." *Journal of Chinese History 中國歷史學刊* 4 (2): 259–75. https://doi.org/10.1017/jch.2020.13.

Fung, Heidi. 1999. "Becoming a Moral Child: The Socialization of Shame among Young Chinese Children." *Ethos* 27 (2): 180–209. https://doi.org/10.1525/eth.1999.27.2.180.

Fung, Heidi, and Benjamin Smith. 2010. "Learning Morality." In *The Anthropology of Learning in Childhood*, edited by David F. Lancy, John Bock, and Suzanne Gaskins, 261–86. Walnut Creek, CA: AltaMira Press.

González-Carvajal, Santiago, and Eduardo C. Garrido-Merchán. 2021. "Comparing BERT against Traditional Machine Learning Text Classification." *arXiv.* https://doi.org/10.48550/arXiv.2005.13012.

Goodwin, Marjorie Harness, and Amy Kyratzis. 2012. "Peer Language Socialization." In *The Handbook of Language Socialization*, edited by Alessandro Duranti, Elinor Ochs, and Bambi B. Schieffelin, 365–90. Wiley-Blackwell.

Gopnik, Alison. 2017. "Making AI More Human." *Scientific American* 316 (6): 60–65.

——— 2020. "Childhood as a Solution to Explore–Exploit Tensions." *Philosophical Transactions of the Royal Society B: Biological Sciences* 375 (1803): 20190502. https://doi.org/10.1098/rstb.2019.0502.

——— 2022. "Children, Creativity, and the Real Key to Intelligence." *APS Observer* 35 (October). www.psychologicalscience.org/observer/children-creativity-intelligence.

Gopnik, Alison, and Elizabeth Bonawitz. 2015. "Bayesian Models of Child Development." *WIREs Cognitive Science* 6 (2): 75–86. https://doi.org/10.1002/wcs.1330.

Gopnik, Alison, and Joshua B. Tenenbaum. 2007. "Bayesian Networks, Bayesian Learning and Cognitive Development." *Developmental Science* 10 (3): 281–87. https://doi.org/10.1111/j.1467-7687.2007.00584.x.

References

Greenhalgh, Susan. 1988. "Intergenerational Contracts: Familial Roots of Sexual Stratification in Taiwan." In *A Home Divided: Women and Income in the Third World*, edited by D. Dwyer and J. Bruce, 39–70. Stanford, CA: Stanford University Press.

Griffiths, Paul, and Stefan Linquist. 2022. "The Distinction between Innate and Acquired Characteristics." In *The Stanford Encyclopedia of Philosophy*, edited by Edward N. Zalta, Spring 2022. Stanford, CA: Metaphysics Research Lab, Stanford University. https://plato.stanford.edu/archives/spr2022/entries/innate-acquired/.

Grimmer, Justin, Margaret E. Roberts, and Brandon M. Stewart. 2022. *Text as Data: A New Framework for Machine Learning and the Social Sciences*. Princeton: Princeton University Press.

Gupta, Akhil, and Jessie Stoolman. 2022. "Decolonizing US Anthropology." *American Anthropologist* 124 (4): 778–99. https://doi.org/10.1111/aman.13775.

Gweon, Hyowon. 2021. "Inferential Social Learning: Cognitive Foundations of Human Social Learning and Teaching." *Trends in Cognitive Sciences* 25 (10): 896–910. https://doi.org/10.1016/j.tics.2021.07.008.

Hamilton, W. D. 1964. "The Genetical Evolution of Social Behaviour. II." *Journal of Theoretical Biology* 7 (1): 17–52. https://doi.org/10.1016/0022-5193(64)90039-6.

Hanneman, Robert A., and Mark Riddle. 2005. *Introduction to Social Network Methods*. Riverside, CA: University of California, Riverside. http://faculty.ucr.edu/~hanneman/nettext/.

Harkness, Sara, Caroline Johnston Mavridis, Jia Ji Liu, and Charles M. Super. 2015. "Parental Ethnotheories and the Development of Family Relationships in Early and Middle Childhood." In *The Oxford Handbook of Human Development and Culture*, edited by L. A. Jensen, 271–91. New York: Oxford University Press. https://doi.org/10.1093/oxfordhb/9780199948550.013.17.

Harrell, Stevan. 1999. "Lessons from the Golden Age of 'China Ethnography.'" In *Anthropological Studies in Taiwan: Retrospect and Prospect*, edited by Cheng-kuang Hsu and Ying-Kuei Huang, 211–40. Taipei: Academia Sinica.

Harris, Paul L. 2021. "Early Constraints on the Imagination: The Realism of Young Children." *Child Development* 92(2): 466–83. https://doi.org/10.1111/cdev.13487.

Headland, Isaac Taylor. 1901. *The Chinese Boy and Girl*. Fleming H. Revell Company.

Henrich, Joseph. 2020. *The WEIRDest People in the World: How the West Became Psychologically Peculiar and Particularly Prosperous*. Farrar: Straus and Giroux.

Henrich, Joseph, Steven J Heine, and Ara Norenzayan. 2010. "The Weirdest People in the World?" *The Behavioral and Brain Sciences* 33 (2–3): 61–83.

References

Hernandez, Jose, and Jing Xu. in prep. "Childhood in Anthropological Texts: Re-Discovering Naturalistic Observations via Natural Language Processing Techniques." *Harvard Data Science Review*.

Hewlett, Barry S., Hillary N. Fouts, Adam H. Boyette, and Bonnie L. Hewlett. 2011. "Social Learning among Congo Basin Hunter–Gatherers." *Philosophical Transactions of the Royal Society B: Biological Sciences* 366 (1567): 1168–78. https://doi.org/10.1098/rstb.2010.0373.

Hirschfeld, Lawrence A. 2002. "Why Don't Anthropologists Like Children?" *American Anthropologist* 104 (2): 611–27. https://doi.org/10.1525/aa.2002.104.2.611.

Ho, D. Y. F. 1986. "Chinese Patterns of Socialization: A Critical Review." In *The Psychology of the Chinese People*, 1–37. New York, NY: Oxford University Press.

Holland, Dorothy and Naomi Quinn, eds. 1987. *Cultural Models in Language and Thought*. Cambridge, UK: Cambridge University Press.

Horowitz, Mark, William Yaworsky, and Kenneth Kickham. 2019. "Anthropology's Science Wars." *Current Anthropology* 60 (5): 674–98. https://doi.org/10.1086/705409.

House, Bailey R., Patricia Kanngiesser, H. Clark Barrett, et al. 2020. "Universal Norm Psychology Leads to Societal Diversity in Prosocial Behaviour and Development." *Nature Human Behaviour* 4(1): 36–44. https://doi.org/10.1038/s41562-019-0734-z.

House, Bailey, Joan B. Silk, and Katherine McAuliffe. 2023. "No Strong Evidence for Universal Gender Differences in the Development of Cooperative Behaviour across Societies." *Philosophical Transactions of the Royal Society B: Biological Sciences* 378 (1868): 20210439. https://doi.org/10.1098/rstb.2021.0439.

Hsiung, Ping-chen. 2005. *A Tender Voyage: Children and Childhood in Late Imperial China*. Stanford, CA: Stanford University Press.

Hyde, Janet S. 1984. "How Large Are Gender Differences in Aggression? A Developmental Meta-Analysis." *Developmental Psychology* 20: 722–36. https://doi.org/10.1037/0012-1649.20.4.722.

Jackson, Joshua Conrad, Joseph Watts, Johann-Mattis List, Curtis Puryear, Ryan Drabble, and Kristen Lindquist. 2021. "From Text to Thought: How Analyzing Language Can Advance Psychological Science." *Perspectives on Psychological Sciences* 17(3). https://doi.org/10.1177/17456916211004８.

Jankowiak, William, Amber Joiner, and Cynthia Khatib. 2011. "What Observation Studies Can Tell Us about Single Child Play Patterns, Gender, and Changes in Chinese Society." *Cross-Cultural Research* 45 (2): 155–77. https://doi.org/10.1177/1069397110394310.

Jiang, Liwei, Jena D. Hwang, Chandra Bhagavatula, et al. 2022. "Can Machines Learn Morality? The Delphi Experiment." *arXiv*. https://doi.org/10.48550/arXiv.2110.07574.

References

Jiang, Tao. 2021. *Origins of Moral-Political Philosophy in Early China: Contestation of Humaneness, Justice, and Personal Freedom*. Oxford and New York: Oxford University Press.

Jones, Andrew F. 2011. *Developmental Fairy Tales: Evolutionary Thinking and Modern Chinese Culture*. 1st edition. Cambridge, MA: Harvard University Press.

Joseph, Suad. 1994. "Brother/Sister Relationships: Connectivity, Love, and Power in the Reproduction of Patriarchy in Lebanon." *American Ethnologist* 21 (1): 50–73.

Jung, Hyang Jin, and Junehui Ahn. 2021. "South Korean Education Under Psychocultural Globalization." *Ethos* 49 (1): 3–10. https://doi.org/10.1111/etho.12297.

Kinney, Anne Behnke. 1995. *Chinese Views of Childhood*. Honolulu: University of Hawaii Press. http://libcat-ind.wustl.edu/?itemid=; iii; b2549756.

——— 2004. *Representations of Childhood and Youth in Early China*. Stanford, CA: Stanford University Press.

Kipnis, Andrew B. 2011. *Governing Educational Desire: Culture, Politics, and Schooling in China*. Chicago, IL: University of Chicago Press.

Kleinman, Arthur. 2011. "Introduction: Remaking the Moral Person in a New China." In *Deep China: The Moral Life of the Person*, edited by Arthur Kleinman, Yunxiang Yan, Jing Jun, Sing Lee, and Everett Zhang, 1–35. Berkeley: University of California Press.

Kleinman, Arthur, Yunxiang Yan, Jing Jun, Sing Lee, and Everett Zhang. 2011. *Deep China: The Moral Life of the Person*. Berkeley: University of California Press.

Klöter, Henning. 2004. "Language Policy in the KMT and DPP Eras." *China Perspectives* 2004 (6). http://journals.openedition.org/chinaperspectives/442.

Kohlberg, Lawrence. 1984. *The Psychology of Moral Development: The Nature and Validity of Moral Stages (Essays on Moral Development, Volume 2)*. 1st edition. San Francisco: Harper & Row.

Kosinski, Michal. 2023. "Theory of Mind May Have Spontaneously Emerged in Large Language Models." *arXiv*. https://doi.org/10.48550/arXiv.2302.02083.

Kuan, Teresa. 2015. *Love's Uncertainty: The Politics and Ethics of Child Rearing in Contemporary China*. Oakland: University of California Press.

Laidlaw, James. 2017. "Ethics/Morality." *Cambridge Encyclopedia of Anthropology*, May. www.anthroencyclopedia.com/entry/ethics-morality.

——— ed. 2023. *The Cambridge Handbook for the Anthropology of Ethics*. Cambridge Handbooks in Anthropology. Cambridge, UK: Cambridge University Press. www.cambridge.org/core/books/cambridge-handbook-for-the-anthropology-of-ethics/378FB10BB7DA9D4650E9516FEB8DABC2.

References

Lambek, Michael. 2010a. *Ordinary Ethics Anthropology, Language, and Action.* New York: Fordham University Press.

———. 2010b. "Toward an Ethics of the Act." In *Ordinary Ethics: Anthropology, Language, and Action*, edited by Michael Lambek, 39–63. New York: Fordham University Press.

Lan, Pei-Chia. 2018. *Raising Global Families: Parenting, Immigration, and Class in Taiwan and the US.* Stanford, CA: Stanford University Press.

Lancy, David F. 1996. *Playing on the Mother-Ground: Cultural Routines for Children's Development.* 1st edition. New York, NY: The Guilford Press.

Lansford, Jennifer E., Patrick S. Malone, Kenneth A. Dodge, Gregory S. Pettit, and John E. Bates. 2010. "Developmental Cascades of Peer Rejection, Social Information Processing Biases, and Aggression during Middle Childhood." *Development and Psychopathology* 22 (3): 593–602. https://doi.org/10.1017/S0954579410000301.

Lemov, Rebecca. 2011. "X-Rays of Inner Worlds: The Mid-Twentieth-Century American Projective Test Movement." *Journal of the History of the Behavioral Sciences* 47 (3): 251–78. https://doi.org/10.1002/jhbs.20510.

LeVine, Robert A. 2010. "The Six Cultures Study: Prologue to a History of a Landmark Project." *Journal of Cross-Cultural Psychology* 41 (4): 513–21. https://doi.org/10.1177/0022022110362567.

LeVine, Robert A., and Sarah LeVine. 2016. *Do Parents Matter?: Why Japanese Babies Sleep Soundly, Mexican Siblings Don't Fight, and American Families Should Just Relax.* New York: PublicAffairs.

Lew-Levy, Sheina, Wouter van den Bos, Kathleen Corriveau, et al. 2023. "Peer Learning and Cultural Evolution." *Child Development Perspectives* 17 (2): 97–105. https://doi.org/10.1111/cdep.12482.

Li, Jin. 2012. *Cultural Foundations of Learning: East and West.* 1st edition. New York: Cambridge University Press.

Lieberman, Debra, and Thalma Lobel. 2012. "Kinship on the Kibbutz: Coresidence Duration Predicts Altruism, Personal Sexual Aversions and Moral Attitudes among Communally Reared Peers." *Evolution and Human Behavior* 33 (1): 26–34. https://doi.org/10.1016/j.evolhumbehav.2011.05.002.

Lieberman, Debra, and Donald Symons. 1998. "Sibling Incest Avoidance: From Westermarck to Wolf." Edited by Arthur P. Wolf. *The Quarterly Review of Biology* 73 (4): 463–66.

Lieberman, Debra, John Tooby, and Leda Cosmides. 2003. "Does Morality Have a Biological Basis? An Empirical Test of the Factors Governing Moral Sentiments Relating to Incest." *Proceedings of the Royal Society B: Biological Sciences* 270 (1517): 819–26. https://doi.org/10.1098/rspb.2002.2290.

References

2007. "The Architecture of Human Kin Detection." *Nature* 445 (7129): 727–31. https://doi.org/10.1038/nature05510.

Loeber, Rolf, Deborah M. Capaldi, and Elizabeth Costello. 2013. "Gender and the Development of Aggression, Disruptive Behavior, and Delinquency from Childhood to Early Adulthood." In *Disruptive Behavior Disorders*, edited by Patrick H. Tolan and Bennett L. Leventhal, 137–60. Advances in Development and Psychopathology: Brain Research Foundation Symposium Series. New York, NY: Springer Science + Business Media. https://doi.org/10.1007/978-1-4614-7557-6_6.

Lonner, Walter J. 2010. "The Legacy of John and Beatrice Whiting for Cross-Cultural Research on Children and Adolescents (Special Issue)." *Journal of Cross-Cultural Psychology* 41 (4): 483–632. https://doi.org/10.1177/0022022110364832.

Lucca, Kelsey, J. Kiley Hamlin, and Jessica A. Sommerville. 2019. "Editorial: Early Moral Cognition and Behavior." *Frontiers in Psychology* 10. https://doi.org/10.3389/fpsyg.2019.02013.

Mahowald, Kyle, Anna A. Ivanova, Idan A. Blank, Nancy Kanwisher, Joshua B. Tenenbaum, and Evelina Fedorenko. 2023. "Dissociating Language and Thought in Large Language Models: A Cognitive Perspective." arXiv.Org. January 16, 2023. https://arxiv.org/abs/2301.06627v1.

Martin, Emily. 1973. *The Cult of the Dead in a Chinese Village*. Stanford, CA: Stanford University Press.

Mattingly, Cheryl, and Jason Throop. 2018. "The Anthropology of Ethics and Morality." *Annual Review of Anthropology* 47 (1): 475–92. https://doi.org/10.1146/annurev-anthro-102317-050129.

Maynard, Ashley E., and K. E. Tovote. 2010. "Learning from Other Children." In *The Anthropology of Learning in Childhood*, edited by David F. Lancy, John Bock, and Suzanne Gaskins, 181–205. New York: AltaMira Press.

McPherson, Miller, Lynn Smith-Lovin, and James M. Cook. 2001. "Birds of a Feather: Homophily in Social Networks." *Annual Review of Sociology* 27: 415–44. https://doi.org/10.1146/annurev.soc.27.1.415.

Metz, Cade. 2021. "Can a Machine Learn Morality?" *The New York Times*, November 19, 2021, sec. Technology. www.nytimes.com/2021/11/19/technology/can-a-machine-learn-morality.html.

Meyer, Jeffrey E. 1988. "Teaching Morality in Taiwan Schools: The Message of the Textbooks*." *The China Quarterly* 114 (June): 267–84. https://doi.org/10.1017/S0305741000026795.

Miller, George A. 2003. "The Cognitive Revolution: A Historical Perspective." *Trends in Cognitive Sciences* 7 (3): 141–44. https://doi.org/10.1016/S1364-6613(03)00029-9.

References

Minturn, Leigh, and William W. Lambert. 1964. *Mothers of Six Cultures Antecedents of Child Rearing*. 1st edition. New York: John Wiley & Sons.

Morin, Olivier. 2015. "How Traditions Live and Die." *Foundations of Human Interaction*. Oxford and New York: Oxford University Press.

Munck, Victor C. de, and Giovanni Bennardo. 2019. "Disciplining Culture: A Sociocognitive Approach." *Current Anthropology* 60 (2): 174–93. https://doi.org/10.1086/702470.

Munroe, Robert L., Robert Hulefeld, James M. Rodgers, Damon L. Tomeo, and Steven K. Yamazaki. 2000. "Aggression among Children in Four Cultures." *Cross-Cultural Research* 34 (1): 3–25. https://doi.org/10.1177/106939710003400101.

Neal, Jennifer Watling. 2020. "A Systematic Review of Social Network Methods in High Impact Developmental Psychology Journals." *Social Development* 29 (4): 923–44. https://doi.org/10.1111/sode.12442.

Nichols, Ryan. 2022. *The Routledge International Handbook of Morality, Cognition, and Emotion in China*. New York: Taylor & Francis Group.

Ning, Rundong, and David A. Palmer. 2020. "Ethics of the Heart: Moral Breakdown and the Aporia of Chinese Volunteers." *Current Anthropology* 61 (4): 395–417. https://doi.org/10.1086/710217.

Obendiek, Helena. 2013. "When Siblings Determine Your 'Fate': Sibling Support and Educational Mobility in Rural Northwest China." In *The Anthropology of Sibling Relations*, edited by E. Alber, C. Coe, and T. Thelen, 97–122. New York: Springer.

Ochiai, Emiko. 2011. "Unsustainable Societies: The Failure of Familialism in East Asia's Compressed Modernity." *Historical Social Research/Historische Sozialforschung* 36 (2): 219–45.

O'Madagain, Cathal, and Michael Tomasello. 2022. "Shared Intentionality, Reason-Giving and the Evolution of Human Culture." *Philosophical Transactions of the Royal Society B: Biological Sciences* 377 (1843): 20200320. https://doi.org/10.1098/rstb.2020.0320.

Österman, Karin, Kaj Björkqvist, Kirsti M. J. Lagerspetz, Ari Kaukiainen, Simha F. Landau, Adam Frączek, and Gian Vittorio Caprara. 1998. "Cross-cultural Evidence of Female Indirect Aggression." *Aggressive Behavior* 24 (1): 1–8. https://doi.org/10.1002.

Peletz, Michael G. 2002. "Ambivalence in Kinship since the 1940s." In *Relative Values: Reconfiguring Kinship Studies*, edited by Sarah Franklin and Susan McKinnon, 413–44. Durham: Duke University Press. https://doi.org/10.1515/9780822383222-018.

Piaget, Jean. 1997. *The Moral Judgment of the Child*. New York: Free Press.

Qiu, Fanxiao Wani, and Henrike Moll. 2022. "Children's Pedagogical Competence and Child-to-Child Knowledge Transmission: Forgotten Factors in Theories

References

of Cultural Evolution." *Journal of Cognition and Culture* 22 (5): 421–35. https://doi.org/10.1163/15685373-12340143.

Quinn, Naomi. 2005. "Universals of Child Rearing." *Anthropological Theory* 5 (4): 477–516. https://doi.org/10.1177/1463499605059233.

Quinn, Naomi, and Claudia Strauss. 2006. "Introduction to Special Issue on The Missing Psychology in Cultural Anthropology's Key Words." *Anthropological Theory* 6 (3): 267–79. https://doi.org/10.1177/1463499606066888.

Railton, Peter. 2017. "Moral Learning: Conceptual Foundations and Normative Relevance." *Cognition, Moral Learning*, 167 (October): 172–90. https://doi.org/10.1016/j.cognition.2016.08.015.

Rothschild, N. Harry, and Professor Leslie V. Wallace, eds. 2017. *Behaving Badly in Early and Medieval China*. Honolulu: University of Hawaii Press.

Santos, Gonçalo D. 2006. "The Anthropology of Chinese Kinship: A Critical Overview." *European Journal of East Asian Studies* 5 (2): 275–333.

——— 2008. "On 'Same-Year Siblings' in Rural South China." *The Journal of the Royal Anthropological Institute* 14 (3): 535–53.

Santos, Gonçalo, and Stevan Harrell, eds. 2016. *Transforming Patriarchy: Chinese Families in the Twenty-First Century*. Seattle: University of Washington Press.

Sarin, Arunima, Mark K. Ho, Justin W. Martin, and Fiery A. Cushman. 2021. "Punishment Is Organized around Principles of Communicative Inference." *Cognition* 208 (March): 104544. https://doi.org/10.1016/j.cognition.2020.104544.

Schieffelin, Bambi B., and Elinor Ochs, eds. 1986. *Language Socialization across Cultures*. New York, NY: Cambridge University Press.

Scott-Phillips, Thomas C., Thomas E. Dickins, and Stuart A. West. 2011. "Evolutionary Theory and the Ultimate–Proximate Distinction in the Human Behavioral Sciences." *Perspectives on Psychological Science* 6 (1): 38–47. https://doi.org/10.1177/1745691610393528.

Shapiro, Jeremy P., Roy F. Baumeister, and Jane W. Kessler. 1991. "A Three-Component Model of Children's Teasing: Aggression, Humor, and Ambiguity." *Journal of Social and Clinical Psychology* 10: 459–72. https://doi.org/10.1521/jscp.1991.10.4.459.

Shepher, Joseph. 1971. "Mate Selection among Second Generation Kibbutz Adolescents and Adults: Incest Avoidance and Negative Imprinting." *Archives of Sexual Behavior* 1 (4): 293–307. https://doi.org/10.1007/BF01638058.

Silverman, Sydel. 2020. "Comments on Omissions and Silences in Ethnographic Research." *Journal of Anthropological Research* 76 (1): 90–94. https://doi.org/10.1086/706943.

Skinner, G. William. 2017. *Rural China on the Eve of Revolution: Sichuan Fieldnotes, 1949–1950*, edited by Stevan Harrell and William Lavely. Seattle: University of Washington Press.

References

Smith, Robert J. 1990. "Hearing Voices, Joining the Chorus: Appropriating Someone Else's Fieldnotes." In *Fieldnotes: The Makings of Anthropology*, edited by Roger Sanjek, 356–70. Ithaca, NY: Cornell University Press.

Sperber, Dan, and Deirdre Wilson. 1996. *Relevance: Communication and Cognition*. 2nd edition. Oxford and Cambridge, MA: Wiley-Blackwell.

Stafford, Charles. 1992. "Good Sons and Virtuous Mothers: Kinship and Chinese Nationalism in Taiwan." *Man* 27 (2): 363–78. https://doi.org/10.2307/2804058.

——— 1995. *The Roads of Chinese Childhood*. Cambridge, UK and New York: Cambridge University Press. https://doi.org/10.1017/CBO9780511586347.

——— 2000. "Chinese Patriliny and the Cycles of Yang and Laiwang." In *Cultures of Relatedness: New Approaches to the Study of Kinship*, edited by Carsten Janet, 35–54. Cambridge, UK: Cambridge University Press.

——— 2010. "The Punishment of Ethical Behavior." In *Ordinary Ethics: Anthropology, Language, and Action*, edited by Michael Lambek, 187–206. New York: Fordham University Press.

——— 2011. "What Confucius Would Make of It." *Anthropology of This Century*, no. 2. http://aotcpress.com/articles/confucius-2/.

——— 2013. "Ordinary Ethics in China Today." In *Ordinary Ethics in China*, edited by Charles Stafford, 3–25. Berg Publishers.

——— 2020. *Economic Life in the Real World: Logic, Emotion and Ethics. New Departures in Anthropology*. Cambridge, UK: Cambridge University Press. https://doi.org/10.1017/9781108673426.

Stengelin, Roman, Rabea Ball, Luke Maurits, Patricia Kanngiesser, and Daniel B. M. Haun. 2023. "Children Over-Imitate Adults and Peers More than Puppets." *Developmental Science* 26 (2): e13303. https://doi.org/10.1111/desc.13303.

Strauss, Claudia. Forthcoming. "What Is (and Is Not) a Cultural Model." In *Cognition In and Out of the Mind: Cultural Models Theory*, edited by Giovanni Bennardo, Victor de Munck, and Stephen Chrisomalis. Palgrave Macmillan.

Strauss, Claudia, and Naomi Quinn. 1997. *A Cognitive Theory of Cultural Meaning*. Cambridge, UK: Cambridge University Press.

Számadó, S., D. Balliet, F. Giardini, E. A. Power, and K. Takács. 2021. "The Language of Cooperation: Reputation and Honest Signalling." *Philosophical Transactions of the Royal Society B: Biological Sciences* 376 (1838): 20200286. https://doi.org/10.1098/rstb.2020.0286.

Szonyi, Michael. 2008. *Cold War Island: Quemoy on the Front Line*. Cambridge, UK and New York: Cambridge University Press.

Tanaka, Stefan. 1997. "Childhood: The Naturalization of Development into a Japanese Space." In *Cultures of Scholarship*, edited by S. C. Humphreys, 21–54. Ann Arbor: University of Michigan Press.

References

Tedlock, Barbara. 1996. "Works and Wives: On the Sextual Division of Textual Labor." In *Women Writing Culture*, edited by Ruth Behar and Deborah A. Gordon, 267–86. Oakland: University of California Press.

Teow, See Heng, and Yang Huei Pang. 2015. "The 1957 Taiwan Riots: Cultural Politics in U.S.-Taiwan Relations in the 1950s." In *Asia Pacific in the Age of Globalization*, edited by Robert David Johnson, 185–98. The Palgrave Macmillan Transnational History Series. London: Palgrave Macmillan. https://doi.org/10.1057/9781137455383_18.

Thelen, T., C. Coe, and E. Alber. 2013. "Introduction." In *The Anthropology of Sibling Relations*, edited by E. Alber, C. Coe, and T. Thelen, 1–26. New York: Springer.

Tobin, Joseph Jay, David Y. H. Wu, and Dana H. Davidson. 1989. *Preschool in Three Cultures: Japan, China, and the United States*. New Haven: Yale University Press. http://libcat.wustl.edu/?itemid=; iii; b1219368.

Tomasello, Michael. 2016. "The Ontogeny of Cultural Learning." *Current Opinion in Psychology* 8 (April): 1–4. https://doi.org/10.1016/j.copsyc.2015.09.008.

———. 2019. *Becoming Human: A Theory of Ontogeny*. Cambridge, MA: Belknap Press: An Imprint of Harvard University Press.

Tomasello, Michael, and Malinda Carpenter. 2007. "Shared Intentionality." *Developmental Science* 10 (1): 121–25. https://doi.org/10.1111/j.1467-7687.2007.00573.x.

Topley, Marjorie. 1974. "Cosmic Antagonisms: A Mother-Child Syndrome." In *Religion and Ritual in Chinese Society*, edited by Arthur P. Wolf, 233–44. Stanford, CA: Stanford University Press.

Trivers, Robert. 1971. "The Evolution of Reciprocal Altruism." *Quarterly Review of Biology* 46 (1): 35–57.

Turiel, Elliot. 2018. "Moral Development in the Early Years: When and How." *Human Development* 61 (4–5): 297–308. https://doi.org/10.1159/000492805.

Ullman, Tomer, and Joshua B. Tenenbaum. 2020. "Bayesian Models of Conceptual Development: Learning as Building Models of the World." *Annual Review of Developmental Psychology* 2 (1): 533–58. https://doi.org/10.1146/annurev-devpsych-121318-084833.

Ward, Barbara E. 1985. *Through Other Eyes: Essays in Understanding "Conscious Models" – Mostly in Hong Kong*. Hong Kong: The Chinese University of Hong Kong Press.

Watson, James L. 1976. "Anthropological Analyses of Chinese Religion." *The China Quarterly* 66 (June): 355–64. https://doi.org/10.1017/S0305741000033749.

Watson, James L., Rubie S. Watson, and Yunxiang Yan. 2019. "A Different Kind of Chinese Family." *Anthropology of This Century*, no. 25. http://aotcpress.com/articles/kind-chinese-family/.

References

Watson, Rubie S. 1985. *Inequality Among Brothers: Class and Kinship in South China*. Cambridge, UK and New York: Cambridge University Press.

Weisner, Thomas S. 1989. "Comparing Sibling Relationships across Cultures." In *Sibling Interaction across Cultures: Theoretical and Methodological Issues*, edited by Patricia Goldring Zukow, 11–25. New York, NY: Springer. https://doi.org/10.1007/978-1-4612-3536-1_2.

Weisner, Thomas S., Ronald Gallimore, Margaret K. Bacon, et al. 1977. "My Brother's Keeper: Child and Sibling Caretaking [and Comments and Reply]." *Current Anthropology* 18 (2): 169–90.

Wellman, Professor Henry M. 2014. *Making Minds: How Theory of Mind Develops*. 1st edition. Oxford and New York: Oxford University Press.

Westermarck, Edward. 1921[1894]. *The History of Human Marriage*. 5th edition. New York: Macmillan.

Whiting, Beatrice, and Carolyn Pope Edwards. 1973. "A Cross-Cultural Analysis of Sex Differences in the Behavior of Children Aged Three Through 11." *The Journal of Social Psychology* 91 (2): 171–88. https://doi.org/10.1080/00224545.1973.9923040.

Whiting, Beatrice Blyth, ed. 1963. "Six Cultures: Studies of Child Rearing." *Journal of Marriage and the Family* 26 (January): 124–25. https://doi.org/10.2307/349404.

Whiting, Beatrice Blyth. 1983. "The Genesis of Prosocial Behavior." In *The Nature of Prosocial Development: Interdisciplinary Theories and Strategies*, edited by D. Bridgeman, 221–42. London: Academic Press.

Whiting, Beatrice Blyth, and Carolyn Pope Edwards. 1992. *Children of Different Worlds: The Formation of Social Behavior*. Cambridge, MA: Harvard University Press.

Whiting, Beatrice Blyth, John Wesley Mayhew Whiting, and Richard Longabaugh. 1975. *Children of Six Cultures: A Psycho-Cultural Analysis*. Cambridge, MA: Harvard University Press.

Whiting, John Wesley Mayhew, Harvard University Laboratory of Human Development, and Social Science Research Council (U.S.). 1966. *Field Guide for a Study of Socialization*. New York: J. Wiley.

Wolf, Arthur P. 1966. "Childhood Association, Sexual Attraction, and the Incest Taboo: A Chinese Case." *American Anthropologist* 68 (4): 883–98.

———. 1968. "Adopt a Daughter-in-Law, Marry a Sister: A Chinese Solution to the Problem of the Incest Taboo." *American Anthropologist* 70 (5): 864–74.

———. 1970. "Childhood Association and Sexual Attraction: A Further Test of the Westermarck Hypothesis." *American Anthropologist* 72 (3): 503–15. https://doi.org/10.1525/aa.1970.72.3.02a00010.

References

1982. "Project Summary for National Science Foundation: Chinese Children and Their Mothers: Cultural and Psychological Aspects of Socialization in a Taiwanese Village." A. P. Wolf's Private Library.

1995. *Sexual Attraction and Childhood Association: A Chinese Brief for Edward Westermarck*. 1st edition. Stanford, CA: Stanford University Press.

2003. "Maternal Sentiments: How Strong Are They?" *Current Anthropology* 44 (S5): S31–49. https://doi.org/10.1086/377668.

2014. *Incest Avoidance and the Incest Taboos: Two Aspects of Human Nature*. Stanford, CA: Stanford Briefs.

Unpublished manuscript. *Chinese Children and Their Mothers*.

Wolf, Arthur P., and Chieh-Shang Huang. 1980. *Marriage and Adoption in China, 1845–1945*. 1st edition. Stanford, CA: Stanford University Press.

Wolf, Margery. 1968. *The House of Lim: A Study of a Chinese Farm Family*. New York: Appleton-Century-Crofts.

1972. *Women and the Family in Rural Taiwan*. Stanford, CA: Stanford University Press.

1978. "Child Training and the Chinese Family." In *Studies in Chinese Society*, edited by Arthur P. Wolf, 221–46. Stanford, CA: Stanford University Press.

1990a. "Chinanotes: Engendering Anthropology." In *Fieldnotes: The Makings of Anthropology*, 343–55. Ithaca, NY: Cornell University Press. https://doi.org/10.7591/9781501711954-014.

1990b. "The Woman Who Didn't Become a Shaman." *American Ethnologist* 17 (3): 419–30.

1992. *A Thrice-Told Tale: Feminism, Postmodernism, and Ethnographic Responsibility*. 1st edition. Stanford, CA: Stanford University Press.

Wong, David B. 2023. *Moral Relativism and Pluralism*. Cambridge, UK: Cambridge University Press. https://doi.org/10.1017/9781009043496.

Woo, Brandon M., Enda Tan, and J. Kiley Hamlin. 2022. "Human Morality Is Based on an Early-Emerging Moral Core." *Annual Review of Developmental Psychology* 4 (1): null. https://doi.org/10.1146/annurev-devpsych-121020-023312.

Wright, Jennifer Cole, and Karen Bartsch. 2008. "Portraits of Early Moral Sensibility in Two Children's Everyday Conversations." *Merrill-Palmer Quarterly* 54 (1). https://digitalcommons.wayne.edu/mpq/vol54/iss1/4.

Wu, David Y. H. 1981. "Child Abuse in Taiwan." In *Child Abuse and Neglect: Cross-Cultural Perspectives*, 139–65. Berkeley: University of California Press.

1996. "Parental Control: Psychocultural Interpretations of Chinese Patterns of Socialization." In *Growing Up the Chinese Way*, 1–28. Hong Kong: The Chinese University of Hong Kong.

References

Xu, Jing. 2014. "Becoming a Moral Child amidst China's Moral Crisis: Preschool Discourse and Practices of Sharing in Shanghai." *Ethos* 42 (2): 222–42. https://doi.org/10.1111/etho.12049.

———. 2017. *The Good Child: Moral Development in a Chinese Preschool*. Stanford, CA: Stanford University Press. www.sup.org/books/title/?id=26737.

———. 2019. "Learning 'Merit' in a Chinese Preschool: Bringing the Anthropological Perspective to Understanding Moral Development." *American Anthropologist* 121 (3): 655–66. https://doi.org/10.1111/aman.13269.

———. 2020a. "Tattling with Chinese Characteristics: Norm Sensitivity, Moral Anxiety, and 'The Genuine Child.'" *Ethos* 48 (1): 29–49. https://doi.org/10.1111/etho.12262.

———. 2020b. "The Mischievous, the Naughty, and the Violent in a Taiwanese Village: Peer Aggression Narratives in Arthur P. Wolf's 'Child Interview' (1959)." *Cross-Currents* 9 (1): 180–208.

———. 2022a. "'The Moral Child': Anthropological Perspectives on Moral Development in China." In *The Routledge International Handbook of Morality, Cognition, and Emotion in China*, edited by Ryan Nichols, 193–214. London: Routledge.

———. 2022b. "Learning Morality with Siblings: The Untold Tale of a Mid-Twentieth Century Taiwanese Family." *Journal of Chinese History* 中國歷史學刊 6 (2): 337–63. https://doi.org/10.1017/jch.2021.31.

———. Forthcoming. "Children at the Margins: Rethinking Anthropological Perspectives about Mid-20th Century Chinese Childhoods." In *Rethinking Childhood in Modern Chinese History*, edited by Isabella Jackson and Yusheng Geng. London: Routledge.

Yan, Yunxiang. 2009. "The Good Samaritan's New Trouble: A Study of the Changing Moral Landscape in Contemporary China1." *Social Anthropology* 17 (1): 9–24. https://doi.org/10.1111/j.1469-8676.2008.00055.x.

———. 2011. "How Far Away Can We Move from Durkheim." *Anthropology of This Century*, no. 2 (October).

———. 2014. "The Moral Implications of Immorality: The Chinese Case for a New Anthropology of Morality." *Journal of Religious Ethics* 42 (3): 460–93.

———. 2017. "Doing Personhood in Chinese Culture: The Desiring Individual, Moralist Self and Relational Person." *The Cambridge Journal of Anthropology* 35 (2): 1–17. https://doi.org/10.3167/cja.2017.350202.

———. 2020. "The Politics of Moral Crisis in Contemporary China." *The China Journal* 85 (December): 96–120. https://doi.org/10.1086/711563.

———, ed. 2021. *Chinese Families Upside Down: Intergenerational Dynamics and Neo-Familism in the Early 21st Century*. Laiden, NL: Brill. http://brill.com/view/title/59613.

References

Yiu, Eunice, Eliza Kosoy, and Alison Gopnik. 2023. "Transmission versus Truth, Imitation versus Innovation: What Children Can Do That Large Language and Language-and-Vision Models Cannot (Yet)?" *Perspectives on Psychological Science* 0(0). https://doi.org/10.1177/17456916231201401.

Yu, Hongbo, Yubo Zhou, and Anne-Marie Nussberger. 2022. "Gratitude Is Morally Sensitive." *Personality and Social Psychology Bulletin*, 50(3): 406–22. https://doi.org/10.1177/01461672221092273.

Index

Adoga ("Big Nose"), 52
adopted girl, 167–74
adoptive mother, 170
Allerton, Catherine, 38, 57, 69
Amir, Dorsa, 13, 222
Anxi, 46
Archer, John, 147
artificial intelligence
    ChatGPT, 18–19
    L.L.M. (large-language-model), 129–33
    morality, 18–19, 137
    training data, 18, 134
Astuti, Rita, 15, 218
authoritarianism, 84, 158, 217, 220

bai-bai, 119, 183, 207
Bamford, Sandra, 179
Banqiao town, 46
banquets, 118
Barrett, Clark, 13, 132
Bateson, Gregory, 137
Bayesian learner, 133
becoming human. *See zuo ren*
behavioral coding, 28–29, 122, 141–43, 192–93
behavioral initiators, 142
behavioral recipients, 142
benshengren, xviii
Björkqvist, Kaj, 145
Bloch, Maurice, 13

Boyer, Pascal, 10, 123
Briggs, Jean, 100
bus attendant, 114

Card, Noel A., 145
Carsten, Janet, 178, 180
Chao, Ruth K, 74
Child Interview, 82–83, 91–92, 127–28
child, innocent, 4, 23, 135
childhood
    Chinese, 20–22, 34, 214–15
    cross-cultural research of, xix, 7, 221–22
    East Asia, 216–17
    memory, xxiii, 216
    representations and discourses, xxiii, 20
childhood cohabitation, 168
childrearing, 5, 21
    agrarian societies, 100
    change, 36
    goal, 94
    method, 96
children's fights, 73–89, 181–82
children's play
    card games, 111
    "crime and punishment", 103–4
    dueling, 146
    games and scenarios, 111
    hide-and-seek, 60, 197
    hopscotch, 111, 146

Index

children's play (cont.)
  marble games, 111
  peer play, xxiv, 103–37
  playing anthropologist, 36–37
  playing house, 56, 60, 112
  playing school, 116–18
  pretend play, 114–21
  rubber bands, 111
child-to-child ties, 34, 106–7
China, postreform, xx, 213
Chinese family, traditional, 101
  obedience, 23, 74
Chinese parenting, *guan*, 74, 95
Chubby Maata, 100
class master, 166–67
Cline, Erin M., 20
coalitional dynamics, 124, 193–98
ColdWar, xviii, 53
Coles, Robert, 160
comforting, 146
Communist, xix, 53–54
  anti-communism, xviii
  anti-communist, xxii
Confucian morality, 215
cooperation and conflict, 121–25, 141–46, 192–93
Cornell University, 41
Croll, Elizabeth, 138
cultural models
  of parenting, 75–76, 82
  theory of, 78, 75, 78
cultural transmission, 9, 13, 120–21, 217–18

D'Andrade, Roy, 11, 75
Dahan River, 46
Dehaene, Stanislas, 10
Diamond, Norma, 22, 75
disobedience, 92–94, 161–73, 205
divisiveness in anthropology, 222
dominance, 2, 122, 144
  through physical coercion, 89
Dunfield, Kristen A, 29, 146
Duryea, Maria, 8, 36, 76, 216

education, nationalist, xviii, 49–50
Edwards, C.P., 8, 136, 142
Eisenberg, Nancy, 145
Ember, Carol, 147
emotional experience, 94, 141
Endendijk, Joyce J., 147
ethnographic epistemology, 35, 64–71, 130–34, 210–11

fairness, 1–3, 122–23, 138
families, working-class, 21
familism, 216
family ties, 109
fantasy, reality-based, 136, 148, 202
favoritism, 63, 123
  parental, 203
fertility, 23, 178, 217
fieldwork
  as an ethical action, 16, 69
  first-person experience, xx, 4
  intermediaries, 38, 55
  journal, 40, 66, 68
first Sino-Japanese war, xviii
Fong, Vanessa, 74
Freedman, Maurice, xx, 138
Fujian, southeast China. *See* Hoklo
Fung, Heidi, 96

gambling, 116, 157
gangsters. *See* lo-mua
Gates, Hill, xiii, xx
gender differences, 142, 145
gender discrimination, 166
gender stereotypes, 141
geopolitical tensions, xviii–xxii, 217
gift-giving, 119
gods, walking, 120
Gopnik, Alison, 18, 130, 133, 223
gossip
  adults, 57, 79, 181, 208
  children, 98, 124, 163, 184
grandparents as caregivers, 46
granting access, 146

Index

Great Leap Forward, xviii, xxii
Greenhalgh, Susan, 138
guan, 167
guardian of Chinese traditions, 22
gunbang zhixia chu xiaozi, 101

Hamilton, William D., 179
Han ethnicity, xviii
harmony, neighborly, 76
Harrell, Stevan, xx, 6, 50, 160
Harris, Paul, 136
helping, 146
Henrich, Joseph, 222
Hewlett, Barry, 135
Hewlett, Bonnie, 135
Hirschfeld, Lawrence, 218
history, intellectual, xix, 6–10, 160, 224–28
Hoklo, xviii
hooligans. *See lo-mua*
House, Bailey, 146
household register system, 46, 228
Hsiung, Ping-chen, 20, 21, 215
Huang, Chieh-Shan, 26, 44, 50, 65
human kinship, double-edged, 179, 210
human mind
  black box, 9, 15
  blank slate, 15, 19, 225
human–machine hybrid approach, 24, 30–32, 70–71, 129–34
humiliation, 101
humor, 102, 112, 113
Hunan, China, xiii, 40

ideology and practice, 220
impartiality, 123
incest avoidance, 168, 227–28
  Westermarck hypothesis, 10
indirect aggression, 145
innate predisposition, 12
intensity, behavioral, 28
intention, behavioral, 28
intentionality

layered, 62, 126
shared, 137

Jankowiak, William, 144
Japanese rule, xviii, 49
Jiang, Tao, 4
jiao hua, 21
Jinmen, xix, 162
Joseph, Suad, 210

KMT (*Kuomintang*), xviii
Kohlberg, Lawrence, 14

Lambek, Michael, 16, 136
Lambert, William, 7
Lancy, David, 136
learning
  active, 6, 17, 214
  behaviorism, 9, 94
  forming internal models, 10–12
  nativism, 10, 17
LeVine, Robert, 7
LeVine, Sarah, 100
Lew-Levy, Sheina, 135, 219
Lieberman, Debra, 178
local surveillance, 158
lo-mua, 154–59
look, dirty, 144
love and attachment, 102

mammalian development, 228
Mandarin, xviii, 48, 49
Mao Zedong, xviii
Martial Law Era, Taiwan, xviii, xxii, 115, 157
Martin, Emily, 75
maternal sentiments, 168
Maynard, Ashley, 177
Mazu, xix
Mencius' Mother, the tale of, 153
methodological pluralism, 24
minor marriage, xx, 8, 167
mixed-methods approach, 27, 70

Index

Model Minority myth, 215
modernization, 49, 216
moral development
    in real life, xvii
    theory of, 14, 17–18
moral discourse, 135
moral emotions, 4
moral expectations, 161
moral experience, 219
    gendered, 138, 168
moral intuitions, 18
moral judgments, 132
moral personhood, 174
moral precepts, 140
moral psychology, 16, 94, 220
moral reasoning, 4
moral sensibilities, 105, 135
moral transgressions, 150
morality
    Chinese, 4, 217
    and ethics, the anthropology of, 16, 99
    everyday, 217
    gendered, 160
    naturalistic view of, 17
    pluralism, 17–18
    transformations, 217
Mother Interview, 78–82
Mother Observation, 82
multi-agent dynamics, 122
multi-child families, 123
Munroe, Robert L., 147

national development, 216
natural experiment, 228
naturalistic observation, 25, 130–31
    Child Observation procedure, 27–28
New Taipei City, xxi, 8
NLP (natural-language-processing), 30–31, 73, 86–88
    BERT, 129–30
    topic modeling, 110–11, 128–29
    word frequency, 85, 110, 190–92
normativity, 134

Older Sister Chen, 5, 26
    ethical entanglements, 61–64
    relation with children, 57–61
One-Child Policy, China, xxiv, 209
ostensive detachment, 123

parental approval, 100
parental authority, 101, 102
parent–child fights, 154
parent–child ties, xxiii, 20
parenting across cultures, 100–101
patriarchy, 138, 175, 220
peer groups, 106
peer leaders, 194
peer learning, 4, 104, 135, 219
Peihotien. See Xia Xizhou
philosophy, Chinese, 4
physical aggression, 122, 147
Piaget, Jean, 14
playful teasing, 146
pocket money, 1, 48, 93
policing, 115–16
polyvocality, 221
positionality, ethnographer, 50–64
PRC (People's Republic of China), xviii
projective test, 26, 65–67
    Doll Play, 173
    as story-telling, 198–205, 136
    TAT, 150–58
projective test, Doll Play, 173
prosocial behavior, 29, 145
prosocial development, 14, 146
prostitute, 47, 152, 165
public shaming, 101
punishment
    as communication, 94
    corporal, 48, 90, 148–50
    emotional arousal, 96
    and its inefficacy, 94–102
    parental ethnotheories, 95

qi, 96
Qing dynasty, xviii

Index

Quanzhou, 46
Quinn, Naomi, 75, 78, 96, 100

randomness, 133
reciprocity, 2, 125, 128, 176–77, 195
red envelopes, 119
religious processions, 119
reputation, 5
reputation-based cooperation, 124
request for access, 145
ROC (Republic of China), xviii, 116

Saxe, Rebecca, 132
schooling, 22, 172–73
    gender, 164–67
scolding, 91, 122, 144
Seattle, xxiii
Second Taiwan Strait Crisis, xix, 54
second-class status, 139
sense-making, 35, 71, 131
sex-selection theory, 147
Sha Ji Jing Hou, 63
Shalun Elementary School, 41, 49
sharing, 123, 146
Sharp, Lauriston, 7
shopping, 48
Shulin town, 41, 50, 151
sibling care, 139, 146, 163–64, 171–72, 194–95
sibling co-residence. *See* childhood co-habitation
sibling relation, 209–11
sibling rivalry, 198–205
sibling solidarity, 209
sim-pu-a. *See* minor marriage
singleton child, xxiv, 143, 209, 213
Six Cultures Study of Child Socialization, xix, 25–29, 142
Smith, Robert, 71
social cognition, 5, 218
  in cultural contexts, 9
  and emotion, 94–99
social exclusion, 145, 196–97

social learning, 9, 13, 135
social network analysis, 31
  behavioral network, 106–8, 187–88
  co-occurrence network, 107, 186–87
  homophily, 109, 185–86
  modularity, 108
  personal network, 186–89
  semantic network, 190
socialization, xiv, 95, 150
  political, 50, 160
socio-emotional intelligence, 132
soldiers, 54
son preference, xx, 23, 146
Stafford, Charles, 15, 100, 127, 214
stepmother, 90
stepsiblings, 178
Strauss, Claudia, 75, 78, 100
Sun Yat-sen, 54

Taipei, 41
Taipei basin, xvii, 46
Taiwanese Hokkien, 48, 49. *See also* Hoklo
Tang-ki (spirit medium), 182
tattling, 73, 82–83, 145
teasing, 126
  aggressive, 72, 127, 140
  playful, 126–32
Tenenbaum, Joshua, 133
text-as-data, 31, 220
theory of mind (ToM), 132
thick description, 134
third-party witness, 123
Tomasello, Michael, 9, 223
traditional Chinese family, 20–23
transcription, 27
troublemaker, 194, 196
Tucheng town, 46

United States, xxiii
uterine families, 139

257

Index

verbal aggression, 122, 144
violence
   learning, 150–60
   the culture of, 158

waishengren, xviii, 25
Wang, Shiqing, 44, 153
Ward, Barbara, 136
weddings, 118
WEIRD societies, 13
Weisner, Thomas, 106, 177
White Terror, 66
Whiting, Beatrice, 7, 142, 225
Whiting, John, 7, 28
Wolf, Arthur, xiii, 97, 178
   aggression and war, 227
   fieldwork memory, 41, 46–48, 51, 83–84, 215–16
   local ideology, 76
   theory, 10, 226–28
   unpublished manuscript, 136, 218–19
   the Wolf archive, 6–8, 24–27

Wolf, Margery, xiii
   Child Training, 147
   Chinanotes, 64, 67–68
   The House of Lim, 36–37, 151–53, 168–69
   A Thrice-Told Tale, 180–81, 210
   The Uterine Family, 173
   Women and Family, 75–76, 138–39, 163
Wong, David, 18
Wu, David YH, 74, 94, 101
WWII, xviii

Xia Xizhou
   economy, 47
   history, xvii–xviii, 45–47

Yan, Yunxiang, 15
yielding, 195
yielding, older to younger children, 81, 89

Zhangzhou, 46
zuo ren, xvii, 4, 229

Printed by Printforce, the Netherlands